Technology and Science in Ancient Civilizations

**Recent Titles in the
Praeger Series on the Ancient World**

TECHNOLOGY AND SCIENCE IN ANCIENT CIVILIZATIONS

Richard G. Olson

Praeger Series on the Ancient World
Bella Vivante, Series Editor

PRAEGER
An Imprint of ABC-CLIO, LLC

A B C CLIO

Santa Barbara, California • Denver, Colorado • Oxford, England

Library of Congress Cataloging-in-Publication Data

Olson, Richard G., 1940–
  Technology and science in ancient civilizations / Richard G. Olson.
    p. cm. — (Praeger series on the ancient world)
  Includes bibliographical references and index.
    ISBN 978-0-275-98936-1 (alk. paper) — ISBN 978-0-313-06523-1 (ebook)
1. Civilization, Ancient. 2. Technology and civilization. 3. Science and civilization. I. Title.
  CB311O46 2010
  930.1—dc22   2009037031

ISBN 978-0-275-98936-1: paper
ISBN 978-0-313-06523-1: ebook

14 13 12 11 10   1 2 3 4 5

This book is also available on the World Wide Web as an eBook.
Visit www.abc-clio.com for details.

ABC-CLIO, LLC
130 Cremona Drive, P.O. Box 1911
Santa Barbara, California 93116-1911

This book is printed on acid-free paper ∞

Manufactured in the United States of America

Table of Contents

List of Figures

Series Foreword

The lives of ancient peoples may seem far removed, socially, linguistically, and especially technologically, from the concerns of the modern world. Yet the popularity of historical subjects on both the big and little screens—*Troy, Alexander, 300*; HBO's *Rome,* the many History Channel programs—demonstrates the abiding fascination the ancient world continues to exert. Some people are drawn to the dramatic differences between the ancient and modern; others seek to find the origins for contemporary cultural features or the sources to provide meaning to our modern lives. Regardless of approach, the past holds something valuable for all of us. It is literally the root of who we are, physically through our actual ancestors, and culturally in establishing the foundations for our current beliefs and practices in religious, social, domestic and political arenas. The same ancients that we study were themselves drawn to their own pasts, often asking questions similar to the ones we pose today about our past.

The books in Praeger's series on the Ancient World address different topics from various perspectives. The ones on myth, sports, technology, warfare, and women explore these subjects cross-culturally, both within the ancient Mediterranean context—Egypt, Mesopotamia, Greece, Rome, and others—and between the ancient Mediterranean cultures and those of the Americas, Africa, and Asia. Others, including the volumes on literature, men, sexuality, and on politics and society, examine their topic more specifically within a Greek or Greek and Roman cultural framework.

All renowned scholars committed to bringing the fruits of their research to wider audiences, each author brings a distinctive new approach to their topic that differentiates them from the many books that exist on the ancient world. A major strength of the first group is their multicultural breadth, which is both informative in its comprehensive embrace and provides numerous opportunities for comparative insights. Likewise, the books in the second group explore their topics in dramatically new ways: the inner life of male identity; the contributions of both women and men to the social polity; the ancient constructions of concepts of sexuality and eroticism.

Bella Vivante
Series Editor, Praeger Series on the Ancient World

Acknowledgments

In addition to those many scholars listed in the bibliography, I owe special thanks to several persons. Chief of those is to Bella Vivante, editor of the Ancient Civilization series for Praeger, who invited me to return to topics that I had not visited for several decades just when I wanted a break from more modern materials. Second is to my Harvey Mudd College colleagues in the Department of Humanities, Social Sciences and the Arts who almost always appeared interested when I approached them with some new factoid that I wanted to regale them with and who then asked why my new bit of information was significant. Students in my Science and Technology in the Ancient and Medieval Worlds classes graciously served as test subjects for several sections of the text, catching many errors. Rudi Volti read most of the manuscript at various stages and has offered good advice, which I sometimes accepted. Individual chapters have been read by Marianne deLaet and Zoyue Wang, and Chang Tan has tried to keep my Chinese names and terms consistent with Pinyin usage. Figures 2.1 and 5.1 through 10.5 were drawn by my architect friend and golfing buddy, Nick Livingston, while all others were prepared by Joseph Emmert.

Several editors at Praeger and ABC-Clio have been friendly and helpful as they prodded and encouraged me to finish in a timely fashion and within a reasonable word limit. These include Brian Foster, Mary Theresa Church, and Elizabeth Potenza. The editorial team at Apex CoVantage is responsible for much of the clarity of the prose. As usual, my wife, Kathy Collins Olson, has been unfailingly supportive. Our new Corgi puppy, Parker, has, however, provided little but distractions.

Richard G. Olson
January 10, 2009

One

On Definitions, Approaches, and Periodization

Imagine a tunnel through a mountain built 2,500 years ago, begun at two opposite ends, constructed solely on basic geometric principles, and which meets in the middle, only two feet off alignment. Or consider an operation done 2,000 years ago to repair a compound fracture of a femur in which a wooden rod was inserted in the bone to stabilize the recovering bone segments. When we become aware of ancient people's technical accomplishments, we marvel at their ability to achieve these results without the benefit of modern scientific advances. This book explores the development of technology and science in the major civilizations of the ancient world, exploring the extent of their achievements and trying to account for how and why different civilizations developed different forms of specific technologies and sciences.

Despite our heavily scientific and technologically oriented world, it may come as a surprise that there has been little agreement on the meaning of these terms. Hence, this chapter begins by examining what is meant by the concepts of science and technology, and just what it is we are looking for when we wish to examine the processes and products associated with them in ancient civilizations. It will continue with an overview of the approach to technology and science in the ancient world represented in this work, set against a few powerful current alternative approaches. Then, it will conclude with a brief history of the seven major cultural areas to be considered: Mesopotamia, Egypt, the Indus Valley, China, early Central America, Greece, and Rome.

DEFINITIONS OF TECHNOLOGY, SCIENCE, CIVILIZATION, AND ANCIENT

Because each of these key terms is a matter of contention among those who write about the history of technology and science, some preliminary discussion of terms will allow readers to be aware of both some of the major ideological battles among historians of ancient technology and science and where I stand on a few important contentious issues.

Technology

In many ways, the least problematic of these central terms is technology, though even this apparently simple term has come in for extensive interpretation (Oldenziel 2006). Prior to 1829, a technology was a book or study about some practical art or craft. Modern usages, which focus on the productive tools and practices themselves, were initiated by Harvard professor Jacob Bigelow in his 1829 *Elements of Technology,* and draw on the ancient Greek term *techne,* which is usually translated into the English terms art or craft, as in "the art of ship making." Well into the 20th century, however, the term was not often used, and where we would now use technology, most people used "mechanic arts," "invention," or "useful arts."

One consideration that complicates our understanding of technology has been well articulated by Wiebe Bijker in his introduction to *The Social Construction of Technological Systems.* Bijker writes:

Technology is a slippery term. . . . Three layers of the meaning of the word can be distinguished. First, there is the level of *physical objects, or artifacts,* for example, bicycles, lamps, and Bakelite. Second, "technology," may refer to *activities or processes,* such as steel making or molding. Third, technology can refer to what people *know* as well as what they do; an example is the "know-how" that goes into designing a bicycle or operating an ultrasound device in the obstetrics clinic. (1989, 3–4)

The knowledge that is presumed to be a feature of a technology here is not the kind of formal theoretical knowledge usually associated with the notion of a science, but instead the kind of tacit knowledge that we mean when we say that someone like Joe Montana knew how to find an open receiver on the football field. In the ancient world, craft know-how was virtually always transmitted orally and/or bodily from master to apprentice and was not written down. It thus left virtually no record. Except in a few cases where we might assume that technologies in contemporary traditional societies involve a continuation of ancient practices, we have no access to this level of ancient technologies. Archeological investigations of ancient civilizations provide the most extensive knowledge of the artifactual dimension of technologies, though occasionally we do have evidence relating to processes used for producing objects, for example, when the remains of potter's wheels and kilns allow us to say something about the processes used for creating pottery.

A recent definition of technology, appearing in the Oxford University Press's *International Encyclopedia of Science and Technology,* raises another issue. It includes the following comment: "Often the term is used to describe any practical application of scientific discoveries in the production of mechanisms and in the solution of problems that confront human beings" (Luck 1999, 353). We will consider the relationships between science and technology much more extensively in the next section of this chapter, but it is certainly the case that few, if any, ancient technologies could reasonably be considered applied sciences. Indeed, ancient sciences were much more likely to emerge out of technological practices, rather than vice versa.

Finally, a definition developed by the distinguished historian of early man, V. Gordon Childe, raises another issue. He writes: "Technology should mean those activities, directed to the satisfaction of human needs, which produce alterations to the material world [along with] the results of those activities" (2004, 155). Since most arts and crafts do involve changes to the material world, it is easy to accept such a definition, but the one extensive list of *techne* which we have from the ancient world—the list of "all the arts that men possess" which Aeschylus's Prometheus presents as his gifts to humankind—includes written language, mathematics, techniques of building in brick and wood, calendrical astronomy, techniques of divination and omenology, the domestication of animals, ship building, medicine, and metallurgy (Aeschylus 1926, 449–471). Of these, at least two—calendrical astronomy and divination, or omenology—do not involve direct alterations to the material world and they meet needs or wants which are not physical but are instead social or psychological.

Rudi Volti has offered a provisional definition of technology that leaves open all of the issues mentioned above, including the relative roles of artifacts, knowledge, and organization, the degree of importance of material goals relative to social, psychological, and organizational ones, the relationship between technologies and systematic, recorded, knowledge of the natural world, and the character of the relationships between technologies and the societies from which they emerge, and I will try to be consistent in using his definition throughout what follows. Volti writes that a technology is: "a system based on the application of knowledge, manifested in physical objects and organizational forms, for the attainment of specific goals" (1995, 6). Just one comment may be important regarding this definition, especially but not solely in connection with technologies of divination. Though a technology may be aimed at a specific goal, its greatest importance may be in connection with unintended consequences. Thus, for example, in the modern world the adhesive that made Post-it Notes possible was initially developed for a completely different purpose. Similarly, in the ancient world, astronomical techniques that were initially intended to predict the outcome of terrestrial events for divinatory purposes served much more effectively for the creation of calendars. In some cases then, it seems that technologies which come into existence for one reason may, by virtue of making new opportunities available, create new demands or needs, and those cases may be of tremendous importance. The human use of fire, for example, almost certainly developed to protect humans from animals or from the cold, but once available regularly, fire provided a way to transform materials to serve a wide variety of human needs—for making bricks and pottery that would not dissolve in water, for creating edible and long lasting cooked food and drink out of inedible and/or easily rotted raw materials, and eventually for creating metal objects out of ores and valuable and useful distilled liquids out of relatively cheap and little desired raw stocks.

Science

If technology is the least problematic of our central terms, science is probably the most problematic because it has long been at the center of heated debates not only among historians from differing interpretive schools, but among self-professed scientists as well. The current controversies regarding the meaning and characterization of science grew out of a World War II and early Cold War conflict between a group of British Marxist scientists and interpreters of science, including J. D. Bernal, Benjamin Farrington, and Joseph Needham, who focused on the social and political contexts for the development and uses of science on the one hand, and a group of scientists and students of science, including Michael Polanyi, Robert Merton, and Vannevar Bush, who sought to focus on the freedom of good science from politics and social needs on the other.

The first group, which founded the Society for Social Responsibility in Science, argued that science emerged in response to the material needs of society and that it was corrupted in the ancient world when it became a kind of game to be played by a social elite freed from productive activity by the exploitation of slave labor or by the creation of a social hierarchy that divorced craft activity from theoretical concerns. The views of J. D. Bernal were and continue to be characteristic of this group and their intellectual descendants, a group that has included the vast majority of students of non-Western ancient technology and science into the present. Bernal writes:

It was the ways of extracting and fashioning materials so they could be used as tools to satisfy the prime needs of man from which first techniques and then science arose. A technique is an individually acquired and socially secured way of doing something: *a science is a way of understanding how to do it in order to do it better.* When we come to examine in greater detail . . . the first appearance of distinct sciences and the stages of their development it will become increasingly plain that they evolve only when they are in close contact and living with the mechanism of production. (1971 Vol. 1, 47 [emphasis mine])

To give the notion that science emerges only out of practical affairs a patina of age, Marxist-influenced historians often refer to the ancient Greek historian, Herodotus, who argued that geometry emerged first in Egypt in response to the need for measuring land (geo–metry) in order to reestablish boundaries after the flooding of the Nile. Modern scholars often challenge the details of Herodotus's claim, but they continue to place the growth of mathematics in practical activities such as brick making (Chattopadhyaya 1986) or commercial record keeping (Nissen, Damerow, and Englund 1993).

If science evolves only in connection with manual activity, then it follows that one can explain why a nascent science stagnated in any particular place by pointing to social forces that tended to separate the hand from the head. Thus, Debiprasad Chattopadhyaya, the distinguished historian of ancient Indian science and follower of Bernal and Needham, argues that early Indic science associated with Harappan culture in the Indus Valley died out after approximately 1750 B.C.E. because of the rise of caste society: "The main cause of the decline of the scientific spirit in India was the entrench-ment of caste society with its disastrous degradation of the social status of the technicians, craftsmen, and other manual workers" (Chattopadhyaya 1989, 9).

Opposed to the Marxist vision of a science intimately involved in produc-tive processes was an openly anti-utilitarian and elitist strain associated with a gentleman amateur tradition that grew during the 18th and 19th centuries and which was articulated in a particularly blatant way by Henry Augustus Rowland, America's first Nobel Prize winner, in his final address as President of the American Physical Society in 1899. Speaking to his fellow physicists, he said:

In a country where the doctrine of the equal rights of man has been distorted to mean the equality of man in other respects, we form a small and unique body of men, . . . whose views of what constitutes the greatest achievement in life are very different from those around us. In this respect we form an aristocracy, not of wealth, not of pedigree, but of intellect and ideals, holding him in the highest rank who adds most to our knowledge or who strives after it as the highest good. . . . Much of the in-tellect of the country is still wasted in the pursuit of the so-called practical science which ministers to our physical needs and but little thought and money is given to that grander portion of the subject which appeals to our intellect alone. (Reingold 1964, 324)

Once again, those promoting a particular view of the motives for the growth and character of science could appeal to an ancient Greek author to sup-port their position. Aristotle's account of the early growth of mathematics, like that of Herodotus, placed its origins in ancient Egypt, but it offers a very different explanation for why it merged there. After describing the origin of the arts in his *Metaphysics,* Aristotle writes: "When all such inventions were already established, the sciences which deal neither with the necessities nor with the enjoyments of life were discovered. And this took place earliest in the places where men first began to have leisure. That is why the mathemat-ical arts were founded in Egypt, for the priestly caste was allowed to have leisure" (981b, 20–25).

My own preference is to offer a definition of science that allows for both utilitarian and nonutilitarian motives and which incorporates the maximum number of features of modern science that can simultaneously be used re-garding ancient activities with relatively few qualifications. The following definition of science, which I first articulated in 1982, will be used through-out this work:

Science is taken to be a set of activities and habits of mind aimed at contributing to an organized, universally valid, and testable body of knowledge about phenom-ena. At any given time [and place] these general characteristics are usually embodied in systems of concepts, rules of procedure, theories, and/or model investigations that are widely accepted by groups of practitioners—the scientific specialists. (Olson 1982, 7–8)

Several comments should be made about this definition. First, especially for the earliest civilizations, for which archeological evidence is often more important than textual evidence, one must infer motives and attitudes because they are not often explicitly addressed. In such cases, I will try to give at least a plausibility argument for such inferences, relating them to textual evidence that might exist in comparison civilizations. Second, the notion of testability may vary widely from one set of local circumstances to another— for many early places and times, the simple fact that a knowledge claim is useful for some purpose may be considered as a test of its legitimacy. In other places and times, meeting formal logical criteria has been a necessary and even sometimes a sufficient test of a science, while in yet other places and times, meeting certain standards of empirical confirmation has been understood to be a necessary element of testing a scientific knowledge claim. Establishing the extent of demand and the ways to provide for empirical confirmation of scientific truth claims is one of the most important ways in which the notion that a scientific community at any place and time establishes—either explicitly or implicitly—its own standards and rules of practice.

Finally, the meaning of universality may vary from local context to local context. With respect to ancient science, the term indicates that scientific knowledge was intended to be applicable to classes of phenomena rather than singular phenomena. Most ancient myths deal with unique events— the creation of the world, the origins of shade tree gardening, the success of a local army in a particular battle, the particular lightning bolt that struck Odysseus's ship, and so on. Scientific knowledge, on the other hand, was intended to explain lightning in general, the long-term repetitive behavior of the celestial bodies, the cause for the growth of all plants, and the like. In modern terms, universality is usually extended to include the claim that scientific knowledge claims should hold for all times and places. Whatever definition of universality we accept, the notion that scientists seek universally valid knowledge does not imply that they ever find it. The Christian admonition to love one's neighbor as one's self is impossible for many, if any, of us to achieve, but it nonetheless shapes the behavior of many Christians. By the same token, even though universally valid knowledge may well be impossible to achieve, the attempt to find it may well influence the behavior of those we would call scientists.

Civilization

By almost all modern secular accounts, humans have existed for at least 500,000, and probably for closer to 2 million, years. Up until just over 10,000 years ago, they all lived in tribal groups of a few dozen adults and subsisted on natural vegetation, usually gathered by women and children, and meat from wild animals, usually hunted by adult males. So, for between 98 and 99.5 percent of human existence, we were primarily hunters and gatherers using stone, bone, and wood tools and living without permanent settlements. Archeological and anthropological evidence suggests some gender-based divisions of labor, the probable existence of special shamanistic functions, and the existence of ritual acts including burials and ceremonies associated with hunting that began no later than 50,000 years ago. Then, around 10,000 years ago, both some plants and some animals were domesticated in relatively dry highland areas where grains such as wheat and barley grew naturally.

The additional food made available by dry land agriculture allowed the growth of fixed settlements, which typically housed 200–500 inhabitants, but occasionally reached populations estimated to be up to 5,000 persons with a significant division of labor at places like Catal Hüyük in southwestern Anatolia and Jericho in Palestine. Archeological evidence suggests the greater specialization of craft activities, such as painted pottery making, cloth making, leather working, the beginnings of metal working, and probably of religious functions as well, though it seems likely that even specialized functionaries also took part in primary food production for much of their time. The fortification of towns, first with stone, and then with shaped-masonry walls, began at Jericho. There is evidence of permanent private houses in open spaces to replace cave dwellings and temporary homes built of local vegetable matter, and the presence of materials that came from distant places indicates the development of extensive trade patterns. Conspicuously absent during this period of growing agriculture and pastoralism is any form of writing or any clear evidence of political hierarchy.

Approximately 5,500 years ago another transformation began to take place—what Gordon Childe labeled the first Urban Revolution (Childe 1950, 3–17), and what we identify as the rise of the first civilizations. Childe listed a series of features that characterized the formation of what he considered to be the earliest cities in Egypt, Mesopotamia, and the Indus Valley. Among the most important was the creation of more extensive settlements with higher population densities (a minimum estimated population of about 5,000 persons in a single settlement of less than one square kilometer has often been accepted as a standard). These cities incorporated classes of persons who were not engaged in primary food production but who were supported by the surplus created by irrigation agriculture and stored in communal granaries. Some of these persons were engaged in traditional crafts and in transporting and selling goods, but others were priests, managers, and military leaders who constituted a ruling class that absorbed a substantial share of the surplus in return for organizing, maintaining and protecting the public works (e.g., canals, granaries, roads, marketplaces, and houses of worship) and distributing the foodstuffs needed to sustain the city's functioning. Cities, moreover, were also characterized by the beginnings of monumental public buildings.

From our perspective, the sixth of Childe's features is particularly important:

They [the ruling class] were in fact compelled to invent systems of recording and exact, but practically useful sciences. The mere administration of the vast revenues of a Sumerian temple or an Egyptian pharaoh by a perpetual corporation of priests or officials obliged its members to devise conventional methods of recording that should be intelligible to their colleagues and successors, that is, to invent systems of writing and numerical notation. Writing is thus a significant, as well as a convenient, mark of civilization. (Childe 1950, 14)

Because there is a sense in which we can say nothing about science in a nonliving culture that left no written records, *for our purposes writing of some kind will be taken as the defining characteristic of civilization in all that follows,* though we will not assume that Childe's account of the origins of writing are necessarily correct for all civilizations.

Childe admitted that many subsequent urbanizations, for example, those in Crete and classical Greece and Rome, did not have to exhibit all, or even many, of the features of the earliest cities because they drew on the experiences of their progenitors. He did, however, suggest that the first cities everywhere, if they were independent of the initial big three, probably emerged in much the same way. This notion was turned into a complete theory of early civilizations by the Sinologist Karl Wittfogel, whose 1957 *Oriental Despotism: A Comparative Study of Total Power* (Wittfogel 1957) extended Childe's analysis to encompass early Chinese and American Pre-Colombian societies. Wittfogel then went on to argue that the need to control and distribute water produced centralized empires and bureaucracies that were hostile to change. Given this situation, the dynamic rise of Western Europe, which avoided the early patterns of urbanization, could be understood as standing out from the background of older hydraulic civilizations.

Almost immediately after Wittfogel's 1957 publication, criticisms of his hydraulic theory of civilization began to appear. Scholars began to qualify and modify it (Adams 1960), though some elements remain in almost all subsequent discussions of the rise of civilizations. All major early civilizations did seem to arise in connection with the movement of agriculture onto the floodplains of rivers and with the consequent increases in agricultural productivity; but some early civilizations, including those of Egypt and the Pre-Columbian Americas produced written records, formal state structures, and monumental architecture long before they produced large cities. Indeed, it is not clear that the Mayan civilization ever produced cities of 5,000 or more inhabitants, nor is it clear that early China or India developed large-scale irrigation technologies like those found in Mesopotamia or Egypt. Even in Mesopotamia, life in cities and the emergence of complex social organization seems to have predated both writing and the beginnings of the large-scale irrigation systems that Childe and Wittfogel had argued necessitated both urbanization and the need for complex social arrangements. Finally, Mesopotamian culture was far from static in terms of its technology and science, and prior to the Akkadian invasions of the late third millennium, the cities of Mesopotamia tended to be independent or competitive with one another rather than constrained by any central imperial apparatus.

My goal will be to avoid accepting at the outset any particular model for how civilization must have arisen, what kinds of political organizations must emerge out of technological demands, and what kinds of political and social hierarchies are more or less likely to promote practical or theoretical innovation. These will be treated as interesting and important but open questions in what follows.

Ancient

Finally, we arrive at the decision of what to count as an "ancient" civilization. Within the Western historical tradition, which traditionally periodizes the past into ancient, medieval, early modern, modern, and contemporary eras, ancient civilization begins in Southern Mesopotamia during the mid-fourth millennium before the Common Era and ends with the fall of the Roman Empire around 476 C.E. Since archeological evidence has yet to suggest that writing appeared anywhere else prior to around 3500 B.C.E., it makes sense to pick up the story of civilization at that time and place. Furthermore, because Western readers have, by convention, looked upon the fall of Rome as the end of the ancient period in the West, we, too, shall accept that notion. But how are we to mark the end the ancient period in India, China, and Mesoamerica, where the fall of Rome had no real significance? In each specific case, I will try to choose a terminal date that makes sense in terms of local historical circumstances.

Approaches to the History of Ancient Technologies and Sciences

The attempt to understand the origins and decline of science in connection with status hierarchies in society has occasionally led Marxist-oriented historians into an alliance with another tradition that has had great importance in connection with the history of science—a tradition associated with the term positivism and the doctrines of the early 19th century French philosopher and historian of science Auguste Comte. For present purposes, the most important feature of Comte's positivism is his Law of Three Stages. According to this law:

Each of our leading conceptions—each branch of our knowledge—passes successively through three different historical conditions: the Theological, or fictitious; the Metaphysical, or abstract; and the Scientific, or positive. In other words, the human mind, by its nature, employs in its progress three methods of philosophizing, the character of which is essentially different, and even radically opposed: viz., the theological method, the metaphysical, and the positive. (Comte 1855, 25)

From this positivist perspective, science and religion must ultimately always be in conflict with one another, and religion can function in relation to science only by establishing barriers to the growth of science—which represents a later and more advanced stage of thought. Marxism, as a materialist and atheistic perspective, shares with positivism its antagonism to religion and Marxist scholars have often appropriated the antireligious arguments of positivist historians, especially when they see priesthoods as initiating the kind of status hierarchies that value intellectual activity over material production. I have argued extensively elsewhere on both theoretical and empirical grounds against the Positivist and Marxist claim that science and religion are inevitably at war with one another (Olson 2004, 5–7). Here it is enough to point out that, in most cases for which we have compelling evidence regarding ancient civilizations, religious and secular medical traditions coexisted in relative peace, and in the case of ancient Greece, the greatest flowering of Aesclepiad (religious) healing and post-dated the highest period of rational Hippocratic medicine, rather than preceded it. There were undoubtedly places and times when it is appropriate to see specific sciences and specific religions in some sort of competition or conflict with one another in the ancient world, but as we shall see, there were also times and places in which religious traditions motivated and propagated scientific knowledge and learning and in which scientific knowledge played a central role in promoting a new religion. In what follows, I will always consider science and religion interactions as matters open to a wide range of interpretations rather than restricted a priori to hostile ones.

Just as Marxist scientists and historians of science found support for some of their key arguments in the anti-theological elements of positivism, those who sought the autonomy of science from social pressures found support in other aspects of positivism. Comte argued that science was pursued for two all but unrelated motives—the satisfaction of a psychological need to dispose facts in a comprehensible order regardless of any notion of utility and the prediction of phenomena in order to be able to act in and on the world. That is, he argued that both nonutilitarian and utilitarian aims operate in motivating scientific activity. But Comte insisted that even if one was developing scientific knowledge for purposes of application, it was only if one could step back and produce a value-free, dispassionate knowledge, that knowledge would provide a completely adequate foundation for subsequent action. What had led the astrologers, alchemists, and medical practitioners of antiquity astray was their passionate interest in the outcome of their investigations. Only by establishing what we now call an objective stance, freed from emotional attachment, can true scientific knowledge be generated. Thus, he wrote in an essay of 1822, "Admiration and reprobation of phenomena ought to be banished from every positive science, because all preoccupations of this sort directly and unavoidably tend to hinder or mislead examination. Astronomers, physicists, chemists, and physiologists [unlike astrologers, alchemists, and physicians] neither admire nor blame their respective phenomena. They observe them" (Lenzer 1975, 54).

Comte and his 19th century followers had generally agreed that, while positive knowledge was the most reliable available at any time and place, it could not achieve the status of absolute and universal truth. Thus, Comte wrote:

The study of the laws of phenomena must be relative since it supposes a continuous progress of speculation subject to gradual improvement of observation, without the precise reality ever being fully disclosed: so that the relative character of scientific conceptions is inseparable from the true idea of natural laws, just as the chimerical inclination for absolute knowledge accompanies every use of theological fictions and metaphysical entities. (Comte 1855, 453)

This recognition is particularly important as we consider scientific knowledge in ancient civilizations, for the fact that from our present perspective ancient authors were either vague or completely wrong does *not* mean that they were not being scientific.

It is important to understand that the question of whether a Marxist-oriented historiography of science or an intellectualist historiography is more nearly correct is not a well formulated or answerable question, because the two traditions *define* science in different ways, one insisting upon the close connection between science and technology and one explicitly insisting upon a separation. Each definition has met the needs of a particular community for a significant period of time, and both traditions have provided important insights into the creation of ancient understandings of the character of the uniformities to be discovered in the behavior of entities in the world. Recently, however, scholars have begun to develop approaches to the history of science and technology which open up, rather than foreclose, questions regarding such issues as the relationships between science and technology at particular places and times and the relationship between religious traditions and scientific ones. There is, of course, not complete agreement among these various scholars regarding how to define science.

Nationalism and the Historiography of Science and Technology

The study of ancient science and technology in some locations has not only been subject to biases induced by ideological commitments to Marxism, positivism, democracy, or intellectual freedom, it has also been subject to nationalistic and/or anti-Eurocentric biases. Ancient documents and artifacts have thus often been interpreted (and possibly distorted) in such a way as to make them appear more consistent with modern cosmopolitan scientific ideas and practices or technological artifacts than might seem reasonable to a less biased interpreter because the authors have wanted to glorify a tradition with which they identify. Gyan Prakash has, for example, discussed the tendency for early Indian nationalists to interpret Vedic (early Hindu) texts in ways that seem implausible to many scholars today in order to find the origins of much scientific knowledge in ancient India (Prakash 1999).

My Own Eclectic Approach

With respect to issues of bias, I take a position often called feminist point of view epistemology. That is, I doubt seriously whether any scholar can be completely objective and unbiased no matter how hard he or she tries. I thus welcome those scholars who openly admit their points of view, for that invites the reader to be particularly careful in evaluating their arguments and evidentiary claims. In this spirit, I should admit that, while I hope that I am not Eurocentric in the sense that I would deny the non-Western origins of many important technologies and scientific developments, I am inclined to be skeptical of claims of great antiquity unsupported by archeological or strong textual evidence because I know that claims of antiquity have been used to give authority to knowledge claims in many cultures. Similarly, I am inclined to favor the idea that comparable artifacts or arguments have independent origins in different cultures unless a strong case can be made for cultural borrowing because I am convinced both that responses to similar problems in similar environments are likely to be similar and because of the important role that contingency plays in history. Again, I find the analogy with evolution suggestive. We know that eyes developed independently in many evolutionary contexts, in each of which chance variations played a large role. For the same reason, we might expect that similar technologies might have developed independently in different places.

Though not a theist, I am a practicing member of an organized religion, so I am inclined to grant religion both positive roles and negative ones in society. I am by temperament what Steven Jay Gould called a lumper, rather than a splitter. That is, I am more inclined to be fascinated by the likenesses among apparently diverse things than to emphasize the differences among apparently like things, so I will probably focus on the similarities between technologies and sciences in different ancient contexts when I can find them, though I will not completely ignore differences. Finally, I seem to have a special affinity for the ironic, so I am inclined to notice and remark on the unexpected and counterintuitive connections among things.

The Structure of This Book and My Choice of Technologies and Sciences to Emphasize

I am particularly interested in technologies and sciences in ancient civilizations for three fundamental reasons, each of which plays a role in the structure of this book. First, mainstream history of science has been written almost exclusively from a Western perspective. Until very recently, even histories of non-Western scientific traditions, including the monumental studies of Chinese science done by Joseph Needham and his collaborators (Needham, et. al. 1954–2004) have primarily reflected Western scientific practices and values. Serious attempts to compare the conditions of scientific knowledge production and use in different civilizations began primarily with a series of explorations of Attic Greek and Chinese science and medicine by G. E. R. Lloyd and by Lloyd and Nathan Sivin, which were initiated fewer than 15 years ago (Lloyd 1996; Lloyd and Sivin 2002); and the first English-language textbook to attempt to integrate the history of science and technology into a world- historical and not exclusively Eurocentric account appeared only in 1999 (McClellan and Dorn 1999).

My goal is to extend the comparative approach initiated by Lloyd and Sivin—though not just their great emphasis on political ideology—beyond China and Greece to most of the major civilizations of the ancient world. This goal has led to the thematic structure of the book in which each chapter explores an isolated technology and science cluster across multiple civilizations rather than a broad range of sciences and technologies in each isolated civilization. I have neither the expertise nor the space to offer the detail achieved by Lloyd and Sivin, but I do hope to offer an approach that is both deeper than that of McClellan and Dorn and more insistently comparative.

Second, my primary interests involve those technologies and sciences that were most centrally implicated in the daily experiences of the citizens of ancient civilizations—those that involved the production and distribution of food, shelter, and clothing as well as their landscapes and mindscapes. These interests are well served by emphasizing the *techne* listed by Prometheus, which include mathematics (chapter 2), written language (chapter 3), astronomy (chapters 4 and 5), divination (chapters 4 and 6), medicine (chapters 6 and 7), construction methods (chapter 8), and metallurgy/mineralogy (chapter 10). To these topics I have added one, the production, distribution, and consumption of food (chapter 9) that Prometheus hints at in *Prometheus Bound* by mentioning the domestication of animals. (Aeschylus 1926, 463–465). In part because the earliest archeological investigations of early civilizations were carried out in connection with military occupations and by European military officers engaging in their hobbies, ancient military technologies have received much attention elsewhere, thus I have felt no need to pay special attention to them, though I have not avoided military considerations where they have been important in connection with construction and metallurgy, for example.

Finally, because I am by training and inclination fascinated by theoretical knowledge as much as or more than by knowledge that is immediately embodied in the daily practices of material production, I have chosen to emphasize the variety of ways in which technological traditions and what I identify as theoretical, or scientific, traditions interacted in ancient civilizations. These emphases are special focal points in chapters 2, 3, 4, 7, and 10.

Historical Background

Before turning to the technologies and sciences of ancient civilizations, we pause here to briefly provide the basic geographical and political settings for what follows. Even if we do not fully subscribe to Wittfogel's hydraulic theory of civilization, there is no doubt that local geography helps to account for important features of each ancient civilization that we will be discussing.

Mesopotamia

Sumerian civilization developed initially in the late fifth millennium near the mouths of the Tigris and Euphrates Rivers, where they produced a marshy alluvial fan as they emptied into the Persian Gulf, which then reached much farther north than it does now. Living in small villages in reed huts, the earliest Sumerians subsisted by farming, fishing, and herding. As time went on, the climate became dryer, and it seems to have become necessary to begin to irrigate fields during the dry season. Since the spring floods of the Tigris and Euphrates Valley were generally short lived and violent, dikes to protect agricultural lands, to divert water into holding ponds, and to provide for irrigation in the dry had to be massive and sturdy—small-scale systems would not do—thus emerged the large cities and social hierarchies suggested by Childe and Wittfogel. At least during the initial period of rapid growth, however, the major cities of ancient Sumer seem to have been largely independent of one another and dominated internally by large temple complexes whose leaders served as the central managers of the agricultural economies and food distribution networks in the name of the gods that they served. The chief priests were literally the "chief tenant farmers of the god X."

Because the Mesopotamian floodplain produced large agricultural surpluses but was relatively destitute of both wood and minerals, temple complexes also entered into trade with peoples as far away as the Indus Valley and the British Isles to get both raw materials and finished goods. In the earliest days, several temple complexes might exist within a single city, though as time went on it became more common for a single temple complex to dominate. By the mid-third millennium, these cities, which were very rich by the standards of the time, became tempting targets for invaders from the hills and for neighboring cities. Organizational leadership tended to pass from the priests to military kings and their retainers, who slowly wrested control of economic resources from the temples. By the late third millennium, Akkadian invaders had assumed military and political control and had formed the formerly independent cities into an empire usually controlled by the king of Babylon, which provided the political, economic, military, and intellectual leadership of the region from around 2000 B.C.E. until the invasion of the armies of Alexander the Great around 330 B.C.E.

Egypt

Around 5000 B.C.E., settlements were established in the Nile River Valley, nearly 900 years earlier than those documented for Mesopotamia. As North Africa became increasingly arid between around 9000 B.C.E. and 5000 B.C.E., people began to settle in the valley of the Nile, the longest river in the world, which carried water down from the mountains in East Africa to the Mediterranean Sea. Because there were major deposits of metals in what is now the desert surrounding the canyon created by the river, these people seem to have brought copper and gold with them. By around 4000 B.C.E., villages dotted the canyon floor over a nearly 660-mile path. The valley varied from less than a mile and a half in width at Aswan to about 11 miles near el-Amarna and then spread out into a marshy delta as the Nile split into many channels north of Memphis and made its way to the sea. During the period between about 3800 B.C.E. and 3200 B.C.E., the villages and towns of southern, or upper Egypt, were first united into small dominions ruled over by chiefs and then into a single kingdom. Northern, or lower Egypt, which constituted the delta region, seems to have been somewhat more loosely organized, but around 3100 B.C.E., northern and southern Egypt were unified under a single king, who became identified as a divine pharaoh.

Though the annual floods of the Nile could vary tremendously in depth and extent, causing serious problems both when they were too high and long and when they were too low and short, the floodwaters typically rose and retreated slowly, arriving sometime in mid-June and departing in mid October, leaving a rich layer of wet silt over the land and the underground aquifers filled. Irrigation ditches were dug to carry water past the normal edges of the river during the dry season, but the only maintenance they usually needed was minor clearing because currents rarely exceeded 10 miles per hour at the center of the river even during the highest floods. There was, therefore, little reason for the agricultural population to congregate in large cities to construct and maintain complex irrigation systems during the Archaic period (c. 3200–2780 B.C.E.), which included the first two dynasties.

During the Early Dynastic period, as the central government became increasingly powerful, large administrative centers became full-fledged cities. This, or Thinis, probably reached around 10,000 inhabitants during the early Old Kingdom period (c. 2780–2130 B.C.E.), which included dynasties 3–6, and Memphis became even larger when the center of government moved there around 2200 B.C.E. The early Old Kingdom period saw Egypt divided into 42 administrative regions, or nomes, each presided over by a provincial governor, or nomarch, whose primary allegiance was to the central government. Initially, these nomarchs tended to move from one nome to another throughout their careers, so they did not develop strong local power bases. During the second half of the third millennium, however, the central government became weaker, probably as consequence of a long dry period with weak floods that decimated the economy. Consequently, local officials grew in strength, leading to a period during which strong families became the hereditary nomarchs of nomes. There was a second flowering of central authority during the Middle Kingdom (c. 1938–1630 B.C.E. and dynasties 11–14) followed by a period of foreign rule over all but a small region around Thebes by a people known as the Hyksos. Thebian leaders recaptured the Nile Valley and Delta, spreading outward into an empire that included part of the eastern Mediterranean during the New Kingdom, which flourished from about 1500 to around 1180 B.C.E. (dynasties 18–20). After that time, Egypt was usually ruled by outsiders—Persians and later, during the Hellenistic Period (from 332–30 B.C.E.) by Greeks, and then, until the end of the Ancient world, by Romans.

India

Very little is known about the background of the Indus Valley civilization, usually called "Harappan," after the first major site excavated. Village culture is evidenced in the large drainage basin of the Indus River and its feeders as early as the seventh millennium. There is little evidence of change prior to around 2750 B.C.E. when an advanced urban civilization seems to have spread rapidly across a huge region approximately 600 miles by 300 miles) with tremendously varied geography. Some regions undoubtedly saw Nile-like seasonal floods, and there is evidence that some crops were planted immediately after the flood, with a probability that other crops—including cotton—were planted during a second growing season. Other regions were covered in dense jungle that had to be cleared for agriculture, while still others seem to have seen floods more like the violent ones that were common in Mesopotamia. Throughout the region, it seems clear that the urban economies were based on food surpluses made available by floodplain agri-culture, though very little evidence of extensive irrigation or of even simple agricultural implements has been found. Nonetheless, huge grain storage complexes were built. These help us to estimate the population of the largest sites at between 35,000 and 42,000 persons.

The Harappan civilization sites, unlike the earliest sites in Mesopotamia or Egypt, were carefully laid out on a north-south and east-west pattern with extremely wide major thoroughfares and narrower side streets. These and other features make it quite probable that they developed independently of their neighbors to the west, even though there is strong evidence that they traded with the Mesopotamians. There is writing carved in brick and stone, but the small number of symbols (around 300) and the short length of all known inscriptions (the longest is 34 characters) have made it impossible to decipher the writing. As a consequence, there are no written records that presently inform us about Harappan religion, trade, or politics. The nearly uniform town planning and the massive architecture associated with public facilities such as baths and granaries suggests the existence of a common imperial government, but gravesites show little evidence of social hierarchy. There are, for example, no royal tombs containing riches and/or retainers, like those that appear in Mesopotamia, Egypt, and China.

The early Indus civilization throughout most of the region collapsed even more rapidly than it rose, almost certainly as a result of both geo-tectonic activity, which shifted river channels, and conquest by an unknown people around 1750 B.C.E. As we shall see, elements of Harappan technology prob-ably persisted, but writing and urban settlements effectively disappeared from northern India for about 1,000 years. During the period between roughly 1750 B.C.E. and 500 B.C.E., there was no writing in India, village-based farming spread eastward into the Ganges basin, and the beginnings of a caste system—initially a four-level system comprised of priests, warrior-nobles, farmers, and craftsmen—and servants is found. Sometime during the second half of this period, a vast oral literature associated with the term *Rgveda-samhita*, and consisting of over 1,000 songs and hymns was composed.

The Vedas were primarily religious, but they also incorporated technical and scientific information and commentaries. This collection was written down by the priestly class with the development of writing sometime around 500 B.C.E. Though there were Persian and, later, Macedonian invasions beginning in the sixth century B.C.E., Chandragupta Maurya unified almost all of India around 311 B.C.E. into an empire that lasted for approximately 100 years. Documentary evidence from this period indicates that there was an extensive irrigation network organized by a state bureaucracy and that the Mauryan Empire had virtually all of those characteristics that Wittfogel suggested were characteristic of hydraulic civilizations—though it was late and short-lived. India was not reunited for nearly 500 years after the collapse of the Mauryan Empire, so its end forms a logical place to end the discussion of ancient India.

China

Like the Indus Valley, the valleys of the Yellow River and its tributaries in what is now China exhibit substantially diverse characteristics. In the West, the smaller valleys of tributary streams constitute upland plateaus in the hill country below substantially higher mountains, while toward the East there is a massive central plain closer to sea level. Both the upland plateaus and the central plain, however, share a basic soil—a very fine black earth called loess, which seems to have been deposited largely by winds during the Pleistocene period (1.8 million–12,000 B.C.E.). This soil, which reaches almost 300 feet in depth in some places of the central plain, is some of the richest soil in the world. Before 2000 B.C.E., archeological records evidence several hunting, herding, and agricultural cultures that still practiced slash-and-burn agriculture (and thus did not establish permanent towns) throughout the region.

Around 2000 B.C.E., population densities increased, stratified societies emerged both in the upland west and in the central valley, and permanent settlements became more common. The western, Yangshao, culture still depended heavily on hunting and produced pottery without the use of a wheel. The eastern, Longshan, culture probably depended on some degree of irrigation for its agriculture, used wheels for the production of its pottery, produced more permanent and larger villages, often surrounded by walls, and used a form of divination based on cracks produced in bone by a heated metal point. This culture spread rapidly southward and eastward into the Yangtze Valley and beyond.

It is likely that many small regions dominated by single powerful individuals existed from around 2000 B.C.E. to around 1600 B.C.E., when most of China was unified under the Shang dynasty, which lasted until 1028 B.C.E. By sometime around 1500 B.C.E., the capital of the Shang dynasty was moved to a site near Anyang where excavation has unearthed both the first Chinese writing and numbering (on about 10,000 oracle bones otherwise identical to the uninscribed Longshan bones) as well as a double-walled city that almost certainly housed at least 20,000 persons. This city was probably an administrative center dependent on the agricultural products of a large number of much smaller villages, such as had emerged earlier in Egypt. As in Egypt, Shang China saw the development of a state structure dominated by a single king or emperor who claimed ownership of all land and surrounded himself with a class of court officials who owed their primary allegiance to him. Members of a noble class held most important positions, while commoners whose service could occasionally raise their status held lower positions. Regions far from the central capital were often ruled by local strongmen who had their own court-official systems and who occasionally challenged the authority of the central state, so there was almost always a condition of warfare somewhere in China.

Around 1028 B.C.E., Wu Wang, a warlord who managed to form an alliance with several tribes from the Western region, defeated the Shang dynasty, and created the Zhou dynasty. The Zhou conquerors established an imperial overlay on top of Shang culture and imported a religion incorporating both Heaven worship and ancestor worship, which became the foundation for all later Chinese religions and sociopolitical ideologies. One consequence of the Zhou military conquest was the partial separation of the Zhou aristocracy, which was in charge of the military presence, from the bureaucratic officialdom and custodians of rituals and morality, composed primarily of scholars from the original Shang population. The Zhou Empire was never very stable, and by around 770 B.C.E., military control of the empire was separated from the Emperor, whose power became largely symbolic and religious and whose function was primarily to serve as an arbiter in conflicts among de facto independent regional lords. From about 480 B.C.E. to 221 B.C.E., there was no single lord capable of uniting a significant portion of China, so this period is known as the Warring States period.

During the Zhou and Warring States periods, the Chinese economy changed dramatically and there was a spectacular flowering of intellectual life that almost certainly benefited from competition among local leaders for distinguished scholars. Increasing agricultural yields based on more extensive irrigation produced the same kind of division of labor and growth of specialized craft production that had occurred centuries earlier in Mesopotamia. Cities grew until they had populations that exceeded 200,000 persons, and merchants who traded both locally and with Western cultures as far away as the Mediterranean became increasingly powerful, even displacing land holding aristocracies in some places. In 256 B.C.E., the last Zhou emperor abdicated in favor of the ruler of the state of Qin, a state in the north-central region of present-day China that was economically advanced and in which the older, land-based aristocracy had been displaced. By 221 B.C.E., the Qin ruler, Qin Shi Huang, had conquered all of the remaining states and had become the effective and titular Emperor of China, creating a new bureaucracy with primary allegiance to him. In order to stamp out the last vestiges of Zhou ideals, in 213 B.C.E. the Qin Emperor ordered all books other than technical treatises burned, so much traditional knowledge and history was lost, though a small amount has recently been recovered from tombs. At roughly the same time, the Qin began to piece together local defensive walls to form the Great Wall of China in order to protect the empire from northern marauders.

With the death of the Qin emperor in 206 B.C.E., a power struggle among many factions eventuated in the rise of a lower class rebel soldier from a farming background, Liu Bang (later given the Imperial name "Gaozu"), who called his dynasty the Han dynasty. Exhibiting the typical farmer's disdain for merchants, Gaozu looked to land-holding families—sometimes descendants of the older Zhou nobility, and sometimes upwardly mobile commoners who had acquired substantial estates—to provide his government officials. Moreover, he and his heirs began to institute a series of examinations for entrance into the ruling bureaucracy that focused on the works of such classical moralists as Confucius and on a canon of technical treatises in mathematics and medicine. This examination system underwent significant changes over time, but it remained in place for over 2,000 years, until 1904 C.E. Though the Han Dynasty lasted only until 220 C.E. and during much of this time factional politics among cliques of prominent families made the imperial government impotent, its governmental authority and structure formed the foundation for all later forms of Chinese government up until the beginning of the 20th century. Its source of authority is described succinctly by Wolfram Eberhard in the following way:

At the head of the state was the emperor, in theory the holder of absolute power in the state restricted only by his responsibility to "Heaven," i.e. he had to follow and enforce the basic rules of morality, otherwise "Heaven" would withdraw its "mandate", the legitimation of the emperor's rule, and would indicate this withdrawal by sending natural catastrophes . . . To draw the Emperor's attention to actual or made-up calamities or celestial irregularities was one way to criticize and Emperor and to force him to change his behavior. (Eberhard 1977, 79–80)

As we shall see, this emphasis on heavenly authority provided a situation in which great effort was given to astronomy and its cognate technology, astrology, toward the end of the ancient period in China, though as we shall also see, that effort was restricted to a very small number of persons within the scholarly elite. After the end of the Han Dynasty, China was not united again until the rise of the Tang Dynasty in 613 C.E., so we will end our discussion of ancient China at this point.

Mesoamerica

Settled farming was not well established in the Americas until around 2000 B.C.E.; then, around 1000 B.C.E., there is evidence of the incursion into the region that now includes Honduras, Guatemala, and southern Mexico, of a people with unusually fine pottery, artwork, and religious practices that included the construction of large temple mounds. These people, the early Maya, engaged in the growing of maize, which tolerates a wide range of growing conditions. Recent satellite pictures show indications that the Mayans drained some marshy regions in the Yucatan Peninsula to create agricultural plots, though no evidence of large permanent cities has been found. Starting around the beginning of the Common Era, however, they built monumental ceremonial centers that included pyramid-shaped structures topped with temples and structures that appear to be astronomical observatories. Many stelae (about 5,000) from the period between the beginning of the Common Era and around 900 C.E. contain written records of important events and indicate the existence of a social hierarchy in which scribes and priests were persons of high status. Architectural features, glyphs in stone monuments, and three extended codices (written on bark treated with lime) that survived the weather and looting by early European conquerors, all evidence both the cultural importance and the sophistication of Mayan astronomy, which we will discuss extensively.

For reasons that are not well known, but which may reflect a rejection of the increasingly sophisticated astral priesthood by the farming population, the great ceremonial sites of the Maya began to be abandoned around 800 C.E. Sometime around 950 C.E., the relatively peaceful Maya were overrun by more warlike cultures from the north and northwest, the Toltecs and Aztecs, whose science was vastly less impressive; so we will focus attention on Mayan culture before about 950 C.E.

Greece

The most advanced ancient civilization in Europe in terms of its science was undoubtedly that of Hellenic Greece between about 600 B.C.E. and 330 B.C.E., and the most advanced ancient civilization in Europe in terms of its technology was undoubtedly that of Rome from about 600 B.C.E. to around 400 C.E., so we will focus attention on these two European civilizations, which had vastly different origins and patterns of development than those discussed so far. Greece, the Aegean Islands, Crete, and the western coast of modern day Turkey had been populated by peoples who engaged in herding and small scale dry-land farming in isolated valleys from long before 1000 B.C.E. Indeed, there is evidence of settlement on the Acropolis of Athens, the region near Corinth, and at the Hill of Troy from the third millennium B.C.E. By the mid-second millennium B.C.E., these peoples engaged in extensive sea trade with Egypt, Mesopotamia, and the western Mediterranean, serving as middlemen and trading olive oil, wine, pottery, and, later, finished leather and metal works, for grain and other finished goods. The relative isolation of population centers produced a collection of small and independent city-states usually ruled by kings who engaged in shifting alliances and who apparently engaged in frequent warfare, as evidenced by the fortification of most towns on the mainland. Their constant interaction with peoples from other cultures led to extensive cultural borrowing in almost all facets of life.

Between about 1200 B.C.E. and 800 B.C.E., two waves of northern invaders, the Ionians and the Dorians, who spoke dialects similar to that of the original Achaean population, swept through Greece and the Aegean, adopting many of the cultural traits of the native population. In each locale, political power tended initially to be shared between the king and a group of land owning noble families who managed estates in which stock rearing and agriculture were mixed, but who could be called upon to provide military service— including service in expeditions for piracy and plunder—when needed. Over time, especially in and around Athens, which will be the region of our most extensive concern, different classes of citizens, based on the income from land (which, in turn, determined what kind of military service one could afford to offer—mounted or on foot) were established. The wealthier classes wrested control from the traditional kings and created what they termed a democratic government, which excluded from power all those who were women or who were merely merchants, craftsmen, or agricultural workers and those who were foreigners (anyone not born to an Athenian citizen) or slaves.

As population densities increased, it became increasingly difficult for local resources to either provide the markets for local industries or the food necessary to support growing populations, and since geography limited local economic expansion, the Greeks sent out colonies into what are now Turkey, the Black Sea region, Sicily, and Italy. With rare exceptions, these colonies emphasized food production, especially from fishing and agriculture, and provided markets for goods produced in places like Athens, which developed major pottery, wine, and olive oil industries. Moreover, with rare exceptions, the colonies that were located on prime agricultural land and with easy access to the sea became wealthier and much more cosmopolitan than their sponsoring cities in Greece, so they provided tempting targets for nearby non-Greek powers.

Beginning around 548 B.C.E., the Persian king, Cyrus, began invading the Greek city-states along the south and west coasts of Anatolia. In 499 B.C.E., several of these cities—led by Miletus—revolted against the new Persian king, Darius, drawing its mother city, Athens, into the conflict. By 494, the revolt was ended with the burning of Miletus, but Darius decided to continue the conflict with the conquest of the Greek mainland—especially of Attica (the region controlled by Athens). In 490 B.C.E., an Athenian force of approximately 10,000 surprisingly defeated a Persian force of nearly 25,000 at the battle of Marathon and the Persians withdrew, to return only 10 years later under the fresh leadership of Darius's son, Xerxes. When Xerxes returned he faced a totally different situation.

The Athenians had used much of the wealth accumulated from the discovery of a rich new vein of silver at the nearby mine at Laurium to build a new fleet, and Athens had acquired leadership of a large league of Greek city-states, all of which now saw Persian domination as a serious threat. This time, the Greek fleet soundly defeated the Persian fleet at the battle of Salamis, and a combined Greek force led primarily by the Spartans defeated the Persian army invading from the north. Athens became the center of an empire of Greek city-states from which she was able to exact tribute for nearly half a century and the center of a flowering of intellectual and artistic life that was unprecedented. A revolt led by Sparta produced the Peloponnesian Wars (431–404 B.C.E.), which undermined the political power of Athens but did little to diminish its leadership in literature and science. That leadership continued at least until Athens was overrun by Phillip, father of Alexander the Great and turned into a puppet state in 338 B.C.E. At this point, intellectual leadership in the Mediterranean world moved to Alexandria in Egypt, during the period between about 330 B.C.E. and at least 150 C.E.

Rome

Rome is located on a series of low hills in the valley of the Tiber River, which flows westward down from the Apennine Mountains, which form a backbone along the east side of the Italian peninsula. This valley forms a rich and wide, but strongly sloping, alluvial agricultural plain dotted with hills, making large-scale irrigation difficult, but providing enough rainfall to grow many crops, especially in lower regions where there is evidence of drainage systems. The Latins settled in the southern part of this region beginning around 800 B.C.E., and beginning around 750 B.C.E., the seven hills that constitute Rome proper became the locus of the largest settlements, which gradually fused into one. The key to Roman history lies in the fact that an aggressive and technologically advanced Etruscan culture, and later, an invading Gallican culture, lay to the north and east of the Tiber Valley, and in the fact that Greek and Carthaginian colonies with expansive interests lay to the south. On the one hand, the Romans traded with these cultures and borrowed heavily from them, yet on the other, they were always being attacked and occasionally overrun by their neighbors. In fact, when Rome was established by combining the settlements on the Palatine Hill with that on the Quirinal, it was almost certainly under the control of an Etruscan king and under the auspices of the Etruscan gods Jupiter, Juno, and Minerva. Between around 750 and around 500 B.C.E., Rome was governed by a king, usually an Etruscan, and a council of wealthy landowning aristocrats, primarily from the indigenous population.

Around 500 B.C.E., the Roman aristocrats rebelled against the king and formed what they termed a republican, oligarchically controlled government, which was then faced with the problem of defending itself against the Gallican forces from the north, so the Roman farmers and herders were forced to become soldiers as well, initially for defensive purposes, but also, as time went on, to engage in preemptive wars of conquest. In 493 B.C.E., the Romans entered into a treaty with all of the other Latin cities of central Italy, pledging mutual support when attacked and the sharing of "All spoil and booty in wars in common" (Dudley 1962, 28). In 390 B.C.E., the Gauls invaded Rome, destroyed much of the city, and departed only after exacting a huge tribute. For nearly 50 years, Rome regrouped and then began a series of wars that brought most of central and southern Italy under Roman control by 293 B.C.E. The cities of the Latin League, who felt that they were not getting their share of the spoils of the Roman wars that they were supporting, tried to rebel early in this period, but they were defeated by Rome in 338 B.C.E. Rome responded in an unusually lenient way that, in theory, became a pattern for the next 500 years. Rome allowed many former enemies to become Roman citizens and gave most others the right to retain their local laws subject only to an obligation to support continuing Roman military actions and to provide annual tribute. By the mid-third century B.C.E., Rome probably had a population of 125,000 and controlled a region of about 52,000 square miles containing 4 million inhabitants. For comparison purposes, Ptolemaic Egypt had a population of about 10 million under the nominal control of a single king.

Starting in 264 B.C.E., Rome was drawn into a series of wars with Carthage when it went to the defense of Messina, in Sicily, at the request of the local rulers. The Punic Wars that ensued ended in 146 B.C.E. with the complete destruction of Carthage and the Roman appropriation of the Carthaginian Empire, which comprised the western Mediterranean including the Iberian Peninsula, what is now southern France, North Africa, and western Egypt. Because Phillip of Macedon had allied himself with Carthage, the Romans also entered into a series of Macedonian Wars, which ended in 148 B.C.E. with the takeover of the Macedonian Empire. Ultimately, the military conquests of the Roman civilization led them to create the largest empire that the world had seen to that time, one that extended from Britain and the German plains in the north to North Africa, including Egypt, to the south, and from Britain in the west to the Persian Gulf in the east at its height, around 116 C.E.

During much of the period from 500 to 30 B.C.E., though its armies were victorious almost everywhere they went, the Roman Republic faced serious class conflicts at home. The plebeian class—all those citizens not in the ruling aristocracy—sought political rights and social equity using secession and the threat of secession to force successive reforms that provided the general population with a strong nominal voice in the government, though effective control tended to remain in the Senate, which was dominated by the aristocracy. A period of severe instability began around 133 B.C.E., when Tiberius Gracchus began to force a redistribution of land into the hands of the plebes. His exhortations to the working class sounds much like the exhortations of socialist leaders in the 19th century:

Wild beasts have their lairs, but the men who fight and die for Italy can call nothing their own except the air and the sunshine . . . Your generals exhort you to fight for hearth and home. You have neither. . . . You fight to defend the luxury of the rich. They call you the master of the world, but you have not one foot of land to call your own. . . . (Dudley 1962, 71)

Tiberius was soon assassinated, as were his principle opponents and his brother, Caius, ushering in a period of almost a century of civil strife, during which party factions within the Senate also intensified, leading to a de facto military coup by Lucius Cornelius Sulla in 82 B.C.E. Sulla had been the general of an army that had put down an Asiatic revolt and then had returned to defeat a marauding Samnite army outside of Rome. Sulla was declared dictator for an indefinite period of time until a new constitution could be passed, and he and his supporters initiated a period of terror during which it is estimated that more than 1,600 people were murdered, largely to the financial benefit of his retainers. The pro-Senate constitution passed under Sulla in 78 B.C.E. lasted less than a year.

New civil strife gradually led to the concentration of power in the hands of Julius Caesar, who became the unprecedented dictator for life until he was assassinated in 44 B.C.E. After some jockeying for position, a young general and Julius Caesar's nephew, Octavian, consolidated power. Then, in 27 B.C.E., after having gained effective control of the Senate and of the armies throughout the empire, Octavian formally renounced his powers and announced the restoration of the Roman Republic. The Senate rewarded him immediately by granting him supreme power over the armies in Gaul, Spain, and Syria. Three days later, he was granted the name Augustus, and the title *princeps* (First Citizen). The Age of Imperial Rome had begun.

Augustus died in 14 C.E., and during a period lasting until 192 C.E., a relatively peaceful Rome was ruled by a series of Emperors of varying abilities. After 192, a new series of coups and counter-coups led toward the final fall of the Roman Empire and of Rome itself. Of the *princeps* following Augustus, Claudius, who reigned from 41–54 C.E., demands our special attention, for under him a series of public works projects incorporating the most advanced technological developments seen in Rome were undertaken. After 116 C.E., the empire began to crumble and Rome succumbed to a series of military coups that eventually led to its the fall in the late fifth century of the Common Era.

Two

Technologies of Computation: Mathematics and Measurement

Record keeping in most cultures almost certainly began with making signs or pictures to denote quantities long before written language developed. Tally marks and collections of dots in petroglyphic art dating from as early as 10,000 B.C.E. very probably recorded the passage of days in lunar months and the counts of animals killed in hunting forays (Murray 1986). Many tribal cultures use knots in rope to record quantities of many things, thus it should not surprise us greatly that the first documents, datable to around 3500 B.C.E., and from the earliest civilization, that of the Sumerians, would be tablets on which several items are depicted along with what appears to be marks to indicate the quantities of those items.

Most of these Sumerian documents, created by pressing a stylus into clay tablets small enough to fit in the hand, also suggest something about the nature of early counting systems because the counting marks are of several kinds: relatively large and deep circular dots, shallower half circles to their right, and smaller, shallower full circles always found to the right of the deeper circles and larger half circles (see Figure 2.1).

More than 5,000 such tablets have been recovered. Although in the earliest tablets there is evidence of several different counting systems, depending on what kind of commodity is being counted (Nissen, Damerow, and Englund 1993), in almost all tablets dating after about 2500 B.C.E., each circle is equivalent to 10 of the half circles to the right of it and to 60 of the smaller full circles to the right of those. Shortly thereafter, when it became common to use wedge-shaped, rather than rounded, styluses for indicating numbers and words, the circles were replaced by a kind of sideways V shape formed by rotating the end of the stylus in the clay; the half-circles were replaced by thin wedge-shaped vertical marks produced by simply pressing the stylus edge into the clay, and the size and depth of the marks became uniform. These marks, because of their wedge-like shape, are called cuneiform, after the Latin *cuneus* for wedge, so Sumerian and subsequent Mesopotamian writing was called cuneiform writing.

Figure 2.1
Early Sumerian Account Tablet. Nick Livingston.

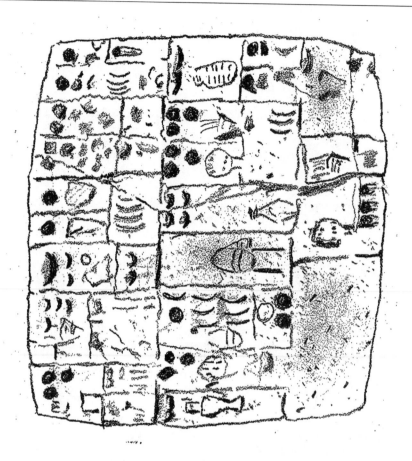

All ancient civilizations used a small number of symbols to represent numbers. Several used one symbol to represent units and another to represent some multiple of a single unit. The Sumerians and the early Indus Valley civilizations used symbols for 1 and 10. The Chinese and Mayans usually used symbols for 1 and 5, while for some purposes they had special number symbols for 20 as well. Early Egyptians had different symbols for 1, 10, 100, 1,000, 10,000, 100,000, and 1 million, a numbering practice followed with minor modifications both by the Greeks and the Romans (see Figure 2.2).

Clearly the choices of 5, 10, and 20 for special symbolic attention derived from the early use of fingers and toes for counting purposes and were inherited from pre-literate times. For some groups, since one hand followed four fingers, it seemed natural to count by ones and multiples of five. Numerous American tribal cultures have names for the numbers one through four and then use their word for hand to express what we would designate by the word

Figure 2.2
Table of Counting Symbols and Representations. Joseph Emmert.

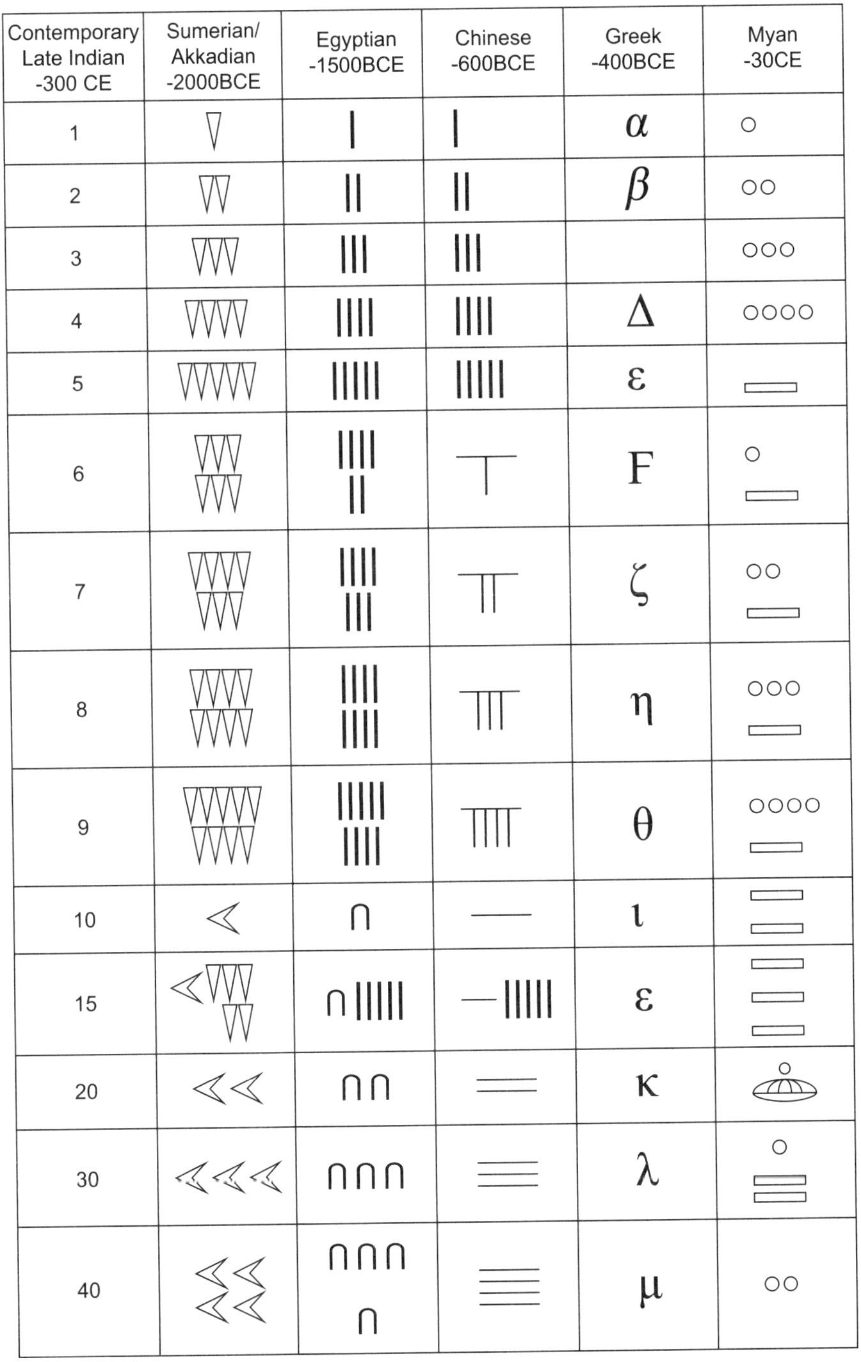

Contemporary Late Indian -300 CE	Sumerian/ Akkadian -2000BCE	Egyptian -1500BCE	Chinese -600BCE	Greek -400BCE	Myan -30CE
1	▽	|	|	α	○
2	▽▽	||	||	β	○○
3	▽▽▽	|||	|||		○○○
4	▽▽▽▽	||||	||||	Δ	○○○○
5	▽▽▽▽▽	|||||	|||||	ε	▭
6	▽▽▽ / ▽▽▽	|||| ||	⊤	F	○ / ▭
7	▽▽▽▽ / ▽▽▽	|||| |||	⊤⊤	ζ	○○ / ▭
8	▽▽▽▽ / ▽▽▽▽	|||| ||||	⊤⊤⊤	η	○○○ / ▭
9	▽▽▽▽▽ / ▽▽▽▽	||||| ||||	⊤⊤⊤⊤	θ	○○○○ / ▭
10	≪	∩	—	ι	▭ ▭
15	≪▽▽▽/▽	∩|||||	—|||||	ε	▭ ▭ ▭
20	≪≪	∩∩	═	κ	(shell symbol)
30	≪≪≪	∩∩∩	≡	λ	○ / ═
40	≪≪ / ≪≪	∩∩∩ / ∩	≣	μ	○○

five (Closs 1986). What we call 6 thus becomes "a hand and one," and 14 becomes "two hands and four or three hands less one." Thus, Mayan numbers were expressed in dot and bar notation, with each bar denoting five dots, and with the dots either above or to the left of the bars. Other groups continued counting on fingers until they achieved closure by completing both hands, making 10 a special symbol, while for some purposes, closure came only with completing all 20 digits on the hands and feet. Some civilizations, including the Greek, had special symbols for 1, 5, 10, and multiples of 10, with symbols compounded of those for 5 and multiples of 10 to indicate 50, 500, 5,000, and so on (see Figure 2.2).

SOURCES OF EVIDENCE REGARDING MATHEMATICS IN ANCIENT CULTURES

As noted above, the earliest evidence relating to mathematics comes from Sumer from about 3400 B.C.E. Because record keeping in Mesopotamia was done on clay tablets that hardened and which were sometimes baked, Mesopotamian records have lasted for millennia and we have tens of thousands of documents containing mathematical operations. The earliest are inventory records, but starting about 2200 B.C.E., thousands appear to be student exercise tablets and tens of thousands more are numerical astronomical tablets that increase dramatically in sophistication over the period from roughly 1600 B.C.E. to 300 C.E. Collectively, these texts reveal the slow development of new mathematical techniques and applications over a much greater span of time in the ancient world than for any other civilization.

Though it is likely that Egyptians had developed many mathematical techniques by the time that the great pyramids were built, circa 2600 B.C.E., the earliest Egyptian textual evidence comes from around 1900 B.C.E. Egyptian records were kept in ink and written on papyrus, a thin, flat material made from the pith from the stem of the papyrus plant. Strips about 18 inches long were laid next to one another with a slight overlap, then another layer of strips was laid over the first, but at right angles to them. The two layers were then pounded into a nearly homogeneous and seamless mat that could be joined to others by beating on overlapping edges. Since papyrus documents were made of organic material, when they were stored in moist places, they generally deteriorated over time, but many of those stored in dry places—often caves in the desert—have survived to the present day.

The Egyptians wrote in two different scripts from very early on, much as printing and cursive writing coexist in our culture. Hieroglyphic script was most often used for formal occasions and involved pictograms that were frequently complex, while the hieratic script was used primarily for informal communication and involved less complex symbols. Mathematical texts used both forms of writing, but for the sake of simplicity I will emphasize only hieroglyphic representations.

The earliest papyrus with mathematical content, the Riesner papyrus, is a set of records from the dockyard and workshops near This in Upper Egypt from around 1900 B.C.E. It includes calculations of the volume of stone blocks in a storehouse, of the volumes of structures along with the number of blocks needed to build them, and accounts of hides, cattle, fish, oil, fowl, and so on. Several short papyri date from around 1700 B.C.E. These include the Moscow papyrus, which contains 25 miscellaneous problems, seven of which are unclear, the Kahun papyrus, which contains a series of unit fractions (fractions in which the numerator is one) produced when two is divided by the first 10 odd numbers, and six problems like those from the Moscow Papyrus, the Berlin Papyrus 6619, which contains two problems involving determining two unknowns given two simultaneous equations, and the Mathematical Leather Roll at the British Museum, which contains a set of 26 problems dealing with finding equivalent expressions for unit fraction sequences. The vast bulk of what we know about Egyptian mathematics comes from a single papyrus, the Rhind papyrus, which was written about 1542 B.C.E., but was apparently copied from a text that dates from about 1800 B.C.E. Apparently a mathematics text for use in scribal schools, it contains 87 problems ranging from very simple addition problems to complex calculations of areas, volumes, and the division of loaves and beer among men, when men from different categories get different amounts (Clagett 1999).

What is striking about this Egyptian evidence is that it all comes from a very small number of sources and from a short period of time. The distinctive character of Egyptian counting systems shows that they were not borrowed directly from another contemporary civilization, though one scholar has recently argued for links between Mesopotamian and Egyptian mathematics during both the earliest phases and the Alexandrian period (Friberg 2005).

The evidence for mathematics in China has a much different character. Numbers appear on Shang oracle bones (i.e., the shoulder blades of sheep and oxen as well as turtle shells on which cryptic predictions about the future were inscribed) from circa 1500 B.C.E., on bronze bells dating from around 1000 B.C.E., and on earthenware pots dating from the Warring States period (475–221 B.C.E.). The latter numbers correspond to a system of calculation to be described in the next section that used counting rods. Many sets of such rods made of bone, bamboo, and ivory have been excavated from the Han period. No text recounting their use exists prior to the fifth century of the Common Era, however a number of bamboo strips containing numbers that appear to be sections of multiplication tables, starting with nine-nines and moving downward to two-twos have been excavated from the Han period, and a few texts purporting to be from the Warring States period incorporate problems that call for addition, subtraction, multiplication, and division. For example, a legal text, *A Treatise on Law,* from around 500 B.C.E. contains the following problem:

A farmer with a family of five has a hundred mǔ (a unit of area) under cultivation. Each mǔ yields a harvest of one and one half dàn (a unit of volume), thus giving one hundred and fifty dàn of cereal. After the tax of fifteen dàn, one tenth of the total, there remains one hundred and thirty-five. Each month, each member of the family consumes one and a half dàn; five persons consume a total of ninety dàn each year.

There remain forty-five. Each dàn is worth thirty coins, a total of one thousand three hundred and fifty. Three hundred coins are used for ceremonials and sacrifices at the ancestors shrine. Thus there are a thousand and fifty left. Each person spends three hundred coins on clothing, so five people spend one thousand five hundred each year. Consequently there is a deficit of four hundred and fifty. (Li and Du 1987, 11–12)

Almost everything else that is known about ancient Chinese mathematics comes from two texts, the *Jiuzhang Suanshu* (*Computational Prescriptions in Nine Chapters*), and the *Zhoubi Suanjing* (*Zhou Dynasty Canon of Gnomic Computations*), initially compiled during the Han period. These became part of a 10-text mathematical canon that was finalized around 620 C.E. and made the basis of Imperial examinations through the 19th century. The *Jiuzhang Suanshu* text, whose 246 problems make it more extensive than any single Mesopotamian or Egyptian text, holds a central place in Chinese mathematics, much as Euclid's *Elements of Geometry* does in Greek mathematics. Its nine chapters cover field measurement, proportional exchanges of different types of grain, proportional distributions to parties with different claims, construction problems, including the calculation of volumes, taxation problems, problems of "excess and deficiency," which deal with contribution and distribution problems when there are remainders, problems that depend upon the solution of simultaneous linear equations, which sometimes eventuate in negative numbers as answers, the use of right-angled triangles for a variety of purposes, and the extraction of square and cube roots of numbers. The *Zhoubi Suanjing* is primarily an astronomical text, but it contains virtually all early Chinese geometrical formulas connected with a variety of right triangles.

Archeological evidence from the Harappan culture of ancient India implies the existence of a system of measurement based on multiples of two and five. Partial sets of what appear to be standard weights representing 1/20, 1/10, 1/5, 1/2, 1, 2, 5, 10, 20, 50, 100, 200, and 500 units have been found in several places. Precise linear measurements are also evidenced in the 15 different sizes of kiln-dried bricks, all of which have sides that are multiples of a single unit (approximately 33.5 mm) and ratios of length, breadth, and thickness of 4:2:1.

The earliest written evidence of Indian mathematical knowledge comes from four Vedic *Śulva-sūtras* (appendices to the Rigvedic writings for calculating how to build altars) ordinarily dated 800 B.C.E. to 400 B.C.E., though the earliest extant text survives from the seventh century C.E. Some pottery inscriptions contain numbers that suggest that the Hindu system of numeration, which eventually passed into Islam and then into Europe as what were called Arabic numerals, gradually evolved from 300 to 800 C.E. Before that time, Indian numbers were indicated by vertical or horizontal lines similar to the counting rod numbers from China, but with no indication of place value grouping.

Evidence for Mayan mathematics comes largely from two codexes written with ink on treated bark, dating from the 13th century C.E., from drawings on pottery dating to the beginning of the Common Era, and from numerous stone *stelae* (pedestal-like monuments) from 50 to 800 C.E.

Finally, evidence for Greek and Roman mathematics is too extensive to explore here in detail. Almost 15,000 fragments of inscriptions and inventory documents indicate that slightly different systems of numeration existed in different Greek cities as late as 320 B.C.E., and that two systems, one called acrophonic and one alphabetic, coexisted in Athens for most of antiquity. More theoretical mathematical texts derive from the sixth and fifth centuries B.C.E., but they are known only from later philosophical writers and from copies written or collected at the Alexandrian Museum between 330 B.C.E. and 400 C.E. Written at Alexandria were Euclid's *Elements of Geometry,* as well as works attributed to Archimedes, Pappus, and other famous mathematicians.

EARLY COUNTING SYSTEMS

In some counting systems, such as those developed in Egypt and adapted for use by the Greeks and Romans, the value of a numerical symbol is usually independent of where it appears. Thus, $\|\cap = \cap\|$ in the Egyptian counting system. The Roman system, like many pre-literate systems, however, used a convention that reduced the number of marks needed to express some numbers, but which also made computational processes more complex. When the symbol for a smaller unit appeared to the right of a symbol for a larger unit, the amount it represented was added to the larger unit; but if it appeared to the left, it was subtracted from the larger unit. Thus while $XI = 11$, $IX = 9$.

When the value of a symbol depends on where it appears in the representation of a number (i.e., to the right or to the left), such that the numbers represented by a given symbol set are constant multiples of those to the immediate right or left, we call that number system a place value system. The multiple of the smaller unit which the same symbol represents displaced by one place defines the number system. When that number is 60, as in late Sumerian civilization and the subsequent civilizations that replaced one another in Mesopotamia after about 2000 B.C.E., we call it a sexagesimal system or a base 60 system. When it is 10, as in early Chinese and Indian civilizations (as well as our own), we call it decimal, or base 10. When it is 2, as in some Vedic Indian texts and in modern computer applications, we call it binary, or base 2; and when it is 20, as in some Chinese and Mayan applications, we call it duodecimal, or base 20.

The simplest number systems from a computational point of view are regular place value systems, as in the fully developed Mesopotamian sexagesimal system and in our own decimal system. The earliest versions of place value systems did not include a place holder like the modern zero. A rough equivalent to zero appeared in the orientation and spacing of the counting rods used by the Chinese, but in the Mesopotamian case, for instance, the number, $[<1 <<11]$, could equal $11 \times 60 + 22 = 682$ or $11 \times 60 \times 60 + 22 = 39,622$ or, most generally, $11 \times 60^a + 22 \times 60^b$, where $a > b$. The choice from among possible values had to be based on the context in which the number appeared.

Only in late Babylonian times was a special sign used to denote an empty place within a number, and the addition of a zero at the end of a number to shift the value of every place to the left did not happen until Greek astronomers at Alexandria developed the practice early in the Common Era. In spite of some claims to the contrary, the zero probably entered Hindu numbers from the Greek astronomers' practice (Van der Waerden 1963).

THE FOUR PRINCIPLE ARITHMETIC FUNCTIONS: ADDITION, SUBTRACTION, MULTIPLICATION, AND DIVISION

The most basic bookkeeping functions in all cultures are related to establishing how many units of a commodity are in an inventory when some determinate amount is brought into the storehouse or disbursed from the storehouse, so the first arithmetic operations to appear are what we would call addition and subtraction problems. Multiplication problems arise naturally in cases in which a given number of units of volume are filled by a certain kind of brick and one wants to know how much volume will be filled by a specified number of bricks, or when a worker can produce a certain quantity of work in a day and one wants to know how much a number of workers can accomplish in a specified number of days. Division problems naturally arise when a given quantity of some commodity must be divided among several persons, or when one knows how much work has to be done in a certain time and how much work each individual can do and needs to know how many workers to assign to the task.

The following figures illustrate how each basic kind of problem is done in the modern decimal system and how it was done in the Mesopotamian sexigesimal system, the Egyptian hieroglyphic system, and the Chinese counting rod system (see Figures 2.3–2.5). Note that none of the common shortcuts that we learn in the decimal system are used, so rather than "carrying" units into a column to the left when the sum of two terms in a column to the right is greater than 10 in the decimal system, we follow the more cumbersome but conceptually prior process of adding one place of the second number to the whole of the first and then adding the next place to the left of the second number to that result, and so on (see explanation below). Complications to Egyptian-style calculations added in the Roman system because of the use of numbers such as IX ("one less than 10") create difficulties which make computations very rare. An algorithm for doing calculations using the Roman system was constructed by Charles Young, et. al., in 1976, but it is not certain that Romans followed this method. A description of the procedures used for each problem follows each table.

Explanation of decimal process:

Step 1: Place smaller number below larger, such that values in the same place are aligned above/below one another.

Step 2: Add the value in the right-hand column of the second number to the entire first number.

Step 3: Move one column left in the second number and add to the result of step 2.

Figure 2.3
Addition Methods. Joseph Emmert.

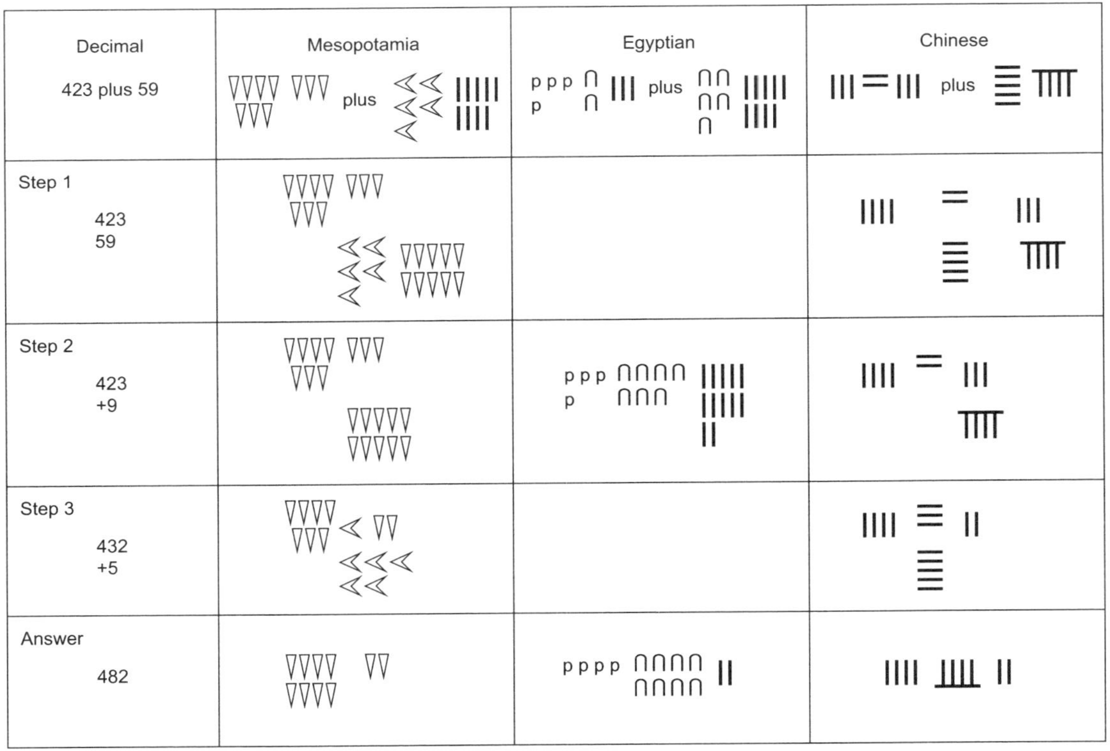

Step 4: Continue by repeating step 3 until all values in the second number have been added. The result of this step is the answer sought.

Explanation of sexagesimal process:

All steps are the same as in the decimal case.

Explanation of Chinese process

Step 1: Same as in decimal system.

Step 2: Starting at the *left* value in the second number, add to the entire first number.

Step 3: Move one column to the *right* and add that value to the result of step 2.

Step 4: Repeat step 3 until all values in the second number have been used. The result is the answer sought.

Explanation of Egyptian Process.

Step 1: Write down the two numbers to be added.

Step 2: Write down, as the preliminary result, the number that has the number of symbols of each kind, as that collected from both numbers to be added.

Step 3: Collect all symbols of the smallest unit present. If there are more than enough to make up a next larger unit, replace the appropriate number of smaller symbols with the larger one.

Step 4: Taking the results of step 3, collect all of the symbols representing the second-smallest value. If there are more than enough of them to produce one of the next larger unit, replace the appropriate number of them with the larger one.

Step 5: Repeat step 4 until all symbols in the preliminary result have been used.

The explanation of subtraction in all systems is similar to addition, except that in each step the value of the second number in each place is subtracted from the previous answer. In the Egyptian case, the number of symbols of each kind in the first number is reduced by the number of symbols of that kind in the second. If there are not enough symbols of a given kind in the first number, one reduces the number of next-highest symbols by one and replaces it with the appropriate number of lower symbols in order to make the required reduction possible.

Only in the Chinese case was it permissible to subtract larger numbers from smaller ones. In that case, the smaller number was subtracted from the larger and the result was recorded as a deficit. In grain cases, for example, one might record an amount of grain owed to the granary by someone rather than an amount disbursed by the granary to someone, or in monetary instances these figures might represent a debt rather than a payment.

MULTIPLICATION

Egyptian multiplication is treated as successive additions of the first number to itself. Start with the first number, this is (1 × the number), add to that the number again, that is (2 × the number). . . . . (*n* × number) until *n* = the

Figure 2.4
Egyptian Multiplication. Joseph Emmert.

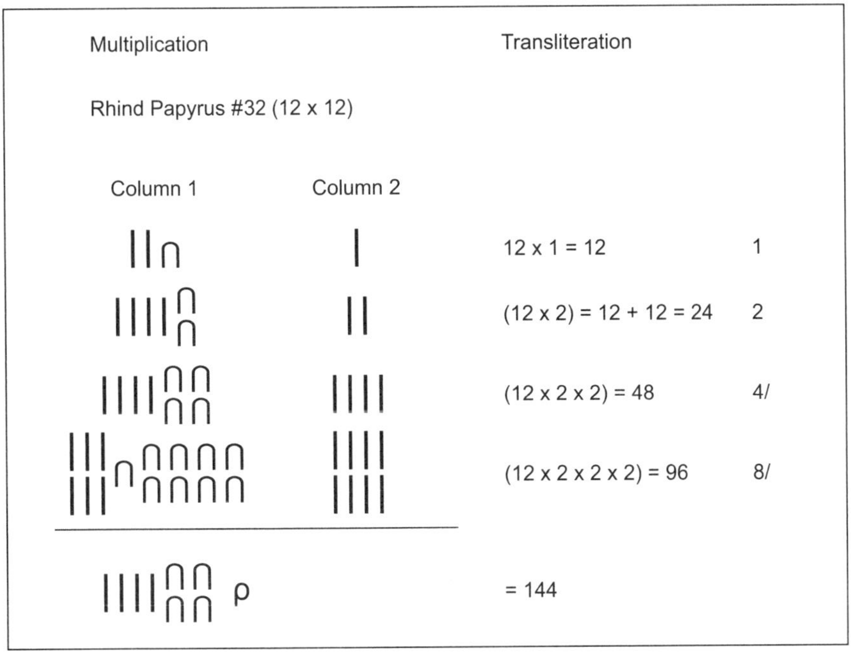

Multiplication   Transliteration

Rhind Papyrus #32 (12 x 12)

Column 1   Column 2

(Column 1 hieroglyphic numerals)   (Column 2 hieroglyphic numerals)

						(hieroglyphs)	12 x 1 = 12	1
(hieroglyphs)	(12 x 2) = 12 + 12 = 24	2
(hieroglyphs)	(12 x 2 x 2) = 48	4/
(hieroglyphs)	(12 x 2 x 2 x 2) = 96	8/

(hieroglyphs)   = 144

multiplier. Shortcut in all systems: when one moves a place value in the second number, shift the place of the multiplicand by one and add that number to itself the number in that place times. So, for, example $20 \times 20 = 200 \times 2 = 200 + 200 = 400$. In the Egyptian system, multiplication by 10^n simply shifts the number signs up by n.

In place value systems, one learns by rote to multiply small numbers up to $(n-1) \times (n-1)$, where n is the base. So for base 10 systems, one learns all multiples from 1×2 through 9×9, and for the sexigesimal system, one must learn multiples through 59×59 (these are probably originally calculated as in the Egyptian system, but for the Chinese case there is evidence that scholars practiced their nine times nine rhymes by the Warring States period. Once these are known, one multiplies each term of the multiplicand by the first term of the multiplier. (Mesopotamians and modern Westerners start from the right-hand end of the multiplier; Chinese counting rod calculators started from the left.) That number is then added to the result of the multiplication of the multiplicand by the second term of the multiplier (accounting for its place value by moving one place left or right, depending on where one started), and so on until all terms of the multiplier have been used.

DIVISION WHERE THE ANSWER COMES OUT EVEN

Division problems are treated as inverse multiplication problems, so that the Rhind Papyrus problem 24 is stated in the following way (when transcribed into decimal notation): add by 80 until you reach 1,120. (i.e., what is 1,120 divided by 80?) Start as if one is doing the multiplication problem (including place value shortcuts) and keep track of the number of additions needed to reach the number to be divided. Since any multiple of a number can be reached by adding successive doublings and multiples of 10 to the original number, the Egyptians started by exhibiting successive doublings multiplications by 10 and listing them in one column with a corresponding number of multiples in a second column. When the sum of some combination of numbers in column 1 = 1,120, then the corresponding numbers in column 2 were added to give the answer. Thus the problem, "what is 1,120 divided by 80?" would be solved by writing

80	1
160	2
320	4/
800	10/

$800 + 320 = 1,120$, so 1,120 divided by $80 - 14$.

DIVISION WHERE ANSWERS DO NOT COME OUT EVEN

With example in the Rhind papyrus 69, serious complications begin: "Add beginning with 8 until you reach 19" (i.e., What is 19 divided by 8?)

Transcription	Analysis		
8	1	Do doublings as before, but $(1 + 2) \times 8 > 19$	
16	2	/	
4	(½)	Try supplemental problem; add beginning with 2 until you get 8, (i.e., take ½ of 8)	
2	(¼)	/	Still cannot get 19, so try ½ of ½ 8, and so on.
1	(⅛)	/	Add in column 1 until you reach 19; take corresponding elements in column 2.
19	$2 + ¼ + ⅛$	Answer is $2 + ¼ + ⅛$	

Note: The answer comes out in terms of unit fractions. The answer 2 and ⅜ would not have been acceptable to Egyptians. All Egyptian fractions with the

Figure 2.5
Chinese Division with Remainder. Joseph Emmert.

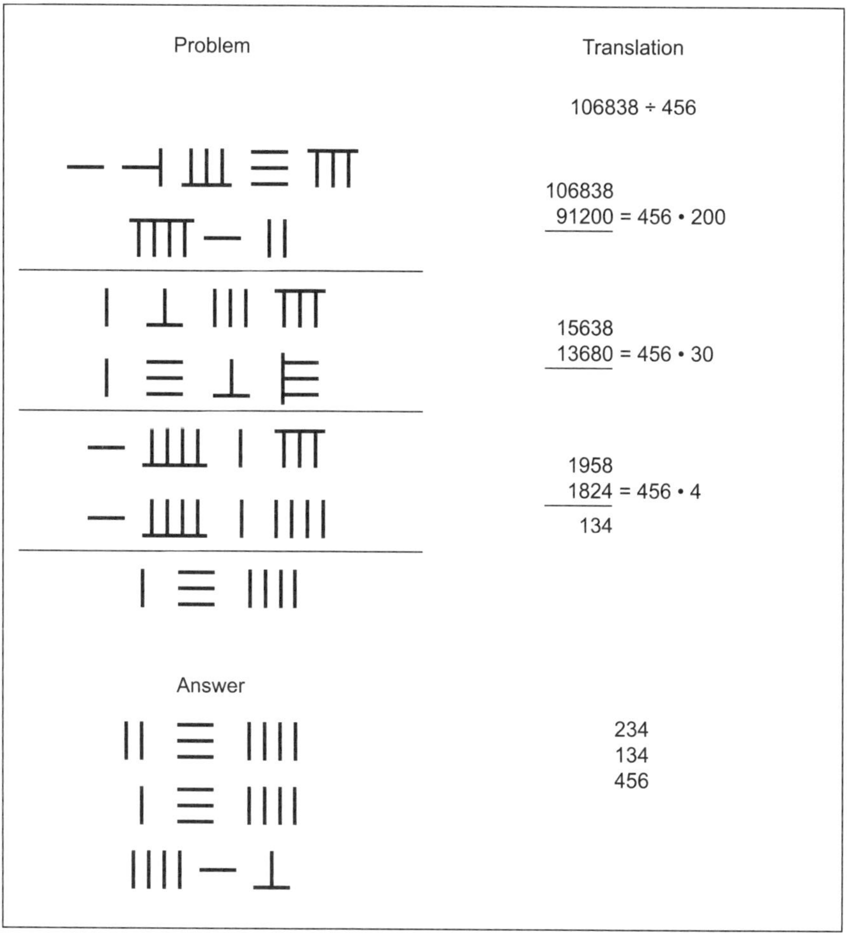

Problem	Translation
	$106838 \div 456$
一 ⼅ 川 三 ⼲ ⼲ 一 ‖	106838 $91200 = 456 \cdot 200$
‖ ⊥ ‖‖ ⼲ ‖ 三 ⊥ ⼃	15638 $13680 = 456 \cdot 30$
一 川 ‖ ⼲ 一 川 ‖ ‖‖‖	1958 $1824 = 456 \cdot 4$ 134
‖ 三 ‖‖‖	
Answer	
‖ 三 ‖‖‖ ‖ 三 ‖‖‖ ‖‖‖ 一 ⊥	234 134 456

exception of ⅔ and ¾, the natural fractions, were expressed as unit fractions. There are several explanations for this situation, all dependant on the relatively literal interpretation of hieroglyphic symbols. The symbol that indicates a fraction to us was interpreted more narrowly as either "the inverse of," or "the nth part of." In either case, there is only one inverse of a number and only one nth part of something divided into n parts. There is a first part, a second part, . . . to the nth part when division has been into n parts. As we shall see, Egyptians tended to be more literal in their linguistic usages than their Mesopotamian counterparts, so these theories have some plausibility.

If the divisor is some multiple of a small odd number, like three or five, halving the divisor may not lead to a finite series of unit fractions, so in the first case, one might use thirds, or the other fifths. But what if the divisor is a multiple of both an odd and an even small number—say 12—then one scribe might choose to express his answer in terms of 3rds, 9ths, 27ths, and so on, while another might choose halves, quarters, eighths, and so on. How could one tell if the answers were equivalent?—only by developing tables of equivalent unit fraction series, which seems to have taken up a significant amount of Egyptian computers' efforts.

One way of doing division that does not come out even in the Chinese system and in the Mesopotamian sexigesimal system is simply to leave the answer as a whole number plus a fraction, the numerator of which is the number left after the last even number of times the denominator can be extracted from the number to be divided. In the Chinese counting rod system, there was a conventional way of representing such a result. Thus, for example, in the case of 106,838 divided by $456 = 234 + 134/456$, the answer would be written:

234

134

456

In place value systems, rather than express a remainder either in terms of unit fractions, or in terms of a single fraction with the divisor as denominator, remainders can be expressed in terms of the sum of one or more terms whose denominators are the base raised to negative powers. In general any place value system of base, N may have places to the right of the units place that are multiples of $N^{-1}, N^{-2} \ldots N^{-n}$ or $1/N, 1/(N^2), 1/(N^3)$, and so on. Thus, for example, $107/12 = 8 + 9/10 + 1/100 + 6/1{,}000 + 6/10{,}000 + \ldots = 8.9166666 \ldots$

A second, and very important, way of handling division problems in place value systems is to treat them as multiplications by the reciprocal. Thus, in a decimal system, division by two is equivalent to multiplication by $\frac{1}{2} = 0.5$. In Mesopotamia, there are many texts of common reciprocals to be used in converting division problems into multiplication problems.

GENERAL COMMENTS ON ARITHMETIC COMPUTATIONAL SYSTEMS IN ANCIENT CIVILIZATIONS

One can easily see that, although addition and subtraction are conceptually simpler in the non-place value Egyptian counting practice because one need not keep track of where a symbol appears in the expression of a number, the complexity of multiplication, and even more, of division problems, becomes a major barrier to rapid calculation in their computational system (and of such Egyptian derivative systems as those of the Greeks and Romans). Without backing up and starting over, there is no way for such a system to evolve into a more efficient one, and the investment in learning the system almost certainly militated against the adoption of alternatives illustrated by trading partners. Efficiency at one stage in computation thus lead into what amounted to a mathematical cul de sac from which there was no effective escape.

On the other hand, in the Mesopotamian case, a culture landed in an extremely efficient place value number system almost by accident (60 happens to be divisible by an extraordinarily large number of factors [2, 3, 4, 5, 6, 10, 12, 15, 20, and 30]; so there is a large number of small whole number reciprocals) when an attempt was made to create a single counting system out of several measuring systems, none of which were, strictly, place value systems. In China as well as in India, decimal place value numbering systems emerged in ways that probably came out of primitive body part-based counting systems, though we know little about precisely why.

The historian of Chinese mathematics, Jean-Claude Martzloff, argues that problems appearing in early mathematical works in all cultures fall along a continuum characterized by four main categories with very blurred edges:

1. Real problems that apply to specific situations and are directly useable.
2. Pseudo-real problems that pretend to address situations of daily life, but are neither plausible nor directly useable.
3. Recreational problems, modeled on riddles, which use data from everyday life in a particularly unrealistic, sometimes grotesque, but always amusing way.
4. Speculative, or purely mathematical problems (1997, 54).

While most of the calculations done by the mathematically literate Egyptians, Mesopotamians, and Chinese were clearly intended to provide techniques that would be useful to officials, even simple calculation processes may give rise to problems that go beyond real problems. Thus, for example, the Han text *Jiuzhang Suanshu* contains the following pseudo-real or recreational problem in the seventh section:

Suppose that a man with many coins enters the land of Shu [Sichuan]. [He trades] and obtains an interest of 3 for ten. First, he sends 14,000 coins [home] then, a second time, 13,000 coins, then a further 12,000 coins, then 11,000, then 10,000. After doing this five times, his capital and interest are completely exhausted. How many coins did he have originally, and how much did the interest amount to?

Answer: 30,468 coins and 84,876/371,293 coins; interest 29,531 coins and 286,417/371,293 coins. (Martzloff 1997, 57–58)

Similarly, the relatively somber Egyptian mathematicians occasionally, though rarely, presented a recreational problem. Thus Rhind papyrus problem number 28 is stated as follows:

Think of a number. Add to it its ²/₃ part. To this sum add its third part. Find a third of this result, and say what your answer is.

Suppose the answer is 10. Then add 1/4 and 1/10 to this ten, giving 13 and 1/2, its third is 9, which added makes 22 and 1/2. Then 1/3 of 22 and 1/2 is 7and 1/2, which added makes 30. Then 1/3 of this 30 is 10. That is how you do it. (Gillings 1972, 184)

EARLY GEOMETRY

The Greek historian Herodotus (484– c. 425 B.C.E.) offers an account for the origins of geometry that places it in Egypt around 1300 B.C.E. and links it to the same kind of administrative practices that gave rise to the computational techniques we have discussed so far:

Sesostris also, they declared, made a division of the soil of Egypt among the inhabitants, assigning plots of ground of equal size to all, and obtaining his chief revenue from the rent which the holders were required to pay him every year. If the river carried away any portion of a man's lot, he appeared before the king, and related what had happened; upon which the king sent persons to examine, and determine by measurement the exact extent of the loss; and thenceforth only such a rent was demanded of him as was proportionate to the reduced size of his land. From this practice, I think, geometry first came to be known in Egypt, whence it passed into Greece. (Smith 1923, 51–52)

Though he probably has the date of origin wrong by at least a millennium, though there were probably multiple places of origin, and though land measurement was probably less important in some places than construction problems, Herodotus was probably correct in seeing the origins of geometry in practical problems of governance such as surveying and construction. However, geometrical texts in Mesopotamia, China, and especially in the Indus Valley show tendencies to go beyond immediate applicability from very near the beginnings of geometrical knowledge.

THE PYTHAGOREAN THEOREM

One important geometrical relationship that had many applications in ancient civilizations is what we know today as the "Pythagorean theorem," which states that, for a plane triangle that contains one right angle (90°), if we let c be the length of the side opposite the right angle (the hypotenuse) and a be the length of one of the other sides while b is the length of the third side, then $a^2 + b^2 = c^2$. One special case of this proposition appears in both Mesopotamian and Chinese texts.

British Museum 14,568 #2 from Mesopotamia circa 300 B.C.E. reads: The flank is 4 and the diagonal is 5, what is the front? Since you do not know, $4 \times 4 = 16$, $5 \times 5 = 25$, remainder, 9. What would I multiply by itself to make 9? $3 \times 3 = 9$. The Front is 3.

Problem 9–3 from the Chinese *Jiuzhang Suanshu* states: Suppose LEG: 4 *chi* [feet], hypotenuse: 5 *chi;* question: BASE?

Answer 3 *chi.*

BASE-LEG rule: LEG automultiplied, by subtracting the result from the hypotenuse automultiplied [then] by extracting the square root of the remainder gives BASE. (Martzloff 1997, 94)

In the *Zhoubi Suanjing,* both the general case and the special 3,4,5 right triangle are also discussed, but in an applied context. Here, we are asked to consider a gnomon, or vertical rod (*Gǔ*) which casts a horizontal shadow (*Gōu*). The line from the top of the rod to the tip of the shadow is called *Xián*. Then:

$$G\bar{o}u^2 + G\ddot{u}^2 = Xi\acute{a}n^2$$

The text says that, "The emperor *Yǔ* can rule the country because of the existence of this *Gōugǔ* theorem" (Li and Du 1987, 29). The reference to legendary emperor Yǔ suggests an early date for this rule, and the reference to its significance for the ruler is supported by a discussion of how the gnomon could be used to discover the heights of objects, the depth of canyons, and the distance of objects from an observer: "Align the gnomon with the plumb line to determine the horizontal, lay down the gnomon to find the height, reverse the gnomon to find the depth, lay the gnomon flat to determine the distance" (Li and Du 1987, 31). If we use the principle that corresponding parts of similar triangles are proportional, which the Chinese used constantly without proof and without explicit statement, we see from Figure 2.6 how the gnomon was used to measure heights, depths, and distances.

One particularly interesting application of the *Gōugǔ* theorem and the similar triangles principle comes at the end of the *Zhoubi Suanjing*. In this section of the text, we are told that the heavens and the earth are both flat and equidistant from one another and that at the summer solstice at Yang Cheng, an 8 *chi* vertical rod casts a 6 *chi* shadow. If one goes south 60,000 miles, the Sun is directly overhead. How far is the Sun from the Earth? Answer, 80,000 miles (see Figure 2.7a). There then follows another problem using the similar

Figure 2.6
The Gnomon and Its Uses. Joseph Emmert.

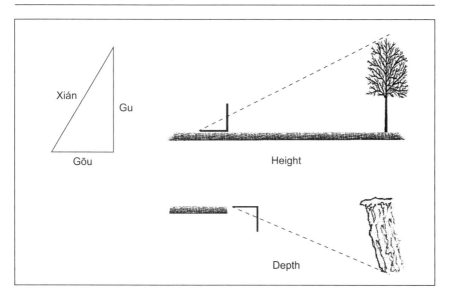

Figure 2.7
Distance to the Heavens and Size of the Sun. Joseph Emmert.

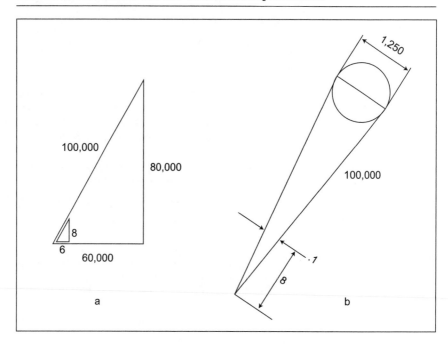

triangles principle. A bamboo sighting tube 8 *chi* long and with a diameter of 0.1 *chi* is used to observe the Sun, which just fills the opening of the tube. What is the diameter of the Sun? (see Figure 2.7b.)

The answer is 1,250 miles (Nakayama 1969).

Not only does the Pythagorean theorem figure in applications in both the Chinese and Mesopotamian traditions, it also figures in the category of pseudo-problems in both traditions. Consider, for example, the following two problems, the first from Selucid era Mesopotamia circa 300 B.C.E. (which follows the pattern of an Old Babylonian problem) and the second from the ninth chapter of the Chinese *Jiuzhang Suanshu*:

A reed is placed vertically against a wall [of equal height]. If it [the top of the reed] moves down 3 cubits, [the other end] moves away by 9 cubits. What is the Reed?

[Let reed be length c, distance away = $a = 9$, $b = c - 3$; $c^2 = 9^2 + (c-3)^2 = 81 + c^2 - 6c + 9$, $6c = 90$, $c = 15$]. (Van der Waerden 1963, 76–77)

Suppose a wall is 10 feet tall and a tree is rested against it so its top is at the top of the wall. If one steps back one foot [at the base of the tree], pulling the tree, the tree falls to the ground [with the top touching the base of the wall]. How big is the tree?

[Let height of tree = c, height of wall = $a = 10$, initial tree base to wall distance = $(c-1)$, $100 + (c-1)^2 = c^2$, $c = 50.5$ ft.]. (Martzloff 1997, 95)

Given the similar ways in which both the special 3, 4, 5 right triangle and the more general Pythagorean theorem appear in the Mesopotamian and the Chinese texts and the temporal priority of the Mesopotamian problems, it is reasonable to ask whether the Chinese might have gained their knowledge of the Pythagorean theorem from Selucid sources. There was trade between China and the Near East along the Silk Road by the mid-Han period, before the two major early Chinese texts seem to have been compiled, so a possibility exists. However, several factors suggest that it is more likely that the Pythagorean theorem was produced independently in the two cultures. First, the reference to the emperor *Yǔ* implies earlier Chinese familiarity with the theorem. More importantly, the initial applications of the *Gōugǔ* theorem are all linked with the similar triangles proportionality principle, which is not present in the Mesopotamian cases. Finally, evidence is fairly strong that trading caravans and ships did not carry scholars during this period, so there is little plausible reason to posit contact between the mathematically literate in the two civilizations.

So far, we have suggested that the Pythagorean theorem was used for applications and for the formulation of pseudo-problems both in Mesopotamia and in China, but there is also evidence of a more theoretical interest in the Pythagorean triplets from a much earlier period in Mesopotamia. A broken tablet at Columbia University designated Plimpton 322 and dating from the Old Babylonian period (c. 1800 B.C.E.) contains several long columns of numbers. Otto Neugebauer noticed that two of the successive columns contained numbers that were the c and b of the Pythagorean triplets where $a^2 + b^2 = c^2$ and that the previous column was c^2/a^2. We now know that all Pythagorean triples are obtainable from the formula $a = 2pq$, $b = p^2 - q^2$, $c = p^2 + q^2$, where $p > q$ and p and q are integers that are relatively prime and not simultaneously odd. This tablet contains the successive Pythagorean triplets generated by the lowest p and q pairs that meet these criteria. Though we have only the sequence of bs, cs, and $(c/a)^2$s, the scribe who created this tablet was almost certainly exploring aspects of number theory, for there is no known practical reason to want to construct a sequence of Pythagorean triplets of this kind (Neugebaeuer 1957).

The *Jiuzhang Suanshu* contains a series of area measurements for figures of varying kinds under the label of "field measurements." Correct formulae for the areas of squares, rectangles, triangles, trapeziums, and circles (for which the area is given as ¼ circumference × diameter). The circumference is then estimated to be three times the diameter, meaning $\pi = 3$.

There are no extended teaching texts for Mesopotamian mathematics comparable to the Rhind Papyrus or the *Jiuzhang Suanshu*, but among the huge number of individual problem texts, we find many that either solve for the areas of such figures as squares, rectangles, triangles, circles, and trapezoids or use the results of such calculations in determining the volumes of cylinders, prisms, and the frustra of cones and pyramids. When they wanted to make theoretical calculations simple, the Mesopotamians used 3 for π, but when real problems had to be solved they occasionally used $\pi = 22/7 = 3.14286$ (modern value approximately 3.14159).

In spite of the dramatic pyramid constructions, the Egyptian geometry represented in the Rhind papyrus was generally less advanced than Mesopotamian geometry in the Old Babylonian period. The formulae for the areas of squares and rectangles are correctly given, and interesting complications are added to rectangular area problems. For example, Moscow papyrus problem 49 tells us that, in a rectangle of area 12, the width is ½ + ¼ of the length. Let h be the length, then $h^2(½ + ¼)=12$, $h^2 = 12\ (1 + ⅓) = 16$, $h = 4$, width $= 3$ (Gillings 1972).

Whether the Egyptians generally had the correct value for the area of a triangle is debated among scholars. Problem 51 of the Rhind papyrus uses the formula A = ½ (*meryet*)(*teper*) where there is general agreement that *teper* should be translated as base. But whether *meryet* should be interpreted as what we call altitude, or "the other side" is problematic. If, as seems to be the case in problem 51, the triangle is a right triangle, either interpretation is correct, but for non-right triangles it makes a difference. Most historians of mathematics are inclined to read *meryet* as altitude (Gillings 1972); but evidence from land contracts as late as 1300 B.C.E. suggests that triangular pieces of land had their areas stipulated as a half one side times the average of the other two, which is not correct even for right angled triangles.

The area of a circle inscribed in a square of side d is given in Rhind problem 50 as $(8/9d)^2$, which is equivalent to $\pi = 3.1605$, which is within 0.6 percent of the modern value of 3.14159. In this case, unlike the Mesopotamian or Chinese cases, we have a reasonably good idea of how this value was obtained. Rhind problem 48 derives the area of an eight-sided figure constructed as in Figure 2.8a. (Note, this is not, strictly speaking, an octagon because alternat-

Figure 2.8
Rhind Papyrus #48—Area of a Circle. Joseph Emmert.

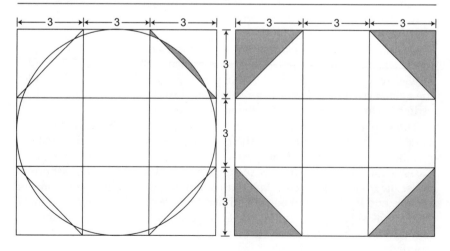

ing sides are 3 and $3 \times \sqrt{2}$ in length.) The area is $(81 - 4 \times 9/2) = 63$ corresponding to a square of side $\sqrt{63}$, which is approximately 8. If we let a side now be d, rather than 9, the approximate area is $(8d/9)^2$. Now, however, consider the relationship between the area of this eight-sided figure and that of a circle inscribed in the square, as shown in Figure 2.8b. The extra area exhibited by the circle in the corner squares is roughly equal to the excess area of the octagonal figure in the side squares, so the area of the circle is approximately that of the inscribed eight-sided figure, producing the 3.1605 equivalent for π.

THE SPECIAL CASE OF EARLY INDIAN GEOMETRY

In the cases of Egyptian, Mesopotamian, and Chinese geometry, it is clear that the measurement of areas of plots of land was an initial motivator, that the measurement of at least some volumes was motivated by the desire to discover the amounts of material needed to fill certain shaped objects or the amount of grain held in silos of given dimensions. In each case, however, some problems indicate a tendency to extend mathematical problems and knowledge beyond the immediately useful, sometimes in a playful manner, and occasionally in a way that indicates an interest in mathematical theory for its own sake. The earliest geometrical writings from India have a quite different character. These writings, the *Śulva sūtras,* appear as appendices to the Vedic religious texts whose dates are generally agreed to be sometime between 800 and 400 B.C.E., with a most probable date of around 600 B.C.E.

On the face of it, they are applied texts that deal with the situation and construction of altars of baked brick subject to certain constraints that we will discuss. Two oddities about these texts is that baked brick was not being used in India when the texts were created, and no altars matching the conditions set down have been excavated.

Harappan civilization, however, did use various sizes of baked bricks. Harappan rectangular bricks generally exhibited constant length-to-depth-to-height ratios, and all linear dimensions were multiples of a single basic unit of length. Moreover, some special wedge-shaped and trapezoidal bricks were made for constructing wells, drains, and circular granary floors. Given the interest in the dimensions and shapes of burnt brick by Harappan artisans and the wide spread assumption that mathematical knowledge must be linked to artisanal traditions shared by many historians of ancient technology, it has usually been hypothesized that the *Śulva sūtras* reflect an oral tradition that goes all the way back to the artisans of Harappan civilization. Thus, the content of the earliest Indian geometry can be traced back to no later than circa 1750 B.C.E. (Chattopadhyaya 1986).

According to those who accept this view, the priestly authors of the *Śulva sūtras* were concerned with getting the construction of their altars done correctly to make their rituals most pleasing to the gods, and they drew on the ancient lore of the brick makers, which had been passed down orally, to accomplish this goal. According to George Thibaut: "Theirs was not the love of disinterested research which distinguishes true science, nor the inordinate craving of undisciplined minds for the solution of riddles which reason tells us cannot be solved: theirs was simply the earnest desire to render their sacrifice in all its particulars acceptable to the gods, and to deserve the boons which the gods confer in return upon the faithful and conscientious worshiper" (Chattopadhyaya 1986, 168). Religious considerations thus motivated an emphasis on precision, but had no impact on technical considerations once they were motivated.

Several altar shapes are discussed in the *Śulva-sūtra* texts, but for all shapes several conditions had to be met: (1) The total area of the initially constructed altar had to be 7-½ *perusa sq.* (where a square *perusa* is a square, each side of which is the length of a man standing with arms uplifted). (2) Each structure was to be made of five layers of brick and to have a total height of one *janu* (knee), so each layer was roughly 4.5 inches high. (3) Each layer had to have exactly 200 bricks. 4. Except at the extremities, no edges of the second layer bricks could be immediately above a seam in the first layer. In addition, special conditions had to be met for each particular shape of altar, necessitating the use of specially shaped and sized bricks. In the most extensively discussed altar, the Falcon altar, for example, the bricks used for the wings have length of 24 *angulas* and the other sides 20 *angulas,* but they must be bent so that the area covered is 54,900 sq. *angulas,* rather than the 57,600 sq. *angulas* that would be covered by rectangular bricks with those dimensions. That is, the acute angles between two adjacent sides has to be less than 90°, making parallelograms, rather than rectangles. This implies a recognition that the area of a parallelogram is its length times height, where height is the altitude of one of the end triangles, rather than the hypotenuse. It also presupposes a way to calculate the length of offset to create the requisite height (19.06 *angulas*), which demands the equivalent of the Pythagorean theorem.

To give just a sense of the kind of problems stated and resolved in the *Śulva sūtra* texts, here are the set explored in the *Baudhayana Śulva sūtra:*

1. How to construct a square, given its side. [This problem requires the construction of a right angle, 2 methods for which are given.]
2. How to construct a rectangle, given its length and breadth [uses the results from 1].
3. To show that the square on the diagonal of a given square has twice the area of the original.
4. To construct a square whose area is three times that of a given square. [First, one constructs a rectangle on the diagonal of the original square with length = diagonal of original and width = side of original, then one constructs a square on the diagonal of that rectangle, since that diagonal = $\sqrt{(1+2)}$.]
5. How to construct a square whose area is the sum of the areas of two squares of different sizes.
6. How to construct a square whose area is the difference between the areas of two given squares.
7. How to construct a rectangle whose area is equal to that of a given square.
8. How to construct a square whose area is the same as that of a given rectangle.
9. How to transform a square into an isosceles trapezoid, whose shorter side is given as lesser than the side of the square.

10. How to construct a triangle with an area equal to that of a given square.
11. How to construct a rhombus equal in area to any given square.
12. How to construct a circle with the area of a given square. [The complex approximation used produces a π equivalent of 3.088, not as good as the ancient Egyptian, Mesopotamian, or late Han values.]
13. How to construct a square with the same area as a given circle.

As this text has been interpreted by Subinoy Ray (Chattopadhyaya 1986), it deserves several comments. First, it incorporates a demand for geometrical constructions and proofs that almost certainly predate any well-attested case in Greece or elsewhere, though none of the *Śulva sūtra* proofs reach the formal rigor of those that we shall see in Greece. Indeed, the general sentiment of Western scholars seems to be that: "It is true that in the sacred geometry of ancient India, known as the *rope rules,* certain geometric facts are stated in the form of *sūtras,* or aphorisms, but these are never proved . . . At best one sometimes comes across some numerical verifications" (Szabó 1978, 186). Nonetheless, it is true that, in setting up the constructions and justifications for the propositions articulated in the *Śulva sūtras,* Indian authors did seek both more explicit assumptions and greater generality of expression than can be found, for example, in Mesopotamian or Egyptian mathematical texts.

Second, looking at the paired problems, 5 and 6, 7 and 8, and 12 and 13 above, from a practical perspective, there is no need to justify both members of the pair, since the first of each pair allows one to accomplish the second calculation automatically. The only reason for demanding justifications for both members of the pair is to achieve theoretical completeness. Finally, from an applied perspective, the value of π implied in 12 and 13 is poor enough that it could lead to serious underestimations of the diameter of a grain silo needed to store a given amount of grain. All of these comments would suggest that these problems are not ones that are likely to have been inherited from Harappan artisans, whose interests were, as far as we know, completely practical and who demanded extreme precision (as suggested in the sets of weights and linear measures that have been excavated).

Coupled with the fact that there is no evidence that alters constructed according the directions in the *Śulva sūtras* were ever built, these comments might lead one to ask if the priestly authors of this geometrical literature ever really expected the altars to be built, or if the whole discussion of burnt brick altars was not primarily an excuse for the authors to explore geometrical theory. There is evidence to suggest that they might not have intended the altars to be built with bricks. Within the contemporary commentaries (*samhitas*) on the *Vedas,* there are several that suggest that "imaginary altars" or "mind-made altars," or "altars made of the organ of speech," were appropriate substitutes for brick-made altars (Chattopadhyaya 1986, 175).

One additional consideration would support the notion that some Vedic priests might have developed an interest in mathematics for its own sake. As Buddhism and Jainism began to replace Vedic religion in India during the sixth century before the Common Era, Jainist priests also demonstrated considerable interest in mathematical topics, though not in the form of commentaries on the construction of altars, because that was not a smokescreen that they could use. Indeed, Jain mathematics was openly abstract and tended to emphasize the theory of numbers. In the Jainist case, the occasion or excuse for discussing mathematics was their philosophy of time and space, which led them to consider not only large enumerable numbers, but also numbers that were innumerable and even infinite. In the course of these discussions, they reached the conclusion that not all infinities are the same and they defined five different kinds of infinity: infinite in one direction, infinite in two directions, infinite in area, infinite everywhere, and infinite perpetually (Joseph 2000). In the *Anuyoga Dwara Śūtra* from circa 200 B.C.E., there is an interesting sample problem regarding how to discover the highest enumerable number. The reader is told:

Consider a trough whose diameter is that of the earth (100,000 *yojanna*) and whose circumference is 316,227 *yojanna*. Fill it up with white mustard seeds, counting one after another. Similarly fill up with mustard seeds other troughs of the various lands and seas. Still the highest enumerable number has not been obtained. (Joseph 2000, 251)

Incidentally, in the statement of this case, π is approximated by the square root of 10, which is substantially better than the previous Indian approximation. In addition, the *Anuyoga Dwara Sūtra* suggests that the Jains had discovered the general rule that $a^m \times a^n = a^{(m+n)}$ and $(a^m)^n = a^{mn}$. In the *Bhagabati Sūtra* from 300 B.C.E., there is an extended discussion of the numbers of permutations and combinations that can be formed from n items taken two and three items at a time. If we designate combinations from n taken three at a time by nC_3 and agree that ab and ba are not different combinations, then $nC_3 = n(n-1)(-2)/1.2.3.$ and $nC_2 = n(n-1)/1.2$. If we think of permutations as arrangements in which ab is not the same as ba, then $nP_2 = n(n-1)$ and $nP_3 = n(n-1)(n-2)$ (Joseph 2000). All of these problems are set in a context of the calculation of numbers so large that actually carrying out the calculations would have been impossible.

For those who insist upon the practical source of ancient mathematical writing, comments on the suitability of imaginary or verbally constructed altars is simply a way around the likely shortage of appropriately trained artisans during the period of construction of the texts. On the other hand, for those of us who admit that most ancient mathematical traditions began in practical demands, but leave open the possibility that there might have been local alternatives, the evidence suggests that what Aristotle wrongly suggested about the origins of Egyptian mathematics might actually have been largely true of the Vedic priests who wrote the *Śulva sūtras*. Aristotle wrote:

When a variety of arts had been invented, some of them being concerned with the necessities and others with the social refinements of life, the inventors of the latter were naturally considered wiser than those of the former because their knowledge was not directed to immediate utility. Hence when everything of these kinds had already been provided, those sciences were discovered which deal neither with the necessities nor the enjoyments of life, and this took place earliest in regions where men had leisure.

This is why the mathematical arts were first put together in Egypt, for in that country the priestly caste were indulged with leisure. (981b)

In Egypt, those who developed and used the earliest mathematics were almost certainly government officials in charge of construction, supplying work gangs, and providing raw materials for activities such as baking and brewing, but in India, the first mathematical texts *were* written by a priestly class whose status within the growing caste society was far above that of artisans. Most Vedic priests were undoubtedly focused on their ritual tasks and uninterested in mathematics; but those few who wrote the *Sulva-sutra-s* may well have been playing with mathematical theory while disguising it as something relevant to their priestly vocations. Furthermore, it seems relatively clear that their successors among the Jainists were continuing the tradition of using religious issues—but in this case their doctrines of time and space rather than the construction of imaginary altars—for doing precisely the same thing.

MORE COMPLEX MATHEMATICAL PROBLEMS

In each of the ancient civilizations there is evidence of mathematical knowledge that went beyond simple calculation and simple geometry. Frequently, except in India, the more advanced mathematical techniques were directly tied to applications; thus, for example, the *Jiuzhang Suanshu* includes the following problem that involves the solution of three linear equations in three variables:

Top-grade ears of rice three bundles, medium-grade ears of rice two bundles, low-grade ears of rice one bundle, makes 39 *dŏu* [of rice by volume]; top-grade ears of rice two bundles, medium-grade ears of rice three bundles, low-grade ears of rice one bundle, makes 34 *dŏu*; top-grade ears of rice one bundle, medium-grade ears of rice two bundles, low-grade ears of rice three bundles, makes 26 *dŏDoneu*. How many *dŏu* are there in a top-grade, medium grade, and low-grade ears of rice? (Li and Du 1987, 46; Martzloff 1987, 252)

We would write:

$$3x + 2y + z = 39$$
$$2x + 3y + z = 34$$
$$x + 2y + 3z = 26$$

Presenting the Chinese counting rod arrangement using our numerals, we can represent this system of equations in the form of a matrix of coefficients:

3	2	1	39
2	3	1	34
1	2	3	26

The goal is now to eliminate the coefficients of two variables in one of the rows by taking two of the equations, multiplying each by some number so that the coefficients are equal, and then subtracting one from the other and substituting the coefficients of the resulting equation for one of the two equations used. The same process is repeated to eliminate the coefficient of the second variable in the equation that now has a zero coefficient for the first. At this point, one can solve the equation for the remaining variable. In the example of the first problem from the chapter on rectangular arrays of the *Jiuzhang Suanshu*, the second row is first multiplied by three and subtracted from double the first row. Similarly, the third row is multiplied by three and subtracted from the first row. Next, the new second row is multiplied by four, and five times the third row is subtracted from it, yielding a matrix in which the third equation is now:

0   0   36   99,

representing $36z = 99$, or $z = 2\,\tfrac{3}{4}$. The middle row is then solved for y, $(y = 4\,\tfrac{1}{4})$, and the top row is solved for x $(x = 9\,\tfrac{1}{4})$. This method continues to be used for eliminating unknowns today; but it was not used in the West until it was discovered by the Frenchman, Jean Borrel in the mid-sixteenth century (Li and Du 1987).

Occasionally, the more complicated problems suggest an interest that goes well beyond application. For example, one of the problems in the Egyptian Berlin papyrus involves what we would call the simultaneous solution of equations of the second and first degrees. Paraphrasing the problem:

The area of a square is 100 [sq. cubits].

This area is the sum of the areas of two other squares the side of one of which is $(\tfrac{1}{2} + \tfrac{1}{4})$ that of the other. Let me know the sides of the two unknown squares.

[In modern notation, $x^2 + y^2 = 100$, $4x - 3y = 0$].

If x were 1, y would be $1/2 + 1/4$ and y^2 would be $1/2 + 1/16$, so $x^2 + y^2 = 1 + 1/2 + 1/16$.

The square root of $(1 + 1/2 + 1/16) = (1 + 1/4)$.

The square root of $100 = 10$.

Divide 10 by $(1 + \tfrac{1}{4}) = 8$, the side of the larger square.

$(\tfrac{1}{2} + \tfrac{1}{4})$ of $8 = 6$, the side of the smaller squarer.

This is clearly a pseudo problem, and the "false" assumption that $x = 1$ offers a strategy that can be applied to solve any problem of the form $x^2 + y^2 = A$, $ax - by = 0$ (Gillings 1972).

A more interesting problem appears in the Mesopotamian Louvre Tablet AO 8862 from the Old Babylonian period:

I have multiplied length and width, obtaining the surface. Then I added to the surface the excess of the length over width [result] 183. Lastly I have added the length and width [result] 27. What are the length, width, and area?

Given: 27 and 183

[Results]: 15 length, 12 width, area 180

[i.e., $xy + x - y = 183$, $x + y = 27$]

Transcription	Analysis
You, in calculating, add 27,	$xy + (x - y) + (x + y) = 210$
The sum of length and width	$x(y + 2) = 210$
to 183 [result] 210	
Add 2 to 27 [result] 29	$x + (y + 2) = 29$
	The problem is now of the standard form,
	$xy' = P, x + y' = a$
	Suppose $x = a/2 + w$, and $y' = a/2 - w$
	$xy' = P = (a/2 + w)(a/2 - w)$
	So $w^2 = (a/2)^2 - P$
You will divide 29 in 2	
[result] 14-½	$a/2 = 14\text{-}½$
14-½ times 14-½ [result] 210-¼	$(a/2)^2 = 210\text{-}¼$
You will subtract 210 from 210-¼	$(a/2)^2 - P = ¼$
(½)^2 = ¼	$\sqrt{((a/2)^2 - P)} = ½ = w$
You will add ½ to the first 29/2	$x = a/2 + w = 15$
[Result] 15, the length. Subtract	
½ from the second 29/2 [result] 14	$y' = a/2 - w = 14$
2, which you have added to 27,	
Subtract from 14 [Result] 12 width	$y = y' - 2 = 12$
Multiply 15 and 12 [Result] 180	$xy = 180 = \text{area}$

—(Van der Waerden 1963, 63–66).

Note that the way in which this problem is stated, adding a length to an area, makes no physical sense because in practice only quantities with the same dimensions can be added to one another, so this is not even a pseudo-problem. For the Old Babylonian scribe, it is, rather, a way of exploring a set of abstract algebraic relationships.

SUMMARY COMMENTS ON MATHEMATICS IN THE EARLIEST CIVILIZATIONS

Several ancient texts in addition to the *Zhoubi Suanjing* suggest how important mathematics was to the intellectual elites of ancient civilizations. For example, in spite of some of the limitations of Egyptian mathematics, the Rhind papyrus announces itself as containing "Rules for enquiring into nature and for knowing all that exists, every mystery, every secret."(Sarton 1952, 37) That is, numeracy was taken as a key to all knowledge. This notion is reinforced by a whole genre of contest texts in which one scribe challenges another or chides him for being unable to accomplish some feat. Most of these texts have mathematical content. Precisely the same kind of challenge texts appear in Mesopotamia, and again they focus in large part on mathematical issues. Even in the Chinese scholarly tradition, which focused on literary classics, numeracy was taken as a key sign of intellectual competence, thus the following story from before the Warring States period:

During the Spring and Autumn period (770–476 B.C.) Duke Huàn of the feudal state of Qí established an "Institute for recruiting distinguished persons" in order to attract people with outstanding abilities. Although he waited quite a while there were still no people applying for positions. After a year a man came along and brought with him a "nine-nines rhyme" as a gift for the Duke and to show his outstanding knowledge. Duke Huàn thought it was quite a joke and said to the man: "You think the nine-nines rhyme demonstrates some kind of advanced knowledge?" The man gave him a sound answer. He said: "As a matter of fact, knowing the nine-nines rhyme is not sufficient to show any ability or learning. But if you appoint me who only know[s] the nine-nines rhyme then there is no doubt that people of ability and skill will queue up for employment." Duke Huàn thought this was a sound argument. So he accepted him and warmly welcomed him. In less than a month many people of ability and skill applied, coming from many places. (Li and Du 1987, 13–14)

It seems clear then, that mathematical knowledge was highly prized in all of those ancient civilizations from which we have evidence, and with the possible exception of Indian civilization during the Vedic period, it is undoubtedly the case that mathematics was initially concerned with practical issues of commerce, governance, and construction. The bulk of the problems known from Egypt, Mesopotamia, and China offer ways to calculate areas and volumes of standardized shapes, how to calculate the provisions needed by groups of men over given periods of time, how to calculate taxes to be levied on different classes of subjects, and so on, yet by around 1800 B.C.E. in Egypt and Mesopotamia, by 600 B.C.E. in India, and by 100 B.C.E. in China, there is evidence that, for some intellectuals, interest in mathematics transcended the practical and reached at least to the production of pseudo-problems that extended practical techniques to impractical situations. The Egyptians and Chinese also began exploring challenging puzzles that depended on mathematical skill, and to a very small extent in Egypt and to a much larger extent in Mesopotamia, it seems as though some members of the scribal class began working on problems that would extend mathematical knowledge in ways that we might identify as speculative or theoretical. Only in the Indian tradition, however, does there seem to be evidence of a demand for some kind of mathematical justifications prior to the Pre-Socratic Greek fascination with logic, which began around 500 B.C.E.

GREEK THEORETICAL MATHEMATICS

Greek theoretical mathematics is so extensive and complex that we can only briefly characterize it here with an emphasis on the major way in which it departed from the mathematical traditions of earlier civilizations. Those interested in greater detail are directed to the works of Asger Aaboe, François Lasserre, Edward Maziarz and Thomas Greenwood, Sir Thomas Heath, Árpád Szabó, and Wilbur Knorr, all of which are listed in the bibliography.

Many, though by no means all, of the mathematical *results* discussed by Greek mathematicians before the great flowering at Alexandria after around 320 B.C.E. were taken over from Egyptian and Mesopotamian sources by Greek intellectuals who lived in cities on the west and southwest coast of Turkey or on the east coast of Italy. Cities like Miletus, Croton, and Elia engaged in trade with Egypt and Mesopotamia beginning in the late seventh century B.C.E. Moreover, we are told by the doxographers that men from those cities, men such as Thales of Miletus and Pythagoras, who supposedly lived at Croton though he was born at Samos, were exposed to the mathematical and astronomical traditions of those cultures. They traveled to Egypt and they brought many of the mathematical results found in Egypt back to Greece. Little is said about travels to Mesopotamia, probably because the antagonism toward that region initiated during the wars with the Persians made it unpopular to grant any credit for things that originated in that area, but results from Mesopotamian mathematics were certainly as important as those from Egypt in the flowering of Greek mathematical theory in the works of Euclid, Apollonius, and Archimedes between 300 and 200 B.C.E.

Far and away the most important feature of Greek scholarly mathematics, and one which differentiates it from all of its predecessors, is its demand for rigorous proofs. As Árpád Szabó writes, "Greek science is concerned not only with stating propositions, but with providing genuine *proofs* of them as well. The role played by proofs is no less important than it is in [21st century] mathematics; in fact, it is the same. Furthermore, Euclid's proofs are for the most part models of their kind and have set the standards of mathematical rigor for generations." (1978, 186) Szabó goes on to argue that the presence of rigorous proofs in Hellenistic Greek mathematics raises two issues:

[One] question that now raises itself is what first gave Greek mathematics the idea that mathematical propositions need to be proved, and how did they become so skilled at proving them that their proofs are still admired today.—A [second] problem is whether mathematicians were originally satisfied with more primitive and less complete proofs than those found in Euclid, and if so, how did the techniques of proof become more highly developed later on. (1978, 186–187)

It is not accidental that Szabó uses the term "science" rather than mathematics in the first sentence quoted above, because many Greek philosophers' desire for absolute certainty regarding their truth claims extended well beyond the domain of mathematics and probably developed outside of mathematics in what we would call natural philosophy today. The search for apodictic certainty that was first exemplified in Pre-Socratic natural philosophy was almost certainly motivated by a set of circumstances that initially had little to do with either natural philosophy or mathematics. I will return to discuss these circumstances more extensively in chapter 7, but for the present it is enough to recognize that those who developed the logical tools needed to produce mathematical proofs were generally teachers of Athenian aristocrats, whose primary desire was to be successful pleaders in the Athenian law courts and political assemblies.

Among these teachers, the most important, in terms of raising interest in mathematics, were undoubtedly Plato and the Pythagoreans, for whom mathematics formed a core element in their cosmologies, but the most important in terms of their contributions to the demands for and techniques of mathematical proof were undoubtedly Parmenides and Zeno, who came to Athens from Elia to teach around 470 B.C.E., and Aristotle, who studied under Plato in Athens. Aristotle established his own school around 335 B.C.E., after Athens became a Macedonian conquest. G. E. R. Lloyd, who along with Nathan Sivin, has written extensively on the comparative contexts for early Greek and Chinese science, argues that the competition for students among teachers in Greece was intense. In that circumstance, "It was success in argument with rivals that secured a reputation, essential not least if you were to make a living as a teacher. In these respects, the tradition of debate itself stands out as the key institution in the situation within which most Greek intellectuals operated" (Lloyd 2002, 135). Faced with the need to develop new techniques of persuasion because of their dissatisfaction with the rhetorical strategies used within the law courts and assemblies, some philosophers sought to find a way to secure incontrovertibility in their arguments.

The level of rigor of these attempts did change over time, and we will use the proof that the square formed on the diagonal of a square has an area equal to double the area of the original square to illustrate certain key features of the change. In his dialogue *Meno*, Plato offers a proof of this claim that represents the character of proofs developed by the Pythagoreans in the late sixth century before the Common Era (even though the *Meno* was written in the mid-fourth century). Plato's goal seems to be to demonstrate that knowledge is nothing but remembering what we knew in a previous incarnation. In order to convince his reader, he questions a slave boy about how to construct a square with area double that of an original square, gradually getting him to recognize the correct answer without ever telling him. For present purposes what is most important about this process is how Meno demonstrates the truth or falsity of the slave's tentative answers. The boy suggests doubling the length of the side of the square first. Meno draws a square with double the sides and shows the boy visually that the area is four times the original (see Figure 2.9a). After other tries, the slave suggests constructing the new square on the diagonal of the old and Meno draws Figure 2.9b, demonstrating visually that the area of the new square contains four triangles equal to the two triangles formed by two sides and the diagonal of the original.

This type of proof had to be abandoned in the face of new challenges to sensory evidence in general, and visual experience in particular. Parmenides (c. 520–450 B.C.E.) and his student Zeno initiated the development of logical techniques, including that of indirect proof, in connection with the *physical* question of whether motion can take place in the real world. We clearly experience motion through our senses, including our vision. Through a set of four paradoxes, Zeno, however, questions whether the motions that we observe can *really* take place. He needs four cases to demonstrate that motion

Figure 2.9
Creating a Square Whose Area is Double That of an Initial Square. Joseph Emmert.

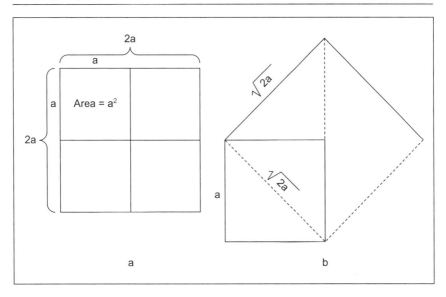

cannot take place either under the condition that time and/or space are in-finitely divisible or under the condition that one or more is finitely divisible. We will use the first case, which assumes the infinite divisibility of space to illustrate the character of his argument. His stadium argument goes like this: if space is infinitely divisible, a runner can never reach the finish line of a race because before he reaches the finish he has to pass the halfway point, but before he can reach the halfway point, he has to get to the quarterway point, and so on, forever if space is infinitely divisible. To pass through an infi-nite number of distances must take an infinite amount of time, thus motion must be impossible under the condition of the infinite divisibility of space. In three other cases, Zeno establishes that motion cannot take place: if time is infinitely divisible, if space is finitely divisible, and if time is finitely divisible.

Several possible conclusions might be draw from these findings. One is that space and time are neither finitely nor infinitely divisible. In some sense this is the modern answer, but that conclusion seemed impossible to most Greek philosophers. Another is that Zeno's form of logic of magnitudes is sim-ply inapplicable to the physical world, but few people other than Aristotle were able to accept this conclusion. The most common conclusion—accepted by Plato and many others—was that the real world is unchanging and mo-tionless and that what we call the physical world is illusory, or an imperfect copy, about which the best we can discover is a "likely story" (Plato 1959, 18).

For present purposes, the most important consequence of this conclusion was that nothing could be *proved* using sensory inputs. The question then became: under what conditions could certainty be attained?

At this point, Aristotle provided an account of how one could achieve a strict demonstration in his *Prior Analytics* and *Posterior Analytics*. Without going into all of the details of Aristotle's theory of sciences which could be certain, several features are worth emphasizing. All such sciences would have to have some terms and propositions assumed to be correct because they were either commonly agreed upon definitions or because they were unchallengeable, or self-evident, propositions. Some of those propositions had to state necessary relationships between well defined terms. Then, all subsequent terms and propositions had to be derivable logically from that initial set or from terms and propositions previously derived logically from that set. Lloyd argues that "the mathematicians in the Euclidean tradition showed what could be done with it [Aristotle's theory of incontrovertible sciences] in practice" (2002, 66).

Euclid's *Elements of Geometry*, which sought to build upon Aristotle's account of argumentative certainty, provided subsequent Greek and later European authors such as Rene Descartes and Thomas Hobbes both with a proof that sciences like that theorized by Aristotle were possible and with a set of suggestions about how the initial definitions and propositions might be constructed. In particular, it provided a model to be emulated by virtually the entire Western mathematical tradition, beginning with Archimedes and Apollonius, who extended the domain of theoretical mathematics beyond what Euclid had covered.

Euclid's *Elements* begins with a set of 23 definitions, from which all other definitions used in the text are derived. It then offers five postulates. Three of these simply assert that a straight line can be drawn between any two points, that a straight line can be continued to any finite distance, and that a circle with any chosen radius can be produced around any given center. The fourth asserts that all right angles are equal, and the fifth (which defines Euclidean geometry as opposed to other geometries developed in the 19th century) states that if a straight line intersects two other straight lines so that the interior angles on the same side make less than two right angles, the other two lines extended will eventually meet on the side on which the angles are less than two angles. Finally, there is a set of five common notions, which include such self-evident claims as "things that are equal to the same thing are equal to one another," and "If equals be added to equals, the wholes are equal" (Heath 1956, vol. 1, 153–155). From this point on, in principle, every proposition in Euclid's *Elements* is a consequence of the logical connection of two or more of these definitions, postulates, and common notions. Diagrams may accompany the proofs of propositions (although the first printed versions of Euclid contained no diagrams), but no proof depends upon the visual inspection of any figure. As a consequence, the proofs avoided the challenges that Parmenides and Zeno had offered to the proof presented by Plato in *Meno*. Indeed, Euclid's mathematical work seemed immune to criticism to his near contemporaries and provided a general model of argumentation that others through the 17th century hoped might be extended to domains beyond mathematics.

Subsequent commentators have shown that, contrary to the ideal, Euclid's *Elements* does use a small number of unstated assumptions. For example, the very first proposition, "On a given finite straight line to construct an equilateral triangle," (Heath 1956, Vol 1., 241) demands the unstated assumption that two circles of radius r, whose centers are a distance $< r$ apart will intersect one another, but such problems had no impact in antiquity.

Three

Technologies of Communication: Written Language, Educational Institutions, and the Character of Natural Knowledge

Though the beginnings of spoken language certainly preceded the origins of computational techniques, written language, at least insofar as it extends beyond the stipulation of commodities or substances more generally, probably developed only after the initiation of computation in Mesopotamia, and the evidence from petroglyphs seems to confirm this sequence for pre-urban cultures. However, evidence from Egypt, India, and China offers no way of determining whether writing and recorded counting developed simultaneously or in some sequence. In all three civilizations, writing and calculating appear simultaneously in the available evidence. In this chapter, we will be asking questions about the early development of writing in ancient civilizations and about whether the character of language, especially written language, can tell us anything about the content and extent of technical and scientific knowledge in early civilizations. In addition, we will ask who became literate, how and why they did so at critical times, and what impact the nature of institutions for the teaching of both literacy and numeracy had on the development of technology and the natural sciences in each civilization. I ventured a brief foray into this last topic at the end of the previous chapter, suggesting that the character of Greek education in the fifth- and fourth-centuries before the Common Era may have produced an unusual interest in the ideas of proof that became central to Greek mathematics. Here, we begin to explore such issues in more detail.

We have almost no information regarding the nature of Harappan language and education, and very little about written Indian language and education before the end of the Maurian empire (around 300 C.E.); nor do we know much about the development of written language and education in Mesoamerica prior to around 1300 C.E. As a consequence, we will concentrate on written language and education in Mesopotamia, Egypt, China, Greece, and Rome because we have significant information about language and education for each of them.

LANGUAGE AND REPRESENTATIONS OF THE WORLD

One central reason for discussing language in a book on science and tech-nology follows from an argument made by the linguists Edward Sapir and Benjamin Whorf. Sapir, Whorf's teacher, articulated a form of linguistic de-terminism in his 1929 essay, "The Status of Linguistics as a Science":

Human beings do not live in the objective world alone, nor alone in the world of social activity as ordinarily understood, but are very much at the mercy of the particular language which has become the medium of expression in their society. It is quite an illusion to imagine that one adjusts to reality essentially without the use of language and that language is merely an incidental means of solving specific problems of com-munication or reflection: The fact of the matter is that the 'real world' is to a large ex-tent unconsciously built up on the language habits of the group. No two languages are ever sufficiently similar to be considered as representing the same social reality. The worlds in which different societies live are distinct worlds, not merely the same world with different labels attached . . . Even comparatively simple acts of perception are very much more at the mercy of the social patterns called words than we might suppose . . . We see and hear and otherwise experience very largely as we do because the language habits of our community predispose certain choices of interpretation. (1929, 209)

Whorf agreed with Sapir to some degree. He held that, "all observers are not led by the same physical evidence to the same picture of the universe. . . ." (1956, 214). Unlike his mentor, however, Whorf distinguished between the physical world per se and our interpretations and representations of it. He wrote in "Science and Linguistics" in 1940:

We dissect nature along lines laid down by our native languages. The categories and types that we isolate from the world of phenomena we do not find there because they stare every observer in the face; on the contrary, the world is presented in a kaleido-scopic flux of impressions which has to be organized by our minds—and this means largely by the linguistic systems in our minds. We cut nature up, organize it into con-cepts, and ascribe significance as we do, largely because we are parties to an agree-ment to organize it in this way—an agreement that holds throughout our speech community and is codified in the patterns of our language. The agreement is, of course, an implicit and unstated one, but *its terms are absolutely obligatory;* we cannot talk at all except by subscribing to the organization and classification of data which the agree-ment decrees. (1956, 213–214)

More recent linguists have attacked the Whorf hypothesis in its strong form on a variety grounds, including the claim that translations between dif-ferent languages would be much more difficult than they are if there were not some species-wide ways of experiencing and cutting nature or at least com-monalities across some range of cultures (Schlessinger 1991). Virtually all languages use color, for example, to describe objects and have ways to distin-guish between bitter and sweet, and all use spatial and temporal categories. It nonetheless seems true that different languages make it easier or more dif-ficult to articulate certain relationships, or to distinguish similar things from one another. Roger Brown and Eric Lenneberg, for example, explored how speakers of one language categorize the color spectrum and how it affects their recognition of colors. In their study, English-speaking subjects were better able to recognize those hues that are easily named in English than speakers of other languages. This finding suggests that linguistic categories influence cognition (Brown and Lenneberg 1954). The suggestion was confirmed by a 1979 study that also demonstrated that, if a language has terms for discriminating between two colors close to one another on the color spectrum, then the actual discrimination/perception of those colors will be affected (Lucy and Shweder 1979). Languages, of course, not only influence the understandings of the world in a given culture, they also reflect that culture's priorities and values, so we have a kind of chicken and egg problem in which language both shapes and is shaped by other cultural factors—it mediates between culture and the physical and social worlds. In many ways, the influence of language on knowledge is probably easiest to see in early written languages that began as pictographic or logographic and either retained that character to a significant extent, as in ancient China, or only slowly took on syllabic and phonological character, as in Mesopotamia and Egypt, for the relationships between sign and thing signed in pictographic languages offer insights into perceived relationships among things in the world that purely phonological signs rarely do. For example, the earliest Chinese symbol for "heavens" or "cosmos" was a stick figure of a man. This relationship between the sign and the thing signed expresses a sense of connection between the human and the cosmic—or the microcosm and the macrocosm—which probably predated the existence of writing in Shang culture, and which, at least in part because of its embedding within written language, never disappeared from pre-modern Chinese thought. Indeed, the connection between man and the heavens lies at the core of virtually all ancient Chinese discussions about both society and nature. In Mesopotamia, on the other hand, the initial symbol for heaven was the crude picture of a star, which was drawn from a visual characteristic associated with the heavens.

The earliest Sumerian pictographs were almost always physically descriptive. On the other hand, while Chinese pictographs were usually descriptive, they occasionally expressed metaphoric or relational connections. The Chinese metaphoric, or associational, language seems to have encouraged a theoretical view of the world that both imposed and explored parallels among different domains of existence—the cosmic, the social, and the human—whereas the nearly exclusively descriptive emphasis in Sumerian language gave little impetus to theorize, focusing instead on description.

Another feature of classical Chinese writing reinforced the tendency to focus on parallels between different orders of existence. Derk Bodde has called special attention to a dominant stylistic pattern of "parallelism and antithesis" in the earliest Chinese literary productions, which was retained into the modern era and which tended to structure scientific thinking and writing as well. I follow his analysis closely here. Consider the first lines of the opening poem in the *Shi Jing* (Songs Classic), which originated sometime during the

Zhou period (1122–771 B.C.E.) and became one of the five Confucian Classics studied by all scholars from the Han dynasty to the early 20th century:

Watchful, watchful, the osprey
On the islet in the river
Comely, goodly, the maiden,
A fit mate for our lord

—(Bodde 1991, 46)

In the original, there is a formal numerical parallelism because each line has four ideographs and because the repeated term in the first line is paralleled by a rhyming pair of terms in the third line; but there is also a *topical parallelism* between the picture of conjugal devotion suggested in the first two lines as the female osprey sits in her nest awaiting the return of her mate and the suggestion of human devotion as the maiden awaits the arrival of the man who is to take her in marriage. "Here," Bodde writes, "in embryo, is the all important 'harmony of man and nature,'" which pervades Chinese cosmological thinking (Bodde 1991, 47).

A second kind of parallelism in which structural parallelism is coupled with *topical antithesis* is also often found in Chinese literary expression. Again, from the *Shi jing:*

Oh, the flowers of the begonia,
Gorgeous is their yellow!
The sorrows of my heart,
How they stab!

—(Bodde 1991, 47)

Here, Bodde argues, is a model for the Chinese view of the universe as "a never-ending flux of interacting [and oppositional] processes, rather than an array of unchanging substances and qualities" (Bodde 1991, 48). This dynamic, oppositional pattern of thought is symbolized by the Yin-yang interaction that characterizes all processes in nature.

At some uncertain point, the Sumerian star pictogram came to mean "god" as well as "heavens." But this signification also took on a very literal meaning consistent with common Mesopotamian practices. Mesopotamian gods were not simply signified by or associated with different stars or planets, as in the later Greek case, rather, the Mesopotamian heavenly bodies became *identified* as gods, leading eventually to a strict form of astral religion and astral determinism that we will discuss in the next chapter. A sophisticated mathematical astronomy was developed in Mesopotamia as a consequence of a dual fascination with celestial divination and calendrical precision, but as one politically dominant group replaced another in the region of the Tigris and Euphrates River Valleys, the Mesopotamians never incorporated their detailed knowledge of astronomical knowledge into a theory of the structure of the universe. As Georges Roux put it, "Babylonian astronomers never tried to assemble the numerous data they collected into coherent cosmic theories, such as the heliocentric system of Aristarchus of Samos or the geocentric system of Hipparchus" (1992, 366). Much the same is true of Mesopotamian secular medicine, which incorporated precise observations of symptoms and applied carefully determined treatments incorporating drugs and manipulations, but which never demonstrated the kind of general theorizing that one finds in China, India, Greece, and even, to a lesser extent, in Egypt.

EARLY AGGLUTINATIVE LANGUAGES—SUMERIAN AND CHINESE AS VEHICLES FOR SCIENTIFIC THOUGHT

Both Sumerian and Chinese began as agglutinative languages (i.e., languages that started with monosyllabic root words for which one could draw pictures; see Figures 3.1 and 3.2), therefore most root words began as the names of things that people experience daily. To produce more complicated meanings, one chose two or more root words which, taken together, suggested the meaning that one wanted and then put them together either by superposition (actually, in China the original signs were written very close to one another either side by side or one on top of the other so that they seemed to create a single compound sign) or by stringing them together sequentially in space (most common in Sumer). In Sumerian, for example, the combination of the pictographs for woman and mountain means "slave," presumably because most slaves were women captured from the surrounding hill tribes. Likewise, the sign for magnet in China combined the signs for pull, iron, and stone, so it is "the stone that pulls iron."

It is significant that the root words in agglutinative languages are combined without inflection, that is, without changing the root word to indicate different grammatical and syntactical functions, so there is no way to know whether a word being used as a noun or pronoun, for example, is singular or plural or whether it is being used in what would be the English language first person or third person. Indeed, there is no way to tell whether many words are being used as what modern speakers would call nouns, verbs, adjectives, or adverbs. As a consequence, no term in an agglutinative language can ever be totally unambiguous. Each must be interpreted within the context in which it is found. Chinese scholars, especially, seem to have reveled in playing on the ambiguities of their language. For example, they often used the rough equivalent of double entendres in modern European languages, so it is often very difficult to tell which of several meanings is meant. Since modern scientific thought seeks to use completely unambiguous, or univocal, terms and expressions, it is difficult to render modern science in classical Chinese or to render classical Chinese expressions into modern scientific statements without significant loss or possible distortion.

In this section and in the preceding one, I have been suggesting that the character of written Chinese language during its formative stages was probably a barrier to thinking about the natural world in ways that are compatible with the descriptive elements of modern Western science, although it may have encouraged theoretical thinking about the natural world in what are sometimes expressed as magical ways (i.e., in ways that emphasize correspondences among different orders of entities) to a greater extent than Sumerian. Thus, it may have been instrumental in promoting its own particular form of natural knowledge, or science, which is not compatible with dominant views of the character of modern science. Joseph Needham, the most prolific Western historian of Chinese science, does not hold this view. He writes:

> There is a commonly received idea that the ideographic language was a powerful inhibitory factor to the development of modern science in China. We believe, however, that this factor is generally grossly overrated. . . . We do not recall any instance where (after adequate consideration) we have been seriously in doubt as to what was intended by a classical or medieval Chinese author dealing with a scientific or technical subject, provided always that the text was not too corrupt, and that the description was sufficiently full. (1969, 38)

Needham's perspective, of course, depends heavily on having his own modern scientific point of view available to control his interpretation of the ancient Chinese texts. (For a more complete version of the views I have been trying to express in opposition to Needham's, see Bodde 1991, 16–96).

AGGLUTINATIVE LANGUAGES AND ISSUES OF CLASSIFICATION

Agglutinative languages offer both important positive features and important negative features when it comes to organizing and classifying information about the world. The positive features are seen most clearly in several sets of Mesopotamian word lists that I will discuss in this section, though they can also be seen in the earliest Chinese dictionary, the *Er ya,* from the very late Zhou or early Han period. This work is a glossary of words arranged under categories such as animals, birds, heavenly bodies, implements, plants, and relationship terms. In most cases, the bulk of words in each category includes the root word for animal, bird, and so on. Thus, the dictionary incorporates the beginnings of a taxonomy of natural and artificial entities embedded within the language. Subsequent Chinese dictionaries, beginning in the late Han period, rejected this organization of words based on what one might call the natural objects or processes to which they referred in order to group words under graphically meaningful categories based on rough similarities of sign shape rather than meaning, giving up the taxonomic character of the *Er ya* and of the Mesopotamian word lists that I turn to next.

In part because we have so many documents related to scribal education from Mesopotamia, in part because successive invaders who became rulers in the Tigris and Euphrates Valleys valued the knowledge developed by the early Sumerian civilization, and in part because Sumerian was a more descriptive language than Chinese, we have many examples of word lists organized according to classes of objects based on sensory characteristics. The earliest word lists are lists of signs and multi-sign words apparently used in Sumerian schools to teach scribes how to write a sign and memorize its pronunciation and meaning. When a single sign had multiple meanings, it was repeated often enough to encompass them all, but the meanings were apparently stated verbally, since they do not appear on the lists (Oppenheim 1977).

As Akkadian began to replace Sumerian around 2200 B.C.E., the initial Sumerian signs were placed in a left-hand column, their meanings were written in a middle column, and the Akkadian translation (written in cuneiform) was in a third column on the right. One set of such word lists translating Sumerian terms into Akkadian at Nippur extends to 40 large tablets (Oppenheim 1977). Even more important for our purposes than these syllabary lists are topical lists consisting only of nouns. One set of such topical lists from the Old Babylonian period contains 22 tablets and includes lists of trees, metals, domestic animals, wild animals, parts of the human body, stones, plants, fish, birds, kinds of beer, varieties of barley, varieties of honey, and other foodstuffs. Each Sumerian term begins with the root word for the category of things described and followed by qualifiers based almost exclusively on observable characteristics, including hardness, color, smell, number, size, and so forth (Oppenheim 1977). For example, within the metals category, 16 forms of gold are listed, 9 of which are distinguished solely by color, and among white stones, five different types are identified based on their degree of hardness and on whether they effervesced in contact with what we know as acids (Forbes 1963, Vol. 7). As time went on, lists that translated Sumerian terms into Akkadian were supplemented with bi- or trilingual translating dictionaries that included translations into Kassite, Hittite, and, eventually, Greek (Roux 1992).

A. Leo Oppenheim has argued that these word lists were all produced principally to make it easier for scribes to learn the language. He therefore warns readers against assuming that "the word lists with names of plants, animals, and stones, are the beginnings of botany zoology, and mineralogy, respectively." Oppenheim may be correct in thinking that the scribes who produced such lists were not explicitly "'organizing' the universe around them" (1977, 248). However, they were, implicitly, doing just that, and they demonstrated a number of characteristics that make Mesopotamian scribal activities look very much like scientific activities. As in the case of Mesopotamian mathematics discussed in chapter 2, activities initially engaged in for practical purposes—in the present case, teaching the language—tended to go beyond the merely practical. In order to make their lists of animals and plants comprehensive, for example, Mesopotamian scholars brought home rare species of plants and animals (Roux 1992) that had no known uses, and they made distinctions based on detailed observations of substances that went far beyond those needed for practical purposes. Moreover, to provide an historical dimension that could have been of little practical value, later Mesopotamian scholars incorporated the Sumerian etymologies of terms relating to the natural world into their dictionaries. Scribes were encouraged in their historical scholarship by such kings as Tiglith-Pileser I (1115 B.C.E.–1077 B.C.E.), who brought together much Old Babylonian literary material, and the Assyrian king Ashurbanipal (685 B.C.E.–627 B.C.E.), who collected a huge library that included not only official government records, but literary and technical texts as well (Roux 1992).

If the list making activities of Mesopotamian scholars imply a curiosity about the world and a persistence in gathering information about it that sometimes went beyond the merely practical to incorporate knowledge for its own sake, a science expressed in lists based principally on physical characteristics has its own important limitations. It does not encourage one to look beneath the surface to find hidden sources of regularity, so it offers little encouragement to synthetic theorizing or even to exploring the parallels between different orders of existence. The Sumerian language does not exclude the exploration of correspondences, but neither does the linguistic structure in itself promote such an exploration.

In China after the *Er ya,* virtually all word classifications through the 18th century followed the pattern set in Xu Shen's *Shuo Shen Jie-zi (Script Explained and Characters Elucidated),* of approximately 100 C.E. This text grouped words under a set of 540 graphically similar elements, rather than by categories based on the entities or actions signified, defining no less than 9,353 separated characters. Thus, it gave no encouragement to the development of an idea of natural classes based on common physical attributes (Bodde 1991). Once again, it clearly did not make awareness of such classes impossible; rather, it simply did nothing to promote taxonomic concerns based on physical characteristics.

AGGLUTINATIVE LANGUAGES, THE EXTENT OF LITERACY, AND THE CHARACTER OF EDUCATION

We have pointed out, by the late Han period, written Chinese involved more than 9,000 separate ideographs, and early Sumerian involved about 3,000. Moreover, each ideograph might have several meanings. Furthermore, when one spoke complex words in an agglutinative language, one vocalized each of the incorporated sounds corresponding to the pronunciation of the root words. Over time, and especially in Sumer, the elements of the compound word sometimes became more closely associated with their sounds than with their original meanings (i.e., they became recognized principally as syllables when they were in compound words). The drawing or pictograph retained its original meaning when it appeared alone, or in some compound words, but it gradually took on a new, purely phonetic meaning in later compound words (in China, at least one element always retained its original meaning, while others might take on phonetic values). The movement from conceptual significance to phonetic value, which was probably completed by around 2000 B.C.E. in Mesopotamia and well before the Zhou period in China, was encouraged by the prior or nearly simultaneous transformation of the original pictographs into more easily formed, more simple, and more abstract ideographs whose pictorial resemblance to the original meaning became ever more remote (see Figures 3.1 and 3.2.).

Figure 3.1
Examples of Chinese Characters. Joseph Emmert.

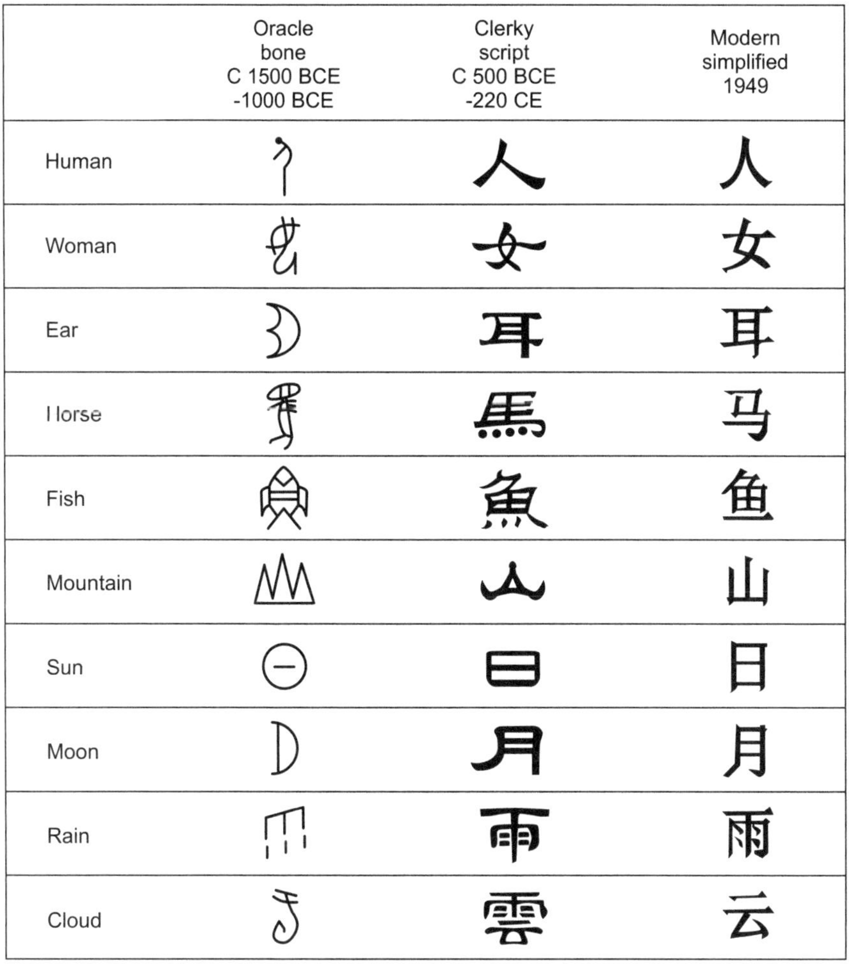

	Oracle bone C 1500 BCE -1000 BCE	Clerky script C 500 BCE -220 CE	Modern simplified 1949
Human		人	人
Woman		女	女
Ear		耳	耳
Horse		馬	马
Fish		魚	鱼
Mountain		山	山
Sun		日	日
Moon		月	月
Rain		雨	雨
Cloud		雲	云

Neither in ancient Sumer nor in ancient China was the meaning of early writing usually made clearer by the use of punctuation marks. This was an even greater problem for Sumerian than for Chinese, because in China the spacing between successive compound ideographs was different from that within the compound words, while in Sumer, no such distinction existed. Thus, any string of five Sumerian signs might indicate five different monosyllabic terms, one five-syllable word, one one-syllable and one four-syllable word in two orders, one disyllabic and three monosyllabic terms in four different orders, two disyllabic and one monosyllabic term in four orders, or a two- and a three-element term in two orders. That is, in theory, any five signs in isolation

Figure 3.2
Mesopotamian Writing. Joseph Emmert.

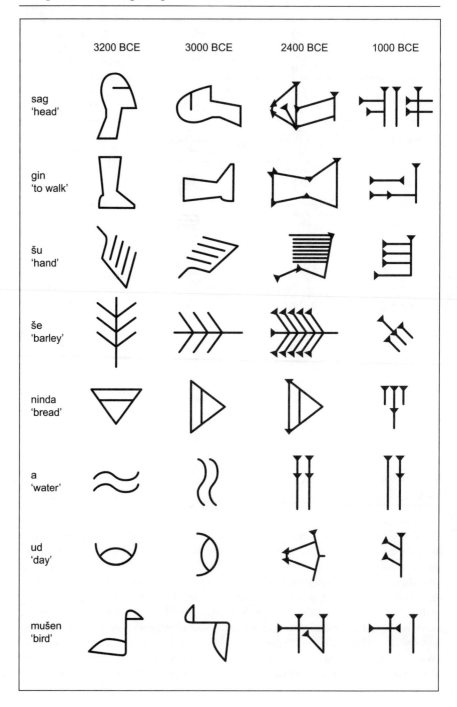

might be interpreted in at least 12 different ways—far more if the decision of whether to read some signs as expressing phonetic rather than cognitive values was left open. Even when a whole range of rules regarding word order and the like are considered, discerning the meaning of a large text given this situation involved an extremely complex process of contextualization and interpretation.

The complexity of the early agglutinative languages, coupled with the need in Sumer to be at least bilingual after around 2300 B.C.E., meant that the time costs of becoming literate were huge. For this reason, a very small fraction of the population was literate. Furthermore, literacy was needed for relatively few roles in society, although some of those roles were extremely important. Among the politically and militarily powerful, including the kings in Sumer and early emperors in China, few seem to have been literate, and among unskilled workers, craftsmen, and artisans there was little need for literacy, though it seems that many physicians, whose social status was roughly that of artisans, were literate. Even among those engaged in many commercial activities—especially transporting goods—literacy seems to have been extremely rare in Mesopotamia and China. Though evidence is virtually nonexistent, one suspects that numeracy was more widely distributed among groups such as artisans and local merchants than literacy because, while negotiations could be carried out orally in vernacular languages, measurements, invoices, and inventories often had to be recorded to be remembered.

Written language seems to have served five basic overt functions in early civilizations. It served to produce records for administrative purposes, to codify laws, to produce rituals and stories that constituted a sacred tradition, to produce records of activities, and, eventually, to produce various forms of scholarship. All of these functions served incidentally to encourage social solidarity within the culture. Far and away the greatest amount of writing in China and Mesopotamia was done for administrative purposes. There is little evidence that records were kept for private commercial enterprises in ancient China. Though this lack of evidence could be because records kept on wood and paper have not survived, whereas records kept on baked clay did, it seems more likely that because the first major commercial enterprises in Sumer were temple-run, and thus collective activities that demanded accountability and the redistribution of gains to members of the community; commercial record keeping became common first in this collective context. When trade became private, or was sponsored by the secular state, the notion that records should be kept was extended beyond the temple context. In China, on the other hand, until the rise of Buddhism during the Han dynasty, there were no religious institutions separate from the state, and Buddhist temples and monasteries rarely, if ever, became sites of economic production. The Han state did, however, have need for some literate and numerate officials. In order to increase its revenues to support military actions against outlying territories, it established government monopolies in salt and iron production around 120 B.C.E. Furthermore, the central government had to maintain close oversight of local officials who wielded tremendous power and authority as tax collectors, recruiters for military and labor services, registrars of land and people, and so on (Hardy and Kinney 2005). Thus, the state had need of some literate administrators, but not for huge numbers of them.

Among the consequences of this situation was that the need for scribes was substantially greater in Mesopotamia than in China. In the Old Babylonian period, when the total population of the Mesopotamian Basin was probably around 2 million, there may have been up to 20,000–40,000 scribes, about 1 to 2 percent of the population. Moreover, Mesopotamian scribes were less subject to the whims of political patrons, in part because there were multiple sources of employment and also because many scribes came from powerful families themselves. One study of 500 scribes who specified their parentage indicates that the fathers of scribes were, "ambassadors, temple administrators, military officers, sea captains, high tax officials, priests of various sorts, managers, supervisors, foremen, scribes, archivists, and accountants. In short, the fathers were the wealthier citizens of urban communities" (Kramer 1959, 3). In one case, however, there is a record of a baby who was "rescued from the jaws of a dog," adopted by a family of means, and sent to a scribal school (Hawkes and Woolley 1963, 662), so parentage did not always seem to be determinative.

Because of the demand for literate scribes and because of the persistence of written evidence in Mesopotamia, there is evidence of multiple schools, or tablet-houses, where scribes were trained and evidence about what they learned and how they learned it. One such tablet-house, at Ur, seems to have been used as a school for over 1,000 years (Hawkes and Woolley 1963). A typical school probably had between 25 and 100 students, from beginners to those who, after two or more years, served as "junior scribes" or "big brothers," assistant teachers who helped the beginners. The head of the school was the "school father," and he was typically assisted by "the scribe of mathematics," "the man in charge of Sumerian," and others, including "the man in charge of the whip," who was charged with maintaining order with the use of corporal punishment (Hawkes and Woolley 1963, 662).

Initially, the curriculum of these schools was heavily oriented toward vocational training in mathematics and in basic writing skills, and the schools were located within temple compounds. Gradually, more and more belles lettres entered the curriculum, tablet houses were located in private residences and governmental buildings as well as temple compounds, and there is some evidence of specialized training either within or after general scribal education. As early as the Old Babylonian period, for example, letters suggest that the city of Isin had schools that specialized in training physicians (Oppenheim 1977). Priests in charge of divination seem to have had special training as well, though it is unclear whether it came through schools or through some kind of apprenticeship.

No women seem to have been admitted to any of the documented scribal schools. There is, however, evidence that there were female scribes, especially in temples dedicated to goddesses. Moreover there is evidence that there were female physicians. Whether these women were privately home schooled or whether tablet houses for women have simply not yet been uncovered is not certain.

In pre-Han China, the bulk of literate persons sought patronage from or employment in the court of some wealthy lord. As the imperial court gradually subjugated other courts, patronage and employment demanding literacy became limited almost exclusively to places in the imperial bureaucracy and to scholars who functioned as teachers. Literacy was largely restricted to a class of minor aristocrats, or *shinen,* although there were exceptions both among the more powerful and among the lower classes. During the Han period, education began as an afterthought, but it gradually took on an increasingly important place. According to the *shiji* (*Records of the Grand Scribe*) of Sima Qian, the first Han emperor, Liu Bang:

sighed over the neglected state of learning and would have done more to encourage its revival, but at the time there was still considerable turmoil within the empire. . . . Likewise during the reigns of Emperor Hui and Empress Lü there was still no leisure to attend to the matter of government schools. Moreover the high officials at the time were all military men who had won their distinction in battle. With the accession of Emperor Wen [in 180 B.C.E.], Confucian Scholars began little by little to be summoned and employed in government. (Hardy and Kinney 2005, 74)

By 136 B.C.E., the Confucian scholars had managed to establish five Confucian classics, *The Book of Documents, The Book of Songs, The Record of Ritual, The Classic of Changes,* and the *Spring and Autumn Annals,* as the standard subject matter for state sponsored study. Twelve years later, Emperor Wu established The Imperial Academy for boys between the ages of 14 and 17. This institution, which had the five Confucian classics as its curriculum, was intended to supply the growing bureaucracy with personnel. Beginning with 50 students in 124 B.C.E., we are told that enrollment reached 30,000 in 220 C.E. Even if we discount the 30,000 substantially, the number of graduates of the Imperial Academy became far greater than the bureaucracy could absorb, and there were other private educational institutions that produced some scholars, creating a literate pool of 160,000–240,000 in a population of nearly 55 million. Consequently, a state-sponsored examination limited to questions about the official curriculum was instituted as a condition for employment. This examination slowly expanded to include the great mathematical classics discussed in chapter 2, as well as the *Analects* of Confucius and a few other texts and commentaries on the core texts. However, its central focus remained on literary texts and moral philosophy. Thus, natural knowledge, while present, remained a marginalized domain in Chinese higher education. With brief lapses and with the subsequent exclusion of very small specialized groups, among which the most important was a select group of court astronomer/ astrologers never amounting to more than a couple of hundred persons, such an examination, based on the same classical texts remained the gateway to governmental positions in China into the early 20th century.

The greatest difference then, between scribal education in Mesopotamia and higher education in China was that the latter was highly centralized and focused on literature and moral philosophy, with a sprinkling of mathematics as time went on. In Mesopotamia, on the contrary, higher education was decentralized and initially focused on technical material. Only later did literary and religious materials enter the curriculum. One consequence was that there was simply a proportionally greater pool of educated persons interested in mathematics and the natural world in Mesopotamia than in China. As we will see in the next chapter, circumstances produced a much more intense and extensive demand for astronomical knowledge in Mesopotamia, which the larger pool of technically trained scribes was able to meet.

In both China and Mesopotamia, literacy provided access to knowledge, and literate scribes and government officials became advisers to political authorities because they were presumed to have special knowledge and ability. This circumstance gave the scribal and scholarly classes a disproportionately large influence in society. At the same time, it is important to note that, especially in China, where patronage for the learned came almost exclusively from the Imperial court, there was a premium on giving advice that would please the emperor, and this almost always meant giving advice that would not destabilize the political regime in power. As a consequence, Chinese intellectual life took on a relatively conservative character. Except during periods of dramatic regime changes, there was little self-interested incentive to disagree with traditional views. Indeed, priority was placed on demonstrating one's allegiance to tradition. Creativity was certainly possible, but only within a widely accepted framework. With respect to fundamental cosmology and fundamental approaches to understanding natural phenomena, this meant that with only minor changes, a single dominant set of theories—to be discussed in subsequent chapters—persisted within Chinese society for more than 2,000 years, from the earliest period in which they appeared until the early part of the 20th century.

EGYPTIAN HIEROGLYPHIC WRITING
AND ITS IMPLICATIONS

Egyptian hieroglyphic writing emerged around 3100 B.C.E. in a context that suggests that the core idea for creating writing probably came from Mesopotamia, but writing in Egypt diverged from that in Mesopotamia very rapidly in several ways. A simplified hieratic form of the original pictographs developed around 2900 B.C.E., but unlike the case in Sumer or China, the original hieroglyphic form was retained for religious and public commemorative purposes until nearly the time of Hellenization, circa 330 B.C.E. (see Figure 3.3).

The hieroglyphic form of writing appeared on monuments, walls of temples, tombs, and palaces, and on ceremonial objects, including utensils, jewelry, and amulets. As a consequence, even when hieroglyphs took on phonetic values, their origins in pictorial representations of specific objects was never completely lost and there was less incentive to examine similarities and differences among natural entities. For example, since there were hieroglyphs based on many specific birds (e.g., falcons, owls, geese, ducks, chicks, etc.), there was no generic "bird" hieroglyph and no incentive to relate one kind of bird to another as there was in Sumer. There are a few early Egyptian lists of related

Figure 3.3
Egyptian Hieroglyphic Writing with Soundings. Joseph Emmert.

HIEROGLYPH	REPRESENTS	PRONOUNCED	HIEROGLYPH	REPRESENTS	PRONOUNCED
	vulture	ah *(father)*		reed	i *(filled)*
	two reeds	y *(discovery)*		arm and hand	broad a *(car)*
	quail chick	oo *(too)* or w *(wet)*		foot	b *(boot)*
	mat	p *(pedestal)*		horned viper	f *(feel)*
	owl	m *(moon)*		water	n *(noon)*
	mouth	r *(right)*		reed shelter	h *(hat)*
	twisted flax	h! *(ha!)*		placenta	kh *(like Scotch 'loch')*
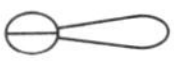	animal's belly	ch *(like German 'ich')*		folded cloth	s *(saw)*
	door bolt	s *(saw)*		pool	sh *(show)*
	slope of hill	k *(key)*		basket with handle	k *(basket)*
	jar stand	g *(go)*		loaf	t *(tap)*
	tethering rope	tj *(church)*		hand	d *(dog)*
	snake	dj *(adjust)*			

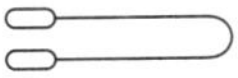

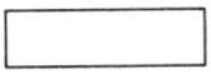

words, but such lists were not generally unified by a single root word as in Sumer. Early attempts to collect words by topic never constituted a major effort and they do not seem to have been continued for long.

The Egyptian language was also inflected, unlike the cases in Sumer and China. Most words had three basic elements: one or more phonograms, each of which might indicate a single sound, a two-sound combination or a three-sound combination; a logogram which indicated the original meaning of the sign; and one or more determinatives that provided a context for deciding precisely how to read the other signs. For example, a short vertical slash after a pictograph indicated that it was to be read as a logogram rather than as a phonogram, and three horizontal slashes indicated that the previous sign should be read as plural. Other symbols indicated what verb tense or what gender was indicated. Finally, though there was no punctuation as we know it, certain symbols at the beginning of a sentence indicated whether the following group of words constituted a declarative sentence or a question. Like Chinese words, Egyptian words were separated from one another by a larger space than separated the elements of a single word. Finally, Egyptian sentences had a regular word order that also served to determine how the words were to be understood. Each simple sentence or independent clause was written with the verb first, subject second, direct object third, indirect object fourth, and (when present) adverb or adverbial phrase fifth.

As a consequence of all these features, Egyptian written language was far less ambiguous than Chinese or Sumerian, and it was able to do with a much smaller number of pictographs. Indeed, up until the Hellenistic period, Egyptian made do with about 600 signs, rather than the more than 3,000 used in Sumer and China. The time investment needed to learn written Egyptian was thus substantially less than that needed to learn Sumerian or Chinese. Consequently, a larger portion of the population probably became literate. Estimates hover around 2–5 percent of the population, rather than the approximately 0.5 percent in China and roughly 1 percent in Sumer. In Egypt, far more occupations were also likely either to demand literacy or have literacy as the norm than was true in China. Thus, in a widely distributed *Textbook of the Hierarchy* written by the scribe Amenemope around 1100 B.C.E., no fewer than 53 of 157 occupations ranging from heir to the throne to vegetable gardener and tender of livestock stalls demanded literacy (Donadoni 1997). While there is no precise way to determine the percentage of employed persons in occupations in which literacy was required or expected, informed guesses exceed 5–10 percent.

It was also the case that literacy provided some status and relief from drudgery. In an often-copied essay from around 1800 B.C.E., a father gives advice to his son:

Put writing in your heart that you may protect yourself from hard labor of any kind and be a magistrate of high repute. The scribe is released from manual tasks; it is he who commands. . . . Do you not hold the scribe's palette? That is what makes the difference between you and the man who handles an oar.

I have seen the metal-worker at his task at the mouth of his furnace with fingers like a crocodile's. He stank worse than Fish Spawn. Every workman who holds a chisel suffers more than the men who hack the ground; wood is his field and the chisel his mattock. At night when he is free he toils more than his arms can do (at overtime work?); even at night he lights his lamp (to work by?). The stone cutter seeks work in every hard stone; when he has done the great part of his labor his arms are exhausted, he is tired out. (Childe 1951, 149)

The largest class of texts from ancient Egypt is religious in nature, and the largest professional category for which literacy was needed was that of priest. Moreover, in Egypt, as in Mesopotamia, with short-lived exceptions, there were many gods and many temples, often independent of the central government, so there was a large priestly class. Many temples incorporated a House of Life, dedicated to teaching, and a House of Books, where manuscripts were collected and copied. Moreover, houses of life sometimes became associated with specific areas of teaching that went well beyond ordinary priestly functions. The one at Heliopolis became renowned as an architectural school, and those at Bubastis, Abydos, and Sais were known for specializing in medicine (Donadoni 1997). By the late Middle Kingdom (c. 1900–1630 B.C.E.) scribal schools also became associated with administrative centers and palaces, which tended to focus on producing civil administrative bureaucrats, centering their training on technical, mathematical knowledge as in Mesopotamia, rather than on literary studies, as in China. By the beginning of the 18th dynasty (1514–1292 B.C.E.), scribal training had even become the norm for leadership positions in the military, and military scribes began to outnumber civilian bureaucrats (Donadoni 1997), so literacy may have reached close to 10 percent of the male population. As in Mesopotamia, there is evidence of a small but significant number of female scribes, but little evidence regarding how they were educated.

GREEK ALPHABETIC WRITING AND ITS IMPLICATIONS

From their earliest appearance in Mycenaean times (c. 1200–1000 B.C.E.) Greek written languages were alphabetic, rather than pictographic. This meant that the Greek student had to memorize only about two dozen symbols, rather than hundreds or thousands. Words were constructed using a small number of signs that carried no meaning other than their sounds, so basic literacy was relatively easy to acquire. On the other hand, until the end of the seventh century B.C.E., Greek culture was primarily an oral culture. Values were inculcated through the singing of poetry by professional bards, and trade was simple enough to be carried out largely on the basis of verbal agreements. Only during the sixth and fifth centuries did written prose become widely important in Greece. In Athens, which will get most of our attention, for example, by the mid-fifth century B.C.E., voting was often done through the use of ostraca, buttons on which the name of a candidate or a proposed action was written. The voter picked up the appropriate button based on what was written on it and placed it in an urn; then officials counted the number of votes for each candidate or action. By 420 B.C.E., written wills had become common; the first political pamphlet dates from 420; and by 400 litigants were required to file written briefs in Athenian law courts and jurors were assumed to be literate.

Most Greek cities probably had private schools to teach basic literacy to boys by the late fifth century. Moreover, pressures to increase literacy continued through the fourth century. Plato proposed in his *Laws,* written about 360 B.C.E., that there should be compulsory schooling at a very basic level for all boys and girls. "The children," he wrote, "must work hard at their letters until they can read and write, but as far as reaching a high level of speed or calligraphy is concerned, those whom nature has not helped along in the prescribed number of years [3] should be released" (Harris 1989, 100). It even seems that, in the fourth century, there were attempts in a few palaces to make publicly funded schooling in basic literacy mandatory for all boys. Diodorus Siculus reports of the lawgiver Charondas of Catana, for example:

He laid down that all the sons of the citizens should learn letters, with the city providing the pay of the teachers; for he assumed that people without means, who could not pay fees on their own, would otherwise be cut off from the finest pursuits. For this lawgiver rated writing [*grammatike*] above other forms of knowledge, and with very good reason. (Harris 1989, 21 & 98–99)

Taking all forms of evidence together it seems likely that, in late fifth-century and early fourth-century Athens, 25–50 percent of adult male citizens could probably read and write at a basic level while some smaller percentage of metics (resident foreigners) and slaves who were engaged in commerce were also literate. Those figures were almost certainly lower in every other city, becoming very small in rural villages.

For our purposes, it is more important to know something about those whose learning went beyond minimal literacy. There is no evidence that higher education in Athens or any other Greek city was part of a path to high-status occupations as in Egypt, Mesopotamia, or China. Indeed, most of the young male Greek citizens who sought education beyond mere literacy were proud of not being engaged in productive economic life, with the possible exception of managing their family estates which were worked by slaves or paid laborers. One consequence of the Greek aristocratic disinterest in productive activities is that written Attic knowledge of the natural world was largely divorced from agricultural or artisanal activities such as architecture, vase making, and ship building, which dominated the economy. Aristotle went so far as to praise the theoretical sciences of natural philosophy and metaphysics specifically because they were about entities that could not be changed or influenced in any way by human beings (Aristotle, *Nicomachean Ethics*).

The focus of most educated Greek citizens was on participation in public life as members of deliberative legislative bodies or in the law courts as jurors or litigants, and what most men sought primarily from their education was rhetorical skill—the ability to convince an assembly or group of jurors that their position was superior to that of an opponent. Undoubtedly, some were genuinely interested in justice, in how to order public life to best serve the citizenry, and in what constituted *arete,* or excellence, in a human being. A few were even interested in understanding the characteristics of the natural world; but since they could bring honor and glory to themselves primarily through oratory and argumentation, instruction in rhetorical skills was in highest demand.

Up until the early fourth century, instruction in these topics was offered in Athens primarily by individuals—often called Sophists—who were usually metics who charged students for taking lessons, although it seems that a few relatively wealthy citizens took up teaching without asking for pay. These independently wealthy teachers, for whom Plato stands as a symbol, looked down on those who sought profit from teaching and claimed a greater emphasis on the content of the knowledge they sought to convey than on the forms of argumentation and presentation. However, they, too, were also deeply interested in how to compel assent to their views, because they feared the power of rhetoric used to support what they viewed as bad policies and judgments rather than good ones, thus they sought to present their positions in the most incontrovertible manner that they could devise (Lloyd 1996). We have already seen in chapter 2 how the demand for certainty played an important role in promoting the increasing rigor of proofs within Greek mathematics. Proof remained the ideal for natural and social knowledge as well, though its attainment outside of mathematics was much more problematic. Probable knowledge grounded in some form of evidence was highly sought as well, and as we shall see, the criteria for such knowledge tended to be developed in connection with medicine and natural philosophy.

Whether they were merely teaching rhetoric or they were promoting deeper knowledge about the good life or the natural world, Greek teachers had to attract students, and while word of mouth from current and past students certainly played a role in attracting students to well established teachers, the major way for new teachers to attract students was by displaying their rhetorical skills in public debate with potential competitors, including those from whom they had learned. Such contests were part of a general cultural pattern of competition among the Greeks. There were wide ranging athletic contests, including the Olympic games. There were local contests among playwrights to have plays put on at the annual Dionysian festival at Athens, local wrestling competitions, musical competitions, and dance competitions, so it is hardly surprising that debates became a form of public competition both between persons from different teaching traditions and among students from a single school to establish who should succeed a retiring master (Lloyd 1996).

Although the primary interest of students was in issues of political and social significance, for reasons that are not well understood, early Greek intellectuals seemed to focus initially on topics connected with understanding the natural world—providing explanations of such phenomena as thunder and lightning, earthquakes, and the origins, structure, and health of human beings, or speculating about what the world is made of and how it came into existence. We will return to these subjects in chapter 7. For now, I simply point out that one consequence of the need for each teacher to distinguish himself from his colleagues and competitors, often through public debate, was that Greek natural philosophy and medicine never settled into a single dominant paradigm or set of interrelated theories and practices as they did in China. Each Greek theorist was obliged to find points of difference with his teacher and his contemporaries.

ROMAN LANGUAGE, LITERACY, AND EDUCATION

Written language entered Italy, probably beginning in the late eighth century B.C.E., from Greece, so all written languages from Italian antiquity are alphabetic. A few Etruscan monuments suggest that writing was well established by the sixth century, but that it played a minimal role in religious, economic, or political life. A handful of Latin inscriptions, largely religious, began to appear in the sixth century, but writing did not become very important outside of religious rituals until at least the third century B.C.E. In spite of the frequent claim that the 12 tablets incorporating Roman Law were placed in the Forum around 450 B.C.E., the first credible evidence of written Roman laws place them around 304 B.C.E., and not until 63 B.C.E. was it required that laws be put into written form (Harris 1989).

As new colonies were founded in Italy between 338 and 218 B.C.E., the need for written record keeping increased, and those needs only grew as Rome's influence expanded toward the end of the Second Punic War. There is evidence of increasing literacy through the third century, with the first documented private school dating from 234 (Harris 1989), but prior to 200 B.C.E. it is unlikely that more than around 2 percent of the Roman population was literate in Latin, while a greater percentage of slaves from Greek-speaking regions were probably literate in their native tongue.

By the end of the Second Punic War in 146 B.C.E., Rome controlled the northern part of the Mediterranean Basin from Spain to Macedonia and Greece and the southern part from Morocco to Egypt. By 117 B.C.E., the empire had reached its greatest size, extending from Britain and Gaul (France and parts of southern Germany) in the northwest to include Egypt, most of what is modern Turkey, and Syria on the east. As a consequence, tribute poured in, and families of the wealthy Senatorial class became increasingly wealthy, while the working class (plebes) suffered economically because cheaper slave labor was being brought in to displace them and socially because they were subject to military conscription but had minimal say in governmental decisions.

Literacy seems to have grown within the senatorial class, and there was a brief flowering of Latin literature during the period from about 100 B.C.E. to 17 C.E. During this period, authors such as Cicero (106–43 B.C.E.), Sallust (86–34 B.C.E.), Livy (59 B.C.E.–17 C.E.), Catullus (87–54 B.C.E.), Lucretius (99–55 B.C.E.), Horace (65–8 B.C.E.), Ovid (43 B.C.E.–17 C.E.), and Virgil (70–19 B.C.E.) fixed the grammatical rules of Latin, increased its vocabulary, and turned it into a language that would remain the dominant language of scholarship in the western world for almost 1,500 years. However, there was no outcry for establishing public schooling and little evidence of private schools in Rome. It is unlikely that literacy rates among the Roman citizens ever reached as high as 10 percent (Harris 1989). There is some late Imperial evidence that the Roman emperors Vespasian (who reigned from 59–79 C.E.) and Hadrian (reigned 117–138 C.E.) encouraged education by relieving school masters of tax burdens, but Caracalla (reigned 211–217 C.E.) removed the exemption for elementary schoolmasters, and there is virtually no evidence of the existence of schools anywhere in the Roman Empire, except in Egypt where long-standing local traditions promoted schooling (Harris 1989). Several literary sources suggest that whatever Roman schools did exist admitted girls as well as boys, and a number of wealthy Roman women are known to have been literate.

Upper class Romans were deeply interested in politics, but they tended to be more engaged in economic activity than Greek citizens of 300 to 400 years earlier. Even in their public life, many Roman politicians tended to be far more interested in providing water, sewers, and roads than in deep principles of political theory. Some, such as Cicero, sought higher education in schools run by Greek teachers, usually away from Rome, but the curricula in these places rarely if ever reached the level of sophistication that it had in Athens or that it did at Alexandria. Moreover, many Roman aristocrats were openly disdainful of the theoretical orientation of Greek intellectuals.

Romans wanted useful knowledge in order to control their physical and social environments. That usually meant learning enough mathematics, natural philosophy, astronomy, and the like to understand examples of outstanding rhetoric, or to engage in such professions as architecture, but not much more. Vitruvius, author of the widely distributed *Ten Books on Architecture* (c. 27 B.C.E.), expressed the prevailing attitude of the educated Roman. After laying out the reasons why an architect should be knowledgeable about a whole range of subjects, he argues, however, that he should not get carried away and attempt to be an expert in any:

An architect ought not to be and cannot be such a philologist as was Aristarchus, though not illiterate; nor a musician like Aristoxenus, though not absolutely ignorant of music; nor a painter like Apelles, though not unskillful in drawing; nor a sculptor such as was Myron or Polyclitus, though not unacquainted with the plastic art; nor again a physician like Hippocrates, though not ignorant of medicine; nor in the other sciences need he excel in each, though he should not be unskillful in them. . . . It appears, therefore, that he has done enough and to spare who in each subject possesses a fairly good knowledge of those parts, with their principles, which are indispensable for architecture, so that if he is required to pass judgement and to express approval of those things or arts, he may not be found wanting. (1960, 11–12)

SUMMARY

Both the character of written language and the character of educational institutions functioned to encourage or discourage certain aspects of scientific thought and activity in ancient civilizations. Where languages were picto-graphic and agglutinative, the difficulty of learning the language was such that only small elites became literate. The character of early pictographs reflected elements of the pre-literate culture. Consequently they tended either to focus attention on the relationship between different orders of existence, and thus on a certain form of theorizing and the creation of an explicit cosmology (i.e., a system that could provide a coordinated system of meanings that linked natural entities and the human world), as in China, or they tended to focus attention on physical relationships among entities of the same kind, creating explicit classification schemes based on similarities, but often ignoring grand unifying schemes, as in Sumer. Education also reflected other cultural orien-tations, so Chinese advanced education focused on literary topics and moral philosophy, whereas early Mesopotamian and Egyptian education tended to emphasize technical material related especially to mathematics and medicine. Finally, because the political system in China became highly centralized and because it was the principle source of all patronage, a premium was placed on agreement among intellectuals and agreement with past traditions, thus ensuring stability rather than conflict within the ruling elite. This relatively conservative character of Chinese intellectual life minimized the kind of com-petition among widely disparate cosmologies that characterized Western in-tellectual life, while it encouraged syncretism and comprehensiveness within cosmology.

Where pictographic language developed ways to inflect the basic logo-graphs, as in Egypt, the language could get along with far fewer symbols than where language remained agglutinative, so learning took significantly less ef-fort and literacy was more widespread than in China or Mesopotamia. It be-came the foundation not only for religious and administrative roles, but also for many artisanal occupations. Scribal education in Egypt thus incorporated much technical material as well as religious and literary material; further-more, it tended to become more specialized than education in China or Meso-potamia, leading to the existence of schools that emphasized medicine, for example, or architecture. The move away from creating new terms primarily by combining root logographs, however, removed the special linguistic incen-tives to theorize or to classify as they arose in China or Mesopotamia. Neither theorizing nor classifying were made impossible within hieroglyphic or hier-atic language, as we will see when we turn to Egyptian medicine in chapter 7, but neither were they encouraged by features of the written language itself.

Alphabetic language, which was imported from Phoenicia into Greece and then from Greece into Italy, reduced the difficulties of learning a written lan-guage, making it possible for a greater portion of the population to become literate. In Greece, and especially in Athens, literacy thus increased dramati-cally among Greek citizens during the sixth through the fourth centuries, as written language became increasingly used in economic, religious, and politi-cal life. Some estimates suggest that, by the late fourth century B.C.E., as much as 25–50 percent of the Athenian citizenry might have been literate. Unlike the large urban cultures of Mesopotamia and Egypt, however, literacy in Greece was rarely associated with any professional role other than educator. Instead, it was often associated with more or less democratic political activity and a class of persons who self-consciously dissociated themselves from productive economic activity to focus on politics, broadly construed. Persons from this class gained status through their successes in arguing within the political assemblies and law courts, so they were often most interested in ways of arguing so that they could persuade their fellow citizens to their points of view. Advanced education in Greece thus tended to focus on rhetoric and on creating ways of arguing that could command assent, almost without regard for the intellectual content of the argument. This led, among other things, to a relative distrust of sensory evidence and to a focus on logic that was most effectively displayed in the development of mathematical proofs in the works of Euclid and his successors and to a concern for establishing criteria for when sensory evidence might be trusted.

The competition for students among Greek educators emphasized debate and created a tradition in which it was important to distinguish oneself from all predecessors and all potential opponents. On the one hand, when applied to explanations of the natural world, this situation led to a progressive character within particular traditions, since the follower of any great teacher had to be able to contribute something new to that tradition, yet on the other, it meant that there was an incentive against differing traditions converging to some widely accepted paradigm because each writer had to find a way to stand out from the crowd. As a consequence, there was never a time in Hellenic Greece, or in the Hellenistic world, when a single explanatory system dominated in any aspect of natural philosophy, as it seemed to in China.

Though written Latin would have been as easy to learn as Greek, the Roman world never saw a spread of literacy comparable to that in Athens in the fourth century B.C.E. Writing came later to Rome than to Athens, and it never became as important in religion, politics, or the economy. Even basic literacy was not widely supported, and those who did receive an education tended to seek practical knowledge rather than theoretical knowledge. As a consequence, though there was a brief flowering of Latin literature during the Augustan age, it is doubtful that literacy even among wealthy Roman citizens ever reached 10 percent. Moreover, with respect to technology and the sciences, technical works on agriculture, architecture, and water delivery systems tended to vastly outnumber theoretical treatises on natural philosophy. Even authors on natural history, such as Pliny the Elder, tended to focus on application rather than on theory.

Four

From Technologies of Divination to the Science of Astronomy

Astronomy emerged in nearly every ancient civilization in connection with at least three interrelated functions: (1) the creation of systems of divination or communication with the divine, based on omen interpretation, that is, systems for anticipating the outcome of proposed actions based on the reading of some set of phenomena or objects, (2) the production of a calendar governing religious ritual, and (3) the institution of an agricultural calendar. Though all ancient, agriculturally based civilizations developed systems for divination, for governing religious practices, and for coordinating religious practices with agricultural events, the sequence in which these functions become linked to knowledge about the Sun, Moon, and what we call the stars and the planets varied from one civilization to another. Moreover, the extent to which these functions promoted the development of a sophisticated knowledge of the motions of celestial bodies varied substantially. Finally, the extent to which astronomical knowledge eventually became a powerful force in shaping other important aspects of the civilization range from minimal, in the case of pre-Hellenistic Egypt, to nearly all-pervasive in Mesopotamia during the Selucid era (313 B.C.E. –200 C.E.) and the immediately preceding centuries.

THE CHARACTER AND FUNCTIONS OF DIVINATION IN ANCIENT CIVILIZATIONS

Every early civilization engaged in the celebration of important events in the life of the community and in the lives of its members. These celebrations usually involved some symbolic ritual enactment of the event, and they often involved some kind of invocation to the gods or spirits presumed to exist in nature to carry out some action that would ensure the successful completion of the event. For example, in Sumer, a new year's celebration was held just before the spring floods began. The central feature of this celebration was the ritual consummation of the marriage of the god of water, Enki, with the earth goddess, Ninmah. The union of the two gods was enacted by the king or the chief priest of the major temple and a selected priestess. This was accompanied both by offerings to the two gods and prayers for the water god to return from his exile from the land and for the subsequent fecundity of the earth goddess. By exhorting the gods, symbolically enacting their union, and by making offerings to them, the people presumably hoped to influence the gods. They sought to bring about Enki's reappearance so that the fertile earth could be impregnated and bring forth next year's crops. Such rituals were seen as crucial to the success of the most important activities of the society, and to fail to satisfy the gods was to invite disaster. On a smaller scale, private intercessory prayer also presumed the willingness of gods to listen to humans and their desire for some kind of quid pro quo, often simply the worship of the supplicant (Frankfort, et. al. 1949).

All ancient civilizations also had some form of divination that involved the interpretation of omens. The interpretation of omens grew everywhere because it was assumed that, sometimes, the gods associated with phenomena arranged things far in advance and could not be convinced to change the determinate course of events. When humans could not convince the gods to direct what might happen to their benefit, the next best thing was to know what was coming so that one could adjust one's actions in order to avoid undesirable outcomes and enhance the likelihood of favorable outcomes. Furthermore, it was assumed that the gods would be willing and able to provide this kind of information through some kind of omen, or sign, which usually needed interpretation by a priestly specialist. Eventually, we will focus in this chapter solely on the interpretation of omens that depended on the behavior of celestial objects, especially on the behavior of the Sun, Moon and Venus, but in order to understand the general character of divination by omen interpretation we will initially look at other significant forms of divination in ancient civilizations as well.

It is important to note that omen interpretation was intended as a practical technology. That is, persons, including political and military leaders, consulted omens in order to direct their own actions toward desirable ends. For example, a military leader would consult an omen in order to determine when or whether to undertake a particular campaign; a priest would consult an omen to determine when a certain religious ceremony should be carried out; a physician would consult an omen regarding whether a particular medical treatment should be used on a patient. In a very few cases, omens might have been causally related to the proposed actions, as when urine inspection might support a particular medical procedure or when certain cloud formations forecast rain. However, we will assume that most ancient omens had no simple direct connection with expected events. How, a skeptical person might ask, could people persist in believing in the efficacy of omen interpretation in the face of the (presumably) random outcomes of subsequent actions? If, for example, military campaigns carried out under favorable omens were as likely to fail as to succeed, would rational military leaders not soon begin to ignore omens?

Contemporary anthropologists such as Stanley Tambiah argue that humans everywhere and at all times have been capable of interacting with the world according to at least two fundamental and complementary orderings of reality associated with the terms *causal* and *participatory*. Causal orderings of the world are "represented by the categories, rules, and methodology of positive science and discursive mathematico-logical reason. The scientific focus involves a particular kind of distancing, affective neutrality, and abstraction to events in the world" (Tambiah 1990, 105). Participatory orderings, on the other hand, are engaged "when persons, groups, animals, places, objects, and natural phenomena are in a relation of contiguity, and translate that relation into one of existential immediacy and contact and shared affinities" (Tambiah 1990, 107). One way of characterizing the participatory orientation to the world is to say that humans live in an "I-Thou" relationship with the world, rather than an "I-it" relationship, attributing personality and human motives to natural entities and imbuing them with both physical and mental powers of many kinds. With rare exceptions, people living in ancient civilizations were far more likely to function participatorally in the world than we are today, although both orientations were available in the ancient world as they are now. Divinatory rituals, including omen interpretation rituals, were a central part of the participatory ordering of the world—an ordering of the world at least initially more concerned with personal relationships than with statistical analyses of outcomes, and one in which direct personal communication with physical objects, the dead, and the gods was believed possible.

From the standpoint of evolutionary theory, it is easy to understand why both orientations to the world persist, even though the participatory orientation may seem to some to make false assumptions about the world. Few today would want to argue that the causal orientation, with its attempt to accurately assess the properties of the external world, is not adaptive. Without this orientation, we would be without most of our modern technologies. On the other hand, as David Sloan Wilson argues:

there are many, many . . . situations in which it can be adaptive to distort reality. Even massively fictitious beliefs can be adaptive, as long as they motivate behaviors that are adaptive in the real world. At best our vaunted ability to know is just one tool in a mental toolkit that is frequently passed over in favor of other tools. . . . Once this kind of reasoning is removed from its pedestal as the only adaptive way to think, a host of alternatives become available. Emotions are evolved mechanisms for motivating adaptive behavior that are far more ancient than the cognitive processes typically associated with scientific thought. . . . We might expect stories, music, and rituals to be at least as important as logical arguments in orchestrating the behavior of groups [and individuals]. Supernatural agents and events that never happened can provide blueprints for action that far surpass factual accounts of the natural world in clarity and motivating power. (2002, 41–42)

With respect to divination in particular, it seems very likely that persons believing themselves to act in concert with the approval or desire of the gods would act with greater motivation and confidence than those believing themselves to be acting against the interests of entities with whom they have a personal relationship, so it is very likely that divination actually did increase the positive outcomes of actions taken after consulting omen interpreters. This is true for much the same reason that persons taking placebos are more likely to heal than those who do nothing—often subconscious processes may improve performance when one feels good about the situation. It is even possible that the kind of self-hypnosis often associated with divining rituals allows persons to access relevant information that is only available through unconscious processes rather than through conscious ones. This kind of access to unconscious processes is especially important in connection with divination by dream interpretation, a technique used extensively in both Egypt and Greece, and one that continues to play a significant role in modern psychotherapies.

There are also other well understood psychological reasons for why humans persist in what skeptics term an "irrational" belief in divination. Even in connection with predictions of events whose outcomes are independent of human agency, human memory functions to remember hits and to forget misses unless meticulous records are kept. Furthermore, ambiguous results are more likely to be seen as hits rather than as misses, and omens are frequently interpreted in vague terms so that almost any outcome is ambiguous (Shermer 1997). Perhaps even more importantly, divination was initially developed largely in connection with public undertakings rather than private ones. When a public agent acted in a way directed by the public interpretation of omens, he was deemed to have acted prudently because he was following public norms. Thus, he could not be blamed if the undertaking was unsuccessful. In much the same way, a bureaucrat acting today in a way consistent with the favored outcome of a statistical analysis of possible outcomes of an action is largely protected against blame because she has followed a culturally sanctioned procedure even if the action does not yield the desired result.

From our present perspective, divination is most interesting because it may be an important stimulus to scientific thinking by directing attention to regularities within selected classes of phenomena and correlations between different classes of phenomena. All forms of omen interpretation begin, according to Erica Reiner "when a fortuitous occurrence and a subsequent good fortune or misfortune" become linked in the mind, "not so much as cause and effect, but as a forewarning and a subsequent event. . . . Such linked pairs, consisting of a protasis (if clause) and anapodosis (forecast), a pair called by the technical term 'omen,' were collected into lists, and these lists eventually developed into large compendia that we call omen series" (1999, 21). Though the initial connection between forewarning and event may have been purely accidental, it becomes useful as an omen when we presume some positive correlation between the behavior of the omen class and the class of events to which human action is directed. This presumption makes it possible for a consistent, nonarbitrary, reading of the meaning of omens by linking the signs to specific events.

After lunar eclipses had been established as an important omen class in Mesopotamia, in 747 B.C.E., King Nabonassar directed his watch keepers to keep records of eclipses and their associated omens:

When the moon is eclipsed you shall observe exactly month, day, night-watch, wind, course, and position of the stars in whose realm the eclipse takes place. The omens relative to its month, its day, its night-watch, its wind, its course, and its star you shall indicate. (Pannekoek 1961, 44)

Though this directive was probably intended initially to make certain that no eclipse omens were missed, rather than to provide data about the timing of eclipses, it is nonetheless the case that the lunar omen series in *Enuma Anu Enlil*, which followed from this directive, led within less than a century to an awareness of the regular appearance of eclipses. A series of four or five eclipses occurred at six-month intervals eight different times between 750 B.C.E. and 650 B.C.E., with quiescent periods between series. Watchers began to assume that, when an eclipse did not appear in the middle of a series of six-month occurrences, it was because it took place during the daylight hours when the moon was below the horizon, and beginning about 675 B.C.E., Babylonian sky watchers began to predict the appearance of eclipses in comments such as the following:

On the 14th an eclipse will take place; it is evil for Elam and Amurru, lucky for the king, my lord, rest happy. It will be seen without Venus. To the king, my lord, I say: there will be an eclipse. From Irasshi-ilu, the king's servant.

To the king, my lord, I sent: 'An eclipse will take place.' Now it has not passed, it has taken place. In the happening of this eclipse it portends peace for the king, my lord. (Pannekoek 1961, 45)

If the moon did not wait for the sun to rise in the morning, then the eclipse could not be seen and the report looked like this:

The eclipse passes; it does not take place. If the king should ask: 'what omens hast thou seen?'—the gods have not been seen with one another. . . . From Munnabitu. (Pannekoek 1961, 47)

As we shall see, the knowledge of eclipse appearances generated through these omen observations would later become integrated with other observational data to create a sophisticated calendar that could predict the first visibility of the new moon (which defined the beginning of a new month) for at least a century in advance. However, the omen texts also seemed to produce a new attitude that led to the production of astronomical diaries starting around 661 B.C.E.. These diaries intentionally recorded lunar and planetary phenomena, correlating them with a huge range of terrestrial phenomena, including the price of barley (Reiner 1999).

Though celestial omens became important early in Mesopotamia, around 2300 B.C.E. , other forms of omens preceded celestial omens even there, and in some ancient civilizations celestial omens never became as important as other forms. In Egypt, for example, the predominant form of omen interpretation involved invoking a god or gods to indicate their answer to a supplicant's questions through the form taken by oil dropped into a copper dish of water. Another common form of divination involved dream interpretation. One directive in the Leyden Papyrus, a Hellenistic text whose content almost certainly dates back to around 1400 B.C.E., tells the supplicant to repeat a long script, which includes the following incantation to the god Ra seven times:

> I pray thee that thou reveal thyself to me tonight and speak with me and give me answer in truth without falsehood; for I will glorify thee before him who is upon the throne, who is not destroyed, he of the great glory. . . . Oh god who is above heaven, in whose hand is the beautiful staff, who created deity, deity not having created him. Come down to me in the midst of the flame that is here before thee, thou of Boel, and let me see the business that I ask about tonight truly without falsehood. Let it be seen. Let it be heard. . . . O great god that is on the mountain of Atuki, Khabato, Takrat, come in to me, let my eyes be opened tonight for any given thing that I shall ask about, truly, without falsehood.

The supplicant is then told to lie down on a rush mat without speaking to anyone, after which the god will answer him in his dream (Harris 1998, 147–148).

The Leyden papyrus also includes a form of numerological divination linked to another potentially scientific domain, that of medicine. It uses the numerical table shown below in connection with the following directions:

> Ascertain in what month the sick man took to his bed and the name he received at his birth. Calculate the course of the moon and see how many periods of thirty days have elapsed; then note in the table the number of days left over. If the number comes in the upper part of the table (above the line) he will live, but if in the lower part, he will die. (Harris 1998, 149)

1	10	19
2	11	20
3	13	23
4	14	25
7	16	26
9	17	27
5	15	22
6	18	28
8	21	29
12	24	30

While the use of such a table as a way of providing a medical prognosis presumably has little or no validity, the search for medical omens seems to have led eventually to the discovery of predictors, such as the character of urine samples, or the strength of the pulse, which were causally linked to the phenomena that they foretold. In that sense, medical prognostication, which was the great strength of ancient medicine almost everywhere, may have grown out of divinatory practices. Only after around 500 B.C.E., and in connection with the spread of Mesopotamian astral omenology (discussed below) into Egypt, did celestial omens become important there.

We have already mentioned that the earliest Chinese writing and numbers are connected with the use of cracks emanating from the location of burned spots on turtle shells and the shoulder blades of animals as omens. Points on the bone or shell were identified with days of the 10-day ritual week, with the cardinal directions, and with certain processes, such as comings (which might be visits, the bringing of tribute, or hostile raids coming from the outside, depending on what kind of question was being asked of the omen), ill-fortune, distressing news, blessings, rains, or harvests (Wang 2000). In addition, the length of cracks indicated whether events predicted should be attributed to distant peoples (*fang*) or to persons nearer to the court (*Si*). The point of a heated bronze rod was pressed into the surface, and the omen was read off based on the points through which the cracks passed and the length of the cracks. The level of detail of the prediction, would, of course, depend on how many symbols were touched by the cracks.

Here are a few sample prognostications from the Shang oracle bones:

1. Crack in day *bingshen*, Gu divining: There will be [a] coming from the West.
2. Divining on the day *guiyou*, In this ten day period, there will be ill fortune coming from the South and bringing disaster.
3. Crack on day *guiyou*, It will rain today. [The rain may come from any direction].

In some cases, not only is the omen entered, but a record of the successfully predicted event is also included. Thus, for example:

4. On day *xinhai,* Nei divining: This first month, *Di* will command rain. On the evening of the fourth day, *jianyin,* [it indeed rained] (Wang 2000, 32–35).

Beginning sometime between the 10th and the 8th centuries B.C.E., most Chinese divination shifted to the use of a set of hexagrams discussed in the *I Jing,* or *Book of Changes,* which became the first of the Chinese classics learned by scholars in the Han Dynasty. Though the process involved in using the *I Jing* for divination is too complex to discuss in detail here, it involved using yarrow sticks to establish a column of six complete (*yang,* or creative) or broken (*yin,* or receptive) lines, yielding 64 possibilities.

Four of the 64 Possible Hexagrams of the *I Jing*

a   b   c   d

Once the particular hexagram was established, divining was accomplished by reading the passage associated with the hexagram in the *I Jing* and interpreting it in the context of the question being asked.

THE RISE OF CELESTIAL OMENS

In Mesopotamia, the earliest form of divination seems to have involved reading the pattern of lobes in the livers of sacrificial animals, which, like the pattern of lines in the human palm, varies from one animal to the next. As early as about 2300 B.C.E., a few passages from Sumer suggest the use of celestial phenomena as omens. In an introductory passage from a myth about the origins of shade tree gardening, which can be dated to around 2300 B.C.E., we read:

He lifted his eyes towards the lands below,
Looked up at the stars in the East,
Lifted his eyes toward the lands above,
Gazed at the auspicious inscribed heaven,
From the inscribed heaven learned the omens,
Saw there how to carry out the divine laws,
Studied the decrees of the gods, . . .

—(Kramer 1959, 72).

And in a dream attributed to Gudea of Lagash (2141–2122 B.C.E.), we find:

She held the shining stylus in her hand, she carried
a table with favorable celestial signs
and was thinking; . . . She announced the
favorable star for building the temple

—(Pannekoek 1961, 38).

A catalog of tablets from around 2200 B.C.E. also suggests that eclipse phenomena may have been used as omens as early as that time, for the first line of one tablet begins, "Who knows the eclipses, the mother of him who knows the incantations" (Kramer 1963, 227).

By around 1800 B.C.E., other forms of divination in Mesopotamia, including the dominant system of interpreting sheep's livers, were seen as under the control of the celestial bodies, as the following beautiful hymn suggests:

They are laying down, the great ones.
The bolts are fallen; the fastenings are in place.
The crowds of people are quiet.
The gods of the land and goddesses of the land,
Shamash [the sun], Sin [the moon], Adad [the storm], and Ishtar [Venus],
Have betaken themselves to sleep in heaven.
They are not pronouncing judgement,

They are not deciding things.
Veiled is the night.
The temple and the most holy places are dark.
The traveler calls on his god;
and the litigant is tarrying in sleep.
The judge of the truth, the father of the fatherless,
Shamash, has betaken himself to his chamber.
Oh great ones, gods of the night, . . .
Oh bow [star] and Yoke [star],
Oh Pleiades, Orion, and the Dragon [?]
Oh Ursa major, Goat [star] and the Bison,
Stand by, and then,
In the divination which I am making,
In the lamb which I am offering,
Put truth for me.

—(Van der Waerden 1974, 58).

B. L. Van der Waerden was almost certainly correct in writing of this poem: "Here it is apparent that the very ancient art of entrail divination is being placed by the poet under the tutelage of the celestial gods. No longer is knowledge of the future to come from the sacrificial lamb itself, nor even from the particular god to whom it is offered, but from the stars, called upon to witness and implant the truth" (1974, 59).

Though it is difficult to conceive of how divination by means of numerology, the patterns made by oil drops on water, patterns of sticks, or even the patterns of cracks in bones or turtle shells might have begun, it is relatively easy to imagine how liver divination began, because the entrails of animals were traditionally offered to the gods when animals were sacrificed in propitiatory rituals, and it would have been easy to notice the correlation between some unusual feature of the offering and some unusual event relating to the request made of the god. It is even easier to imagine how unusual celestial events, which have an important emotional impact, might come to be associated with events that immediately followed, thus the interest in eclipses and in other significant lunar phenomena.

Once diviners' attention had been drawn to celestial events by phenomena associated with the Moon, it was not long before they began to observe phenomena associated with the third brightest object in the sky, the planet Venus, which was linked to the critically important goddess of fertility, Ishtar. Thus, in Mesopotamia around 1581 B.C.E., we get a list of observations of the heliacal risings of Venus for 21 years with associated prognostications. (The heliacal rising of a celestial object occurs when it rises over the horizon in the east just before the Sun rises and obliterates its visibility. Likewise, a heliacal setting is when the object sets in the west just long enough after the Sun sets to be visible briefly before it disappears.) Many of these observation/prognostication passages unsurprisingly deal with harvests, which depend upon the fertility of the earth. For example, one from year 10 of the series reads as follows: "If, on the 10th of Arahsamma Venus disappeared in the east, remaining absent two months and six days in the sky [because it was circling behind the Sun as viewed from the Earth], and was seen on the 16th of Tebitu in the west, the harvest of the land will be successful" (Van der Waerden 1974, 50).

Ishtar was an extremely troublesome goddess as well, so Venus omens were also frequently associated with dire predictions linked to disease and warfare. Among omens from the massive series of 7,000 celestial omens, *Enuma Anu Enlil*, for example, we find the following: "If Venus appears in the east in the month Airu and the Great and Small Twins [star groupings] surround her, and she is dark, then will the King of Elam fall sick and not remain alive" (Van der Waerden 1974, 49). As we shall see, Venus phenomena were observed and used as omens in both China and Mesoamerica, among the Maya, shortly after eclipses began to be used as omens, though in those cultures they were not linked to a fertility goddess.

Within approximately 20 years after the initiation of Venus observations, Mesopotamian astronomical observers initiated a new practice that was to have huge implications for subsequent Mesopotamian civilizations. Based on the series of Venus appearances and disappearances that had been observed, they recognized a pattern that allowed them not simply to observe, but also to predict the future appearances and disappearances of the planet. In a text that can be dated to within a few years of 1561 B.C.E., there is a section of observations and omens that looks much like earlier Venus omen texts, but that section is followed by a section in which the position descriptions include future as well as past events.

For example:

If, in the month Nissannu on the second day, Venus arose in the east, there will be need in the land. *Until the 6th Kislimu she will stay in the east, on the 7th Kislimu she will disappear. Three months she remains out of the sky. On the 7th Sadaru will Venus appear again in the west,* and one king will declare hostilities against the other. (Van der Waerden 1974, 55)

The predicted visibility and invisibility periods in this section do not perfectly match what modern theories say those periods would have been, but they observe a perfectly regular pattern in which a visibility period of eight months and five days is followed by an invisibility period of three months. That, in turn, is followed by a visibility period of eight months five days and by an invisibility period of seven days. This four-element cycle is then repeated.

The significance of the capability that this texts symbolizes is hard to overstate. From this time forward, Mesopotamian astral priests, unlike any other diviners, could not only interpret omens, they could tell in advance what those omens were going to be. They could open up a virtually unlimited perspective into the future, and this gave them tremendous prestige. Over time, the impulse to observe and theorize regarding the detailed motions and interactions of more heavenly bodies, fed by the successes of the Venus predictions and the later predictions of eclipse phenomena, drew the Mesopotamian astronomer-priests into increasingly precise and comprehensive theories of the motions of the Sun, Moon, and all known planets. As a consequence, the astral elements within traditional Mesopotamian religion became increasingly important relative to gods associated with water, the earth, storms, canals, and so on. Moreover, divination became increasingly important relative to rituals that asked the gods to listen and respond to human needs and wants, for the absolute regularity and predictability of celestial motions made it clear that the astral gods could not or would not listen. They simply went on their way, doing precisely what they had always done.

In the next chapter, dealing with the production of religious and agricultural calendars, we will follow some of the detailed developments of astronomical theory both in Mesopotamia and in the other early civilizations, but it is worth signaling here how the increasing knowledge of astronomy shaped the ongoing development of Mesopotamian religion and society.

Up until about 400 B.C.E., astral priests continued to use divination primarily to determine auspicious and inauspicious times for undertaking various actions, so there was a presumption that humans could still choose to act, if not in defiance of the celestial gods, at least in cooperation with them and using the information that divination provided. Moreover, prognostications tended up to this time to focus on public events rather than private ones. However, around 400 B.C.E., the practice of casting horoscopes for individuals based on the celestial configuration on their date of conception began, implying that even the behavior of private persons was determined by the stars. The Hellenistic historian W. W. Tarn has very nicely summarized a crucial cultural consequence as horoscopic astrology reached its most sophisticated levels:

The stars, and above all, the planets, obviously moved in the vault of heaven according to fixed laws; and a doctrine of "correspondence" had arisen—this was the vital matter—according to which the heavens above and the earth beneath were the counterpart of each other, and what happened in the sidereal world was reproduced on earth. But the movements of the sidereal world were fixed; if, then there was a correspondence, what happened on the earth was also fixed; and men's actions, too, were fixed, for man was a microcosm, a little world, the counterpart of the great world, or universe, and his soul was a spark of that celestial fire which glowed in the stars. From this sprang one of the most terrible doctrines which ever oppressed humanity, the Babylonian *Heimarmene,* or Fate, which ruled alike stars, earth, and men; all their motions were fixed by an immutable Power, non-moral, which neither loved nor hated, but held on its course as inexorably as the planets across the firmament. (1952, 345–346)

This vision of a rigidly determined universe spread widely and rapidly through the Mediterranean Basin into Greece, Alexandrian Egypt, and even Rome. Thus, we hear from the Greek historian Nemesios of the Greek Stoic philosophy, which emerged in Athens around 320 B.C.E.:

The stoics explain: the planets return to the same celestial sign, where each individual planet originally stood . . .; in certain times the planets bring conflagration and annihilation of all things; then the world starts anew from the same place, and while the stars turn again the same way as before, each individual thing will . . . be restored unchanged; then there will again be a Socrates and a Plato . . . everything will be the same and unchanged down to the minutest details. (Van der Waerden 1974, 162)

The Roman historian Appian tells a story about the founding of the city of Selucia, near Babylon, by Alexander's general, Selucus Nicander. The general wanted his city to surpass the ancient capital of the region, so he consulted the Babylonian astral priests regarding the best hour to begin construction on the new city. But the priests, fearing that the new city would outshine their own, named an unlucky hour. Selucus assembled the workmen and told them to wait until he gave the signal for construction to begin, but they inexplicably started before his signal.

The heralds who tried to stop them were not able to do so. . . . Selucus, being troubled in his mind, again made inquiry of the *magi* concerning his city, and they, having first secured a promise of impunity, replied, "that which is fated, o king, . . . neither man nor city can change, for there is a fate for cities, as well as for men." (Cramer 1954, 11)

We have very limited evidence from the Maya regarding how they regarded their calendar cycles, which also incorporated astronomical parameters, but what we do have suggests a close parallel to the divination emphasis in Mesopotamia. At several Mayan sites there are documents that detail the events associated with the accession of a new ruler and project those same events into the past and future for rulers who were or will be born on the same calendar cycle days (Lounsbury 1978).

In China, as in Mesopotamia, celestial omens relating to the Sun, Moon, and planets grew in importance over time. As a consequence, increasingly precise observations were made, and by the early Han period, eclipse phenomena were predicted. However, several circumstances—both technical and cultural—led to a much different use of and attitude toward celestial omenology in China than in the West. For technical reasons that we will discuss when we discuss calendrical astronomy, ancient Chinese astronomical predictions were not as accurate as those in Mesopotamia, and by the Han period celestial events were not considered as omens unless they were *not* predicted. In Mesopotamia, if an expected eclipse was not seen—which could happen because of cloud cover or because, as the astronomers soon theorized, the eclipse occurred under the horizon—the usual statement was that because the omen did not appear, there would be no prediction. In Han China, to the contrary, if a predicted eclipse *did* happen, there was no omen. Only if an eclipse appeared when not expected was the phenomenon taken as an omen. Similarly, comets and supernovae were accepted as omens in China because their appearances could not be anticipated.

While there was a presumed parallel between terrestrial and celestial phenomena in China, celestial omens emphasized apparent irregularities, rather than an oppressive determinism, because the omen signs violated rather than affirmed the orderly behavior of predictable phenomena. Moreover, to the extent that there was a presumption of causation related to the celestial-human parallels, it was presumed in China that celestial omens reflected terrestrial events rather than vice versa. Beginning sometime during the Zhou Dynasty, the Chinese emperor was understood to be chosen by the heavens to be responsible for governing the human inhabitants of the terrestrial world. Furthermore, by the early Han period, it was assumed that when the people accepted his rule, omens would appear verifying their acceptance of the ruler's legitimacy:

The man who received a kingly position because Heaven gave him great support and made him the king must receive signs that are not produced by human effort [i.e., the hexagrams discussed in the *I Jing*] but rather arrive by themselves. These signs are the verification of receiving the Mandate. When people all under Heaven submit themselves with one heart to such a king as if they were submitting to their parents, then Heavenly omens arrive responding to such sincerity. (Wang 2000, 150)

Though some astral omens might confirm the authority of the reigning monarch, most unusual celestial events—comets, for example—were viewed as signs of corruption in the court and as possible indicators that the favor of the heavens might be transferring to some other ruler. As a consequence, though it was important for the emperor to get good information about celestial omens, the emperor also had an interest in restricting access to such information, lest an omen encourage rebellion against his regime. As a result, although the Chinese court had an astronomical bureau from the Han period onward, access to astronomical learning was rigorously restricted. By the Song Dynasty all reports of the Astronomical Bureau were confidential reports to the emperor, and officers in the bureau were not allowed to transfer out, nor were their children. Moreover, anyone who taught astronomy to unauthorized persons was subject to capital punishment (Huff 1993).

Mayan writing is not well enough understood for us to have a clear idea of how celestial omenology played a role in Mesoamerican civilization, but it is the case that lunar data were collected beginning around 357 C.E. and that theoretical systems for eclipse prediction and subsequently for predicting the phenomena associated with Venus were developed by 668 C.E. While some of the lunar cycle observations might, in principle, have been made in order to create a Moon-based calendar, as we shall see, the Mayans established a 20-day month as the basis for their calendar sometime before 30 C.E., and they never changed. Additionally, there is a section of the *Dresden Codex,* our most comprehensive Mayan astronomical text, that links heliacal risings and settings of Venus to simple prognostications (Lounsbury 1978).

In India, from some time around 1500 B.C.E. until the arrival of Greek astronomy around 200 B.C.E., lunar phenomena were used to establish auspicious days for performing sacrifices and engaging in fasts. There is, however, no evidence of extended lunar observations during this period, nor is there evidence that attention was paid to Venus or any other planet. Moreover, as we shall see, Indian calendrical astronomy was too crude to form the basis for any predictive theories regarding lunar motions. Similarly, though the Moon and planets were occasionally mentioned in Egyptian omen texts, they played a small role, and Egyptian astronomy never developed much sophistication until Greek-Mesopotamian hybrid theories were produced at Alexandria.

Finally, horoscopic astrology became important in Greece and Rome, motivating some of the Greeks' and Romans' interest in astronomy. Indeed, Ptolemy, the second-century astronomer whose *Almagest* became the foundation for most subsequent Islamic and medieval European astronomy, also wrote the *Tetrabyblos,* which became the foundation for almost all subsequent astrological theory.

REBELLION AGAINST ASTRAL DETERMINISM AND THE RISE OF TRANSCENDENT DEITIES IN THE WEST

All of the civilizations that we have been considering incorporated beliefs in spirits or gods associated with natural entities and engaged in rituals that asked those gods to bend their wills to meet human desires. In the words of John Hermann Randall, they were involved with "gods that listened" (Randall 1970, Table of Contents) to their wishes, but the extreme form of astral determinism associated with late Mesopotamian astral religion deprived people of the comfort of such gods, leading to several responses.

The first, which appears, among other places, in the myth of Er described in book 10 of Plato's *Republic,* accepts the deterministic astral influences on the physical world, identifying the eight heavenly bodies (the Sun, Moon, Venus, Mercury, Mars, Saturn, Jupiter, and the sphere of the fixed stars) as the "spindle of necessity." Moreover, Plato accepts the doctrine of the "great year" that assumes that every time the stars come into the same relationship with one another, precisely the same events will recur, but then Plato, like the early Mesopotamian astral priests, insists that each human soul is free to choose its own fate. Lachesis, "the daughter of necessity," speaks to the souls as they come before her:

Souls of a day, here shall begin a new round of earthly life, to end in death. No guardian spirit will cast lots for you, but you shall choose your own destiny. Let him to whom the first lot falls chooses first a life to which he will be bound of necessity. But virtue owns no master: as a man honors or dishonors her, so shall he have more of her or less. The blame is his who chooses; Heaven is blameless. (1959, 617D–617E)

A second response, which appeared first in the works of the Greek philosopher Epicurus around 300 B.C.E., argued that humans fear gods of their own making, and that a true understanding of the causes of natural events—especially celestial events—would do away with the need for and belief in such gods. Thus, in his "Letter to Herodotus," Epicurus wrote:

there are three things that account for the major disturbances in men's minds. First, they assume that the celestial bodies are blessed and eternal yet have impulses, actions, and purposes quite inconsistent with divinity. Next, they anticipate and foresee eternal suffering . . . Finally, they suffer all this, not as a result of reasonable conjecture;

but through some sort of unreasoning imagination; and since in imagination they set no limit to suffering, they are beset by turmoil as great as if there were a reasonable basis for their dread, or even greater. But it is peace of mind to have been freed from all this . . . and when we have learned the causes of celestial phenomena and of other occasional happenings, we shall be free from what other men most dread. (1964, 33)

This view has been revived in the modern world, but it had very limited importance in the ancient world.

Far and away the most important response to astral determinism in antiquity came not out of the Greek philosophical tradition, but initially out of the experiences of farmers in what is now southern Iraq as astral religion became ever more deterministic. These Mandean Gnostics could neither deny the power of the official astral deities nor tolerate the deterministic doctrine associated with them, for the astral priests told them that the stars determined when to plant and when to harvest, even if the conditions on the ground were not suitable. Their response was to bewail the influence of the celestial gods, to posit the existence of a great, good, listening and transcendent God (i.e., one outside of the physical universe controlled by the astral deities), and then to appeal to that god for escape from the domination of the stars. Their rebellion shows forth particularly powerfully in the following lamentations from about 200 B.C.E.:

The seven [planets] and the twelve [signs of the Zodiac] become my persecution.

The Seven will not let me go my own path. How I must obey, how endure, how must I quiet my mind! How must I hear of the seven and the twelve mysteries, how must I groan! How must my mild Father's Word dwell among the creatures of the dark.!

O how shall I rejoice then, who am now afflicted and afraid in the dwelling of the evil ones! O how shall my heart rejoice *outside the works which I have made in this world!* How long shall I wander and sink within all the worlds?

The evil ones conspire against me. . . . They say to one another, In our own world the call of Life shall not be heard, it [the world] shall be ours. . . . Day in, day out, I seek to escape them, as I stand alone in this world. I lift mine eyes unto Manda d'Hayye [the Alien, transcendent god of the Mandeans], who said unto me, Soon I come to thee. (Jonas, 1963, 66–67)

Here, it seems, lie the beginnings of a whole series of religions, including Christianity, Mandeanism, Manicheanism, and Mithraism. Since the farmers were unsuccessful in fighting the demands of the state-mandated religion, they retreated into otherworldly religions whose adherents renounced the physical world and sought salvation by escape into a spiritual world where the god that listened lived. In 1 John, 2:15–16, we find the sentiment common to all:

Love not the world, neither the things that are in the world. If any man love the world, the love of the Father is not in him. For all that is in the world, the lust of the flesh, and the lust of the eyes, and the pride of life, is not of the Father, but is of the World.

Though evidence about the relationship of astral priests to the common man within Mayan civilization is far less extensive, New World scholars have suggested that the transformation of classical Mayan civilization may also have been related to the divorce between the agricultural foundations of the society and the growingly esoteric astronomical and astrological doctrines of the priesthood. Thus, G.H.S. Bushnell writes:

In AD 800 the last hieroglyphic inscription was carved at Copan. No further building was done and shortly afterwards the hierarchy disappeared. During the century which followed, the same thing happened at Quiriguá, Piedras Negras, Tikal, Uaxactún and the other southern centers [of Mayan civilization]. We do not know why this happened, but the most probable reason is that their religion had grown away from the people, the cult of time was being developed for its own sake, and much of what went on in the sanctuaries did nothing to promote the fertility of the fields. The peasants continued to cultivate the valley, but the Acropolis was abandoned to the Forest. (1961, 382)

Five

Calendars, Time Keeping, and the Increasing Complexity of Astronomy

All early civilizations, with the exception of the Mesopotamian and Indian, initially organized their cycles of religious observances in ways that were independent of astronomical phenomena and only sometimes relatively loosely linked to agricultural cycles. Over time, however, because these civilizations were fundamentally agrarian, because agricultural years correspond relatively closely to the annual appearance of certain celestial phenomena, and because in many places omenology called special attention to the heavens, calendars became regulated by celestial phenomena in all early civilizations.

Both in Shang China and in the earliest Mayan period, ritual calendars were initially established that were completely independent of any natural phenomena. The ritual cycle used in the Chinese oracle bones is a 60-day cycle of six 10-day weeks, for example, and the earliest ritual cycle used by the Mayans was a Sacred Round, or almanac, in which 13-day weeks, or *kins* were fit into 20-day months, or *uinals*, giving a cycle in which both day of the *kin* and day of the *uinal* terms repeated after 260 days.

THE EARLIEST EGYPTIAN CALENDAR

Although there have been some suggestions that there was a primitive Egyptian calendar based on lunar months that began with the day after the old crescent of the waning moon could no longer be seen (Clagett 1995), the earliest Egyptian calendar for which there is unambiguous evidence is one in which an agricultural year (presumed to be 365 days long) is broken into three seasons, each containing four 30-day months of three 10-day weeks, with a five-day new year's festival added at the end of the year. This civil year, established around 3000 B.C.E., began with the rising of the Nile flood, which initiated the inundation season. This season was followed by the season of planting and growth, and then by one of harvest and low water (Clagett 1995). Note that this calendar had no astronomical content. This civil year was maintained as the official year in Egypt up until 144 C.E., and Western astronomers up to and including Copernicus used it for long-term calculations because it was the only constant length year established in the Western world (Neugebaur 1942).

Because the Nile flood could easily be 10 days earlier or later than that suggested by the average period of recurrence, it would have taken on the order of a century to recognize that the 365-day year was about 0.25 days short of an agricultural year and that the civil year would slide through the agricultural year at the rate of one cycle every 1,460 years. By the time that this recognition was formally acknowledged (around 2600 B.C.E.), the civil year was so well established that it was continued for official governmental purposes. The "first of the year" began the civil calendar, but starting around 2600 B.C.E. a second, agricultural, calendar, which began with the "opening of the year," was initiated. The opening of the year began when the flood actually arrived at the capital of Egypt, so it remained correlated with agricultural activities. That this was so is indicated by a text from around 1870 plus or minus six years B.C.E. that gives the civil date on which the opening of the year occurs as during the fourth month of the second season (Clagett 1995). This date is consistent with the presumption of a 1,460-year cycle of civil years moving through the agricultural seasons.

THE INITIAL INCORPORATION OF ASTRONOMICAL ELEMENTS INTO CYCLICAL RITUAL CALENDARS: EGYPT AND INDIA

The Egyptian calendar incorporated its first astronomical element around 2780 B.C.E. in connection with a text that stated that the star Sothis (modern Sirius) is herald of the new year and of the flood (Clagett 1995). This text is almost universally interpreted to mean that the star Sothis rose heliacally just before the annual flood of the Nile and that, because its appearance was more regular than the annual flood, it would henceforth mark the beginning of the year. Since heliacal risings can only occur at even day intervals, the choice of the heliacal rising of Sothis had to be after either 365 days or after 366 days. In fact, the average Sothis period is almost exactly the same as the average solar year (they are off by one day in 1,460 years), so to keep the civil year consistent with the Sothis year, one day would have to be added to a 365-day year every four years; however, the Egyptians chose not to do this, allowing the Heliacal rising of Sothis to migrate through the civil year as the agricultural year did.

Just as an agricultural calendar grew in parallel with the civil year, a calendar of religious ritual based on a better approximation to lunar months than the official 30-day months of the civil calendar was created because priestly ceremonial duties were often related to the phases of the moon. The average lunar month is 29.53 days, or very close to 29.5 days, so by around 2000 B.C.E. we begin to see Egyptian religious ceremonial calendars in which 30- and 29-day months alternate so as to keep rituals close to the appropriate phases of the Moon. Twelve such lunar months are 354 days long, while the solar year is over 365 days. A lunar calendar can be kept loosely in phase with a solar calendar by intercalating (adding) a 13th month to some years—as happened in Mesopotamia and Greece—but there is no textual evidence of such inter-calations in Egypt before a new, Greek-based calendar was created in 144 C.E. (Clagett 1995).

A final astronomical element entered pre-Hellenistic Egyptian timekeeping sometime before 2100 B.C.E. Given the choice of the heliacal rising of Sothis to signal the beginning of the year, Egyptian calendar keepers began to use the heliacal rising of other stars—later called *decans,* by Egyptologists—to signal the beginnings of each 10-day week during the year. After 10 days, a new star would be chosen to indicate the new week, and the star of the previous week would become the star of the watch before dawn. Ten days later, the initial star would become the star of the second watch before dawn and so on. Diagrams of successive *decans* became so fascinating that, for a period of nearly 200 years beginning around 2100 B.C.E., they were used to decorate sarcophagi (Clagett 1995).

Model of Decans Decorating a Coffin Lid

First 10-day week	Second 10-day week	Third 10-day week	Fourth 10-day week
X			
X-1	X		
X-2	X-1	X	
X-3	X-2	X-1	X

When chosen to indicate successive 10-day weeks, the *decans* produced 12 watches between sunset and sunrise. Thus, in *The Book of Amduat,* which dates from the end of the Old Kingdom, the Sun passes through 12 hours during the night (Clagett 1989). Assuming symmetry between daylight and dark, the Egyptians produced the 24-hour days which we continue to use.

In India, the earliest known calendar is discussed in the *Vedanga Jyosta,* which exists in two early and obscure or corrupt versions (Chattopadhyaya 1996). The orbit of the Moon was divided into 27 equal arcs, called *nakastras,* and there are 27 month names corresponding to the *nakastra* names as well. The winter solstice was identified with the star beta Delphini (which has led to a tentative date of around 1500 B.C.E. for the parameters given in the text). The solar year is taken to be 366 days, so 5 solar years is 1,830 days. Sixty-two lunations (from first visibility to first visibility of the moon) are taken to be 1,830 days (giving an average month length of 29.16 days, compared to the modern value of 29.53). Furthermore, 67 sidereal lunar months results in 1,830 days (a sidereal lunar month being the time that the Moon takes to return to the same place measured against the background of the stars). In order to keep the lunations coordinated with the years, each 1,830-day cycle, called a *yuga,* had to contain three 12-month years and two 13-month years. To get this to happen, one intercalated month was placed after the 30th month of the cycle and one after the 61st month.

A *yuga* began when the Sun, Moon, and winter solstice all met at beta Delphini. After each 1,830 days in the theoretical calendar, the same situation again occurred and the next *yuga* began. This system governed the order of sacrifices within the Vedic tradition and persisted, with one very minor shift in the day of the start of the year, from its origins into the second century B.C.E. in spite of the fact that the ritual calendar bore little relation to the observed astronomical phenomena within a century of its origins.

EARLY EGYPTIAN CLOCKS AND SUNDIALS

Celestial observation conditions in Egypt occasionally make it difficult to see the stars at night and thus to determine watch lengths. To deal with this problem, by around 1470 B.C.E., Egyptian timekeepers devised a new technology for determining the passage of relatively short periods of time. They invented water clocks in which the dripping of water out of a small hole in the bottom of a specially designed bowl indicated a watch or hour (Clagett 1995). Very quickly they recognized that the night is shorter during some times of the year than during others (i.e., that watch hours measured by their new clocks varied from relatively long at the winter solstice to relatively short at the summer solstice). The initial Egyptian response was to adjust how much water they put in their clocks, depending on the season, to keep both night and day 12 variable hours each (Clagett 1995). Other civilizations, including all modern industrialized civilizations, led by the Mesopotamians, would choose to keep their hour length constant and insist that day and night lengths, as measured in hours, fluctuate seasonally.

Starting about 1425 B.C.E., Egyptian daylight hours were measured using solar shadow clocks. These clocks used the length of the shadow of a gnomon, which only crudely approximated hourly intervals except at the vernal equinox, for which the clocks were calibrated (Clagett 1995). Within about 200 years after the first use of shadow clocks, the Egyptians had begun to use sundials to measure the hours, not by shadow length, but by the angular position of the shadow of the vertical gnomon. Unlike later Greek and Roman sundials, the lines radiating from the base of the gnomon were straight and at equal angular distances from one another, so again the dials indicated unequal hours— longer near dawn and dusk than near noon, even at the equinoxes. In spite of the fact that the Egyptians developed instruments that measured variable length hours, there is evidence from the 12th century B.C.E. that they were beginning to think of shifting to a 24 equal-hour system, though that was never formally accomplished.

MORE COMPLEX ASTRONOMICAL ELEMENTS IN CYCLICAL CALENDARS: MAYAN ASTRONOMY AND CHINESE ASTRONOMY IN THE HAN PERIOD

Sometime before around 500 B.C.E., the Mayans incorporated a 365-day cycle, which scholars call the vague year, into their calendar. Whether this cycle was drawn initially from the agricultural year or was an approximation based on astronomical phenomena is uncertain. Mayan temple architecture incorporated site lines that allowed the observation and timing of solstices and equinoxes, including the zenith passage of the Sun at the summer solstice, which provided a precise way to determine the solar year length, so it is difficult to imagine the use of such observations over even a short period of time leading to such a crude value for the solar year as 365 days. Indeed, some scholars interpret a tablet from Palenque as indicating that 1,508 vague years equal 1,507 solar years, giving a solar year length of 365.2422 days, compared with the modern value of 365.2420, but this value for the year was achieved long after the vague year had been adopted for calendrical purposes.

Because 365 and 260 (the number of days in a Sacred Round) have 18,980 as their lowest common multiple, when dates were given as places in the Sacred Round and places in the vague year, they repeated after 52 vague years or 73 sacred rounds, giving a Calendar Round.

In order to establish the distance between two dates in different calendar rounds, the Mayans counted by a system of days, 20-day months (*uinals*), 360-day *tuns*, 360 by 20-day *katuns*, and 360 by 20 by 20-day *baktuns*. Why this calculating system was used is unclear because it violated the place value convention that was used for non-astronomical quantities. The more natural counts would seem to have been days, 20-day months, 20^2 day tuns, 20^3 day katuns, 20^4 day baktuns, and so on.

Given that any two dates within a single calendar round are given by the triplets (t_o, v_o, y_o) and (t, v, y), where t is the day number, v is the month in the sacred round, and y is the day in the vague year, then the distance between any two dates in the same or different Calendar Rounds is n_1 kin, $+ n_2$ uinals $+ n_3$ tuns $+ n_4$ katuns $+ n_5$ baktuns, where

$$t = (t_o - n_5 - 2n_4 - 4n_3 + 7n_2 + n_1) \text{ [mod 13] ([mod 13], or modulus 13, means}$$
$$\text{subtract all multiples of 13) from the number.}$$
$$v = (v_o + n_1) \text{ [mod 20]}$$
$$y = (y_o + 190n_5 - 100n_4 - 5n_3 + 20n_2 + n_1) \text{ [mod 365] (Closs 1986, 309).}$$

Though this algorithm reproduces the calendar distances indicated in Mayan texts, at this point we have no idea regarding how the Maya themselves calculated these distances.

The *Dresden Codex* is a Mayan text written with ink on treated bark now located in Dresden, Germany and datable to around 1200 C.E., from which most of our knowledge of the Mayan calendar and astronomy comes. In this text, early dates are established by giving their Calendar Round position and their distance from the presumed origin of the universe, 13 *baktuns*, or approximately 5,200 *tuns* before the creation of the codex (i.e., around 4000 B.C.E. The earliest Mayan stone inscriptions can be dated by this system to about 31 B.C.E. (Closs 1986).

So far, we have discussed no unambiguously astronomical element in the Mayan Calendar, but by 375 C.E., there are tablets that include not only the *kin*, *unial*, and vague year positions for a given day, but which also indicate the phase (age) of the Moon and its position in a lunar sequence of six months.

The age of the Moon may take on any value between 1 and 30, but successive lunations alternate between 29 and 30 days with an occasional extra 30-day month, giving an average month a length of 29.53061 days. The observations (or calculations—there is still disagreement) reported in these tablets soon led in Mesoamerica, as in Mesopotamia and in China (discussed below), to the construction of tables that predict the possibility of lunar and solar eclipses.

The path of the Moon is sometimes above that of the Sun and sometimes below, and we call the distance above or below the Sun's path, or ecliptic, the "latitude of the Moon." When the lunar path crosses the path of the Sun, we call it a node, and it happens to be the case that there are three lunar nodes in almost exactly 520 days, so it is probably the case that the use of a 260-day Sacred Round within which the Moon crossed the path of the Sun precisely six times over four cycles led by chance to a recognition of this lunar phenomenon and to the recognition that eclipses only take place when lunar latitudes are relatively small (i.e., when the Moon is near the nodes of its path). (see Figure 5.1). At the same time, eclipses can only take place when the Moon and Sun are near what we call opposition (lunar eclipses) or conjunction (solar eclipses, that is, when they are directly opposite from one another relative to the Earth, or when they are directly in line with one another. Eclipses, thus, depend upon both the longitudinal periods of lunar and solar motion (i.e., the periods taken for completion of motion along their paths) and the latitudinal motion of the Moon. By 668 C.E., Mayan astronomers had recognized that there was a 405-lunation cycle in which lunar eclipse possibilities recur at either six- or five-month intervals such that in every 69-month period there are three sequences of six-month intervals and three five-month intervals (Lounsbury 1978). At some point before the construction of the materials in the *Dresden Codex*, Mayan astronomers further recognized that 405 lunations was about 1/9th of a day short of the 11,960 days initially posited for the completion of the full cycle, or that their eclipse possibility cycle was off by about one day in every 299 years, so they adjusted the cycle by simply advancing the lunation cycle by one day.

The latitude, or nodal, cycle chosen by the Maya is also more than 1.5 days off after 69 internodal intervals, or 14.5 days in nine repetitions of the complete cycle. This meant that the eclipse prediction tables would have begun to lose their effectiveness about 33 years after their initiation, but there is no indication that this problem was ever formally addressed. Why a much smaller difference in the lunation cycle was recognized and corrected for while the larger latitude problem was not is an unsolved problem in understanding Mayan calendrical astronomy.

The possibilities of solar eclipses are governed by all of the same considerations that regulate lunar eclipse possibilities, but we now know that solar eclipses are much more difficult to predict because lunar eclipses are produced when the Earth gets between the Sun and Moon, while solar eclipses occur when the Moon is between the Earth and the Sun. The shadow of the Earth cast on the Moon is much larger than the shadow of the Moon cast on the Earth. Indeed, the shadow of the Moon on the Earth is never large enough

Figure 5.1
Conditions Allowing Total and Partial Lunar Eclipses. Nick Livingston.

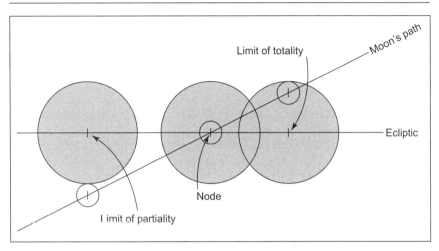

so that a solar eclipse is seen everywhere on the Earth, while many lunar eclipses seem to be total as viewed from anywhere on the globe. Whether the Mayans had any understanding of the causes of eclipses, we do not know.

As in Mesopotamia, when Mayan astronomical observers began to focus on lunar phenomena, they naturally saw Venus, the third-brightest object in the sky, and began to track its path. The *Dresden Codex* contains Venus cycle tables that represent two stages of theoretical development. In the first, five schematic Venus cycles are presented. Each begins with the first visibility of Venus in the morning and has an initial visibility period of 236 days. Venus then becomes invisible for 90 days. Visibility as the evening star begins on day 327 and lasts for 250 days. Invisibility starts again on day 577 and lasts 8 days, giving a 584-day complete cycle (the modern value is 583.92 days) (Lounsbury 1978). This schema is off by about 0.08 days per year, but heliacal risings and settings are not very precise because they depend upon a number of factors affecting visibility, so the 584-day cycle would have seemed adequate for some time. Over a century, however, it would be off by eight days. Over a century or so, the precise difference between the 584-day cycle and the more exact 583.92 value was established in the Mayan culture, and a scheme for subtracting 24 days from each 301 Venus cycles was instituted (Lounsbury 1978).

According to the *Shu jing*, or *The Book of Documents*, compiled sometime around 400 B.C.E., the mythical Chinese Emperor Yao established what was to become the Imperial Astronomical Bureau during the Han Dynasty: "He ordered Xi and He to accord reverently with August Heaven, and its successive phenomena, with the sun, moon and the stellar markers, and thus respectfully to bestow the seasons upon the people" (Cullen 1996, 3). He directed their sons to observe the equinoxes and solstices, and then he gave Xi and He the following further direction: "The period is three hundreds of days, and six tens of days, and six days. Use intercalary months to fix the four seasons correctly, and to complete the year" (Cullen 1996, 4). Several things are explicit or implicit in these few words. They acknowledge that calendrical astronomy is a subject of imperial concern, they direct observations of several kinds, they direct the astronomers to set a calendar that approximates the solar year length at 366 days, as was the case in India when the *Shu jing* was compiled, but the text acknowledges that this value is inexact. Finally, it mandates a luni-solar calendar in which intercalary months are to be used to keep the calendar adjusted to the seasons.

We have already seen that astronomy and the calendar became a special concern of the Emperor in part because he was the mediator between the heavens and humanity and because disorder in the heavens was a sign of corruption in the human order, for which he was responsible. The prediction of celestial phenomena such as eclipses and first visibilities of critical stellar objects, such as Venus, reduced the number of unexpected and therefore disorderly events. As Nathan Sivin has written, a system for predicting the dates of characteristic phenomena of the Sun, Moon and planets was important because

the ability to predict moved celestial events from the realm of the ominous to that of the rhythmic and intelligible. The Emperor was thus enabled to know Nature's *Tao* so that his social order might be kept concordant with it. Failure of the official system to predict was necessarily a sign of moral imperfection, a warning that the monarch's virtue was not adequate to keep him in touch with the sacred rhythms. The Chinese theory of the natural order and the political order as resonating systems . . . imposed on the history of astronomy an insatiable demand for increased precision—far exceeding, in the area of the calendar, any conceivable agricultural, bureaucratic, or economic necessity. (Sivin 1995, II–7)

Furthermore, one of the ways in which the Emperor was understood to maintain the cosmic order was through carrying out rituals at the appropriate times, thus it was important to know precisely when astronomical phenomena, including the solstices and equinoxes and the phases of the Moon, would occur, in order that no critical sacrifice or celebration should be missed because its timing had not been anticipated. At the same time, the Emperor did not want the general populace to know of disturbances in the heavens because they might interpret them as signs of heavenly disfavor toward his regime. So, in China, astronomical knowledge was restricted to a very small number of persons, and Astronomical Bureau reports of unexpected events were made directly to the Emperor and not to any other members of the court bureaucracy.

We saw that during the Shang period the basic ritual cycle was a 60-day cycle produced when 10 "heavenly stem" names were paired with 12 "earthly branch" names according to a scheme that produced 60, rather than 120, combinations. The first Chinese luni-solar calendrical systems are datable to the

Qin Dynasty, beginning around 222 B.C.E. These systems retained the 60-day ritual cycle, but also incorporated a period of 365.25 days for the solar year and 29 and 499/940 days for the lunar month.

At the beginning of the Han Dynasty, that system was replaced by the Grand Inception system, which maintained all of the period relationships of the earlier system but which started the calendrical scheme of days, months, and years on December 24, 105 B.C.E., a day which was counted simultaneously as the day of the winter solstice, the first day (i.e., the day of conjunction of Moon and Sun) of the Astronomical First Month, and the first day of the 60-day cycle for recording days. Indeed, the very small errors in period relations rarely became important in China because each emperor tended to establish his own system merely by starting the system running anew using current observed positions, so long-term errors based on inaccurate period relations rarely had a chance to develop.

Within about 100 years, this relatively simple system was replaced by the Triple Concordance System, which changed the period relations very slightly to make the solar year 365.2502, or 365 385/1539 days and the lunar month 29.53086, or 29 and 43/81 days. Since both of these periods are just slightly further away from accepted modern values than those used in the Grand Inception System, one might ask why the change was made. Christopher Cullen is almost certainly correct in arguing that the change was made to make 81 the divisor in the fractional day of the lunar month because 81 was numerologically significant. It was both the largest number of the nine-nines rhymes and the number of standard volume units (*cun*) in the pitch pipe that defined the Chinese musical scale (Cullen, 1996). In this system, an Epoch Cycle was defined as that cycle in which time of day, year, lunation, and 60-day cycles all repeated exactly. The first three repeated every 1,539 years, or 19,035 lunations, or 56,120 days, which was called a Concordance cycle. But to make this number of days evenly divisible by 60, it had to be tripled, making the Epoch cycle 1,686,360 days equal 4,617 years, or 57,105 lunations.

More importantly, the Triple Concordance System pushed back the beginning date of the calendar to a grand conjunction of planets some 31 Epoch cycles, or more than 4,000 years, before the establishment of the Han Dynasty, in order to account for the current places of the planets (a grand conjunction occurs when all planets are lined up with one another within a single station of the heavens. The Chinese divided the sky into 28 very roughly equal stations defined by easily recognized star clusters, much like the Western signs of the zodiac, but spaced around the celestial equator rather than along the path of the Sun). In order to establish the point at which a grand conjunction occurred, the Chinese had to have established the synodic periods of all five planetary motions. (A synodic period is the time it takes for an object to pass from the place of one equinox or solstice back to the place of the same equinox or solstice. For the Sun, this defines a solar year.) The Chinese established the synodic periods by counting the even number of times a given planet passed the summer solstice during some even number of solar years. Given these periods, they established the Great Planetary Conjunction Cycle of

138,240 years, which was the time between two successive conjunctions of all five planets.

The Triple Concordance System also incorporated a method for eclipse prediction based on the awareness that 23 lunar eclipses occurred during every 135 lunations. This cycle was called the Phase Coincidence Cycle, but to confuse the issue, the Phase Coincidence Cycle did not use the new solar year and lunation periods, but instead went back to the periods used for the Grand Inception System in which there are 235 lunations in 19 (365.25 day) years. This cycle, called the Rule Cycle, is identical to the Metonic Cycle used by around 450 B.C.E. in Mesopotamia and Greece. It implies that, in every 19-year period, there must be twelve 12-month years and seven 13-month years. In order to bring an even number of eclipses into an even number of years and days, the Chinese created what they called the Coincidence Month of 27 Rule Cycles, which equaled 6,345 lunations, or 513 years. Finally, in order to integrate the calendrical cycle with the eclipse prediction cycle, they used the relationship that nine Coincidence Months equals 4,617 years.

In Nathan Sivin's interpretation of the use of this eclipse material, Chinese astronomers began with the first visible eclipse of a cycle and added 5 and 20/23-month intervals, always rounding off to the nearest full moon. If a predicted eclipse was not seen, but one occurred either 5, 6, 11, or 12 months later, the prediction was counted as successful. If, on the other hand, an eclipse was seen at any time not predicted, it was counted as a failure. Sivin has shown that, using his criteria of success or failure, the system was consistently successful immediately after its creation but that it obviously failed in at least 2 out of 10 cases by around 50 C.E.

One feature of all the cyclical calendrical and eclipse prediction systems discussed so far is that they assumed that the motion of every heavenly body through its cycle as viewed from the observer's location on the earth was constant. We will see in the next two sections that producing theoretical lunisolar calendars and eclipse predictions that did not fail over at least a century would depend on dropping this assumption and allowing for variable, but still regular, motions of celestial objects.

THE INCORPORATION OF VARIABLE MOTIONS INTO CYCLICAL CALENDARS AND PREDICTIVE TABLES: THE SELUCID CALENDAR IN MESOPOTAMIA

The earliest calendars in the region around the Tigris and Euphrates River Valley were luni-solar agricultural calendars regulated by agricultural processes and by observed celestial phenomena. Months, which started with the observed first visibility of the new moon, were coordinated with the growing season, and the names of several were derived from the agricultural activities which took place in them. Thus, for example, at Nippur around 2400 B.C.E., the 4th month was the month of Seed Corn the 8th was the month of Opening Soil with the plow, and the 12th month was that of Barley Harvest. As the month of barley harvest approached, a priest would go into the fields and, if the grain was nearly ready to harvest, he would declare the next month to be Barley Harvest Month. If it was not nearly ready, he would add a month to the year and declare the next month to be the Month Preceding Barley Harvest. In many ways, this was the best imaginable agricultural calendar because it allowed constant adjustment based on local growing conditions. The barley harvest could virtually always be made to take place during the month named for it, but as astral deities became increasingly important in Mesopotamia, there seems to have been a growing desire to govern the year solely through astronomical phenomena.

Around 1000 B.C.E., the intercalary month was moved to follow Barley Harvest (Langdon 1935) and a related text says, "The star Dil-gan appears in the month Nisan [the first month of the Babylonian year]; when the star stays away, the month must" (Pannekoek 1961, 31). Now the decision to intercalate a month was made retroactively based on an astronomical, rather than an agricultural, event. If Dil-gan did not rise helically during Nisan, that month was declared to have been a pre-Nisan month, and the next month became Nisan, the first month of the year. Sometime shortly after 600 B.C.E., the observation of Dil-gan was dropped and intercalations based on the Metonic Cycle of 235 lunar months in 19 solar years was adopted. Each 19 years was, henceforth ,to have twelve 12-month years and seven 13-month years, and a formula for deciding where the intercalary months should be placed was established, decoupling the calendar from all but one observational element, the observation of the new moon to begin a month (Parker and Duberstein 1942).

From the standpoint of a ritual calendar that was supposed to be correlated with lunar phases, however, this calendar was still not completely satisfactory because the first days of new lunar months still had to be based on the observation of the new moon, and when observing conditions were bad for several days, the beginning of the month could be substantially delayed. Thus, planning for complex public rituals could not begin far in advance. Beginning in 574 B.C.E. and continuing through 270 B.C.E.—well after the invasions of Alexander the Great—two new types of calendar texts offered the possibility of *predicting* the first visibilities of the new moon long into the future. The possibility of creating such texts almost certainly depended on the prior discovery, based on observations of lunar positions intended to provide for eclipse prediction, that not only did 223 lunations and 242 latitude, or Draconic, months coincide, but in that same period, there were also 239 variable velocity cycles or anomalystic months, during which the apparent velocity of lunar motion increased and decreased, returning to its original value. This period is that of the Saros cycle.

Transcriptions and analyses of nearly 200 of these texts were largely completed by Otto Neugebauer by 1955 (Neugebauer 1955), though as is the case with Mayan and ancient Chinese astronomy, some problems remain unresolved and the analysis involves some conjectures. All of the texts look basically like that depicted in Figure 5.2, that is, they are tablets in which the front (obverse) and back (reverse) each contains 10 columns of sexagesimal numbers. In the 96 tablets of Type A, the second column of the obverse contains numbers that increase by the same increment until they reach a maximum, then decrease until they reach a minimum, and then repeat, producing what may be called a "linear zigzag function." In the 80 tablets of Type B, the numbers in the second column remain the same for six rows, then they change to another value for six rows, then they return to the original value for six rows, and so on, creating a "step function." Scholars interpret this second column in each type of text as representing the apparent motion of the Sun during the month indicated in the first column of the same row in degrees per month, so both break with the pattern of constant velocity assumptions made by the early astronomy of every other early civilization. Though complicated, the Selucid calendar was the most accurate ancient calendar, capable of predicting first visibilities (assuming perfect observing conditions) for a century or more, and its superiority was due largely to the fact that it incorporated estimates for the variable velocities of the sun and moon as observed from the earth.

A HYPOTHETICAL "SELUCID CALENDAR TEXT"

The following discussion offers a brief and somewhat simplified discussion of Type A texts and is derived from Neugebauer's interpretations. It is intended to give those readers who have some mathematical and astronomical knowledge a sense of how sophisticated and complex Selucid astronomy was. Those who have not developed some astronomical knowledge may want to skim this discussion or move on to the next section. For a more detailed understanding of these texts, one should consult Neugebauer 1955 or 1957.

It is probably easiest to understand the calendar texts by working through a hypothetical problem predicting the first visibility for some month. We will take month 5 in Figure 5.2 as our target month, which will allow us to predict the first visibility of the new moon in month 6. Consider Figure 5.2. Column T simply gives ordinal numbers to allow the reader to keep track of what month is being considered. Thus, the top row, which starts with 12, contains information about the last month, which began in 2006. Column A gives the Sun's velocity in degrees per month during the month identified with the number in Column T. The average value of this function is 29; 6, 19, 20°/month, and the period of the function is 12; 22, 8, 53, 20. If the period length for the function had come from the Metonic cycle, it should have been 12; 22, 6, . . . But the period used varies from that by about 1 day in 20,000. This does not, however, mean that the Babylonian astronomers had discovered a more refined period relation by observation. What they apparently chose to do was to take the observed maximum and minimum velocities in the yearly cycle and then, in order to keep calculations relatively simple, they adjusted the monthly differences in velocity to be exactly $|0; 18, 00|°$/degrees per month (the $|x|$ notation denotes the absolute value of x, which is the same for $+x$ and $-x$). Given these three parameters, the period was fixed at 12; 22, 8, 53, 20. Looking at Figure 5.3a, Column A for month 5 should be the value for month 4 plus 0; 18, 0, or 28; 37, 21+0, 18, 00=**28; 55, 21.**

Figure 5.2
Hypothetical Babylonian Calendrical Tablet. Nick Livingston.

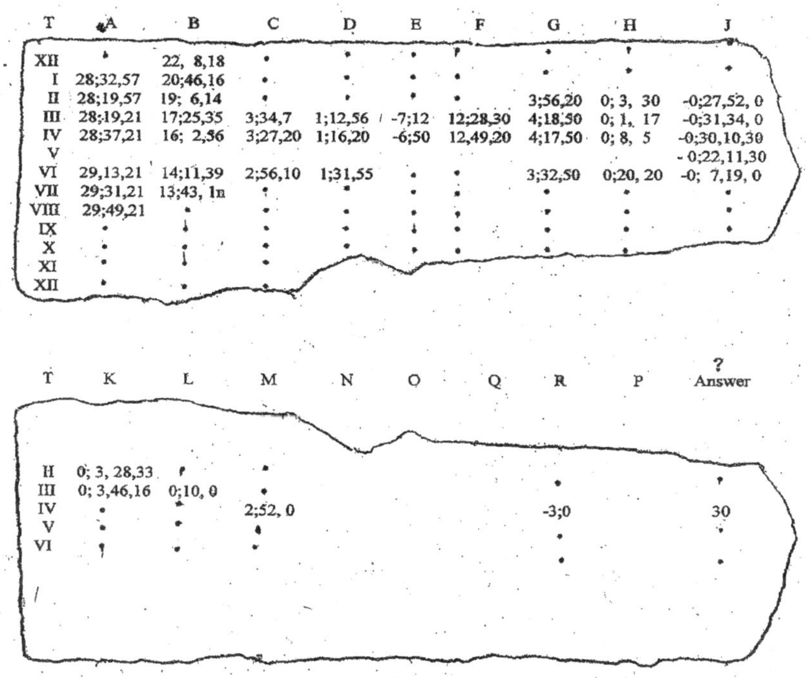

T	A	B	C	D	E	F	G	H	J
XII	•	22, 8,18	•	•	•	•	•	•	•
I	28;32,57	20;46,16	•	•	•	•			
II	28;19,57	19; 6,14	•	•	•	•	3;56,20	0; 3, 30	-0;27,52, 0
III	28;19,21	17;25,35	3;34,7	1;12,56	-7;12	12;28,30	4;18,50	0; 1, 17	-0;31,34, 0
IV	28;37,21	16; 2,56	3;27,20	1;16,20	-6;50	12,49,20	4;17,50	0; 8, 5	-0;30,10,30
V									- 0;22,11,30
VI	29,13,21	14;11,39	2;56,10	1;31,55	•	•	3;32,50	0;20, 20	-0; 7,19, 0
VII	29;31,21	13;43, 1n	•	•	•	•	•	•	•
VIII	29;49,21	•	•	•	•	•	•	•	•
IX	•	•	•	•	•	•	•	•	•
X	•	•	•	•	•	•	•	•	•
XI	•	•	•	•	•	•	•	•	•
XII	•	•	•	•	•	•	•	•	•

T	K	L	M	N	O	Q	R	P	? Answer
H	0; 3, 28,33	•	•				•		•
III	0; 3,46,16	0;10, 0	•				•		•
IV	•	•	2;52, 0				-3;0		30
V	•	•	•				•		•
VI	•	•	•				•		•

Column B gives the place in the zodiac (the belt of stars which brackets the path of the Sun and is broken into twelve 30° signs) where the conjunction of Moon and Sun would occur if the lunar velocity was constant and the solar velocity was given by Column A. This position is calculated by adding the distance traveled by the Sun during the month for which we seek the length to the position for the prior month, [mod 30] and indicating the appropriate sign. Thus, for month 5 the value is 28; 55, 21+16; 2, 56 Leo=14; 58, 17 Virgo.

Column C gives the day length at the point in the zodiac at which the first estimate of the conjunction (Column B) takes place. This value will be used later to determine the time between the conjunction given in Column B and the time of the next sunset, which is when the first visibility of a new moon might take place. Like the Egyptians, but somewhat later, the Babylonians recognized that day lengths varied with the seasons. Sometime after 700 B.C.E., the periods of daylight were correlated with signs of the zodiac, with Aries 8° taken as the vernal equinox, or point at which day and night are equal as daylight periods are lengthening. Times are given in equal "large hours, (H)," each equivalent to four modern hours. It seems as if these times were empirically observed. They reach a maximum of 3; 36 H at the place of summer solstice

Figure 5.3
Diagrams Helpful for Interpreting the Selucid Calendar Text -1. Nick Livingston.

(a) Solar Velocity in Degrees per Month (first approximation).
(b) Day Length in Large Hours at Point of Conjunction.
(c) Lunar "Latitude" above or below the Path of the Sun.
(d) Lunar Velocity at Conjunction (first approximation).

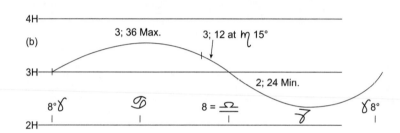

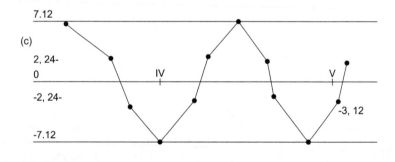

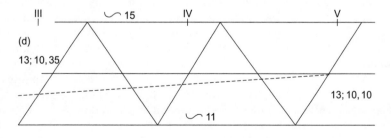

and a minimum of 2; 24 H at the place of winter solstice, fitting roughly on what we would now call a sine curve whose mean value is 3H, or 12 of our hours. At 14; 58, Virgo, the day length was taken to be **3; 12 H** (see Figure 5.3b).

Column D gives one half the night length at the point for which Column C was calculated. It is assumed that the approximate conjunction of Column B occurs at midnight, so the time between the conjunction and the first possibility of a new moon will be one half the night plus the daylight time. The value of Column D is thus given for any month by ½(6H−C), which in our case is ½(6H−3; 12H)=**1; 24H.**

Column E is a departure from the usual arrangement of texts of Type A, but it always appears in texts of Type B and its results are used later in Type A texts. Why it does not appear in all texts of Type A is one of those minor mysteries regarding Babylonian astronomy that has not yet been solved. The phenomena that Column E seems to describe is the angular distance of the Moon above or below the path of the Sun in degrees. That is, it describes the latitude of the Moon, which was so important in determining when lunar eclipses would be possible. The maximum displacement of the Moon from the path of the Sun was taken to be |7; 12°|. Babylonian astronomers apparently found that lunar latitudes did not fall exactly on a zigzag function with constant slope, so they used a pattern using two different slopes in which the absolute value of the differences between successive positions was greater near the mean value and smaller near the extremes with the slope changing at |2; 24°| (see Figure 5.3c). The period for Column E is 0; 55, 17, 18 months, so 242 latitude months equals 223 synodic months. From Figure 5.3c, one can see that for the month we are interested in, the lunar latitude is—**3; 12°.**

Column F gives the velocity of the Moon on the day of the conjunction at B. These velocities, like the solar velocities from Column A, constitute a linear zigzag function, but with a period of 0; 55, 59, 6 months or 27; 33, 20 days. This value follows from the observation, again used for eclipse predictions, that 239 lunar velocity periods, or anomalistic months equals 223 lunations (synodic months), or 242 latitude (draconic) months. From Figure 5.3d, we see that for month 5, **F=13; 10, 10.**

Column G uses the result of Column F to improve the estimate of the time of the actual conjunction before the coming first visibility of the new moon. If the Moon is traveling faster than its mean velocity on the day of the conjunction, it will overtake the Sun at an earlier time than if it were traveling at its mean speed. Column G takes this into account and gives the actual time between conjunctions in large hours in excess of 29 days. The mean value of G plus 29 days gives the mean synodic month the value 29 days; 3, 11, 50 H, or 29.53055 days, compared with the modern value of 29.5306 days. The value of G for month 5 is **3; 55, 20** (see Figure 5.4a).

The next two columns, H and J, provide a correction term for the month length based on a more refined assumption about the velocity of the Sun. If the Sun is moving faster than its speed from Column A, the Moon will take longer to catch up and the month will be longer. Conversely, if the Sun is moving more slowly, the Moon will catch up sooner and the month will be shorter.

Figure 5.4
Diagrams Helpful for Interpreting the Selucid Calendar Text -2. Nick Livingston.

(a) Time of "Actual" Conjunction in Large Hours in Excess of 29 Days.

(b) Correction of Time of Actual Conjunction Based on Second Approximation for Solar Velocity.

(c) Correction of Time of Visibility for Distance of Moon above the Horizon.

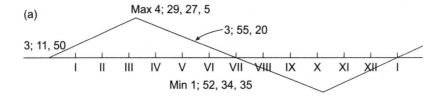

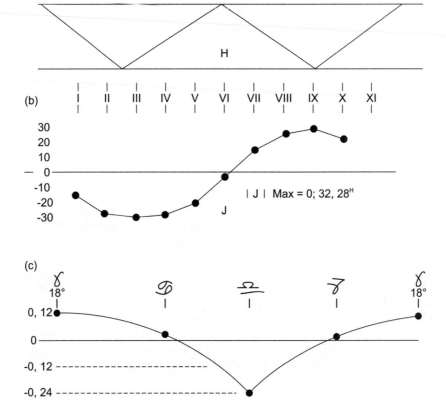

For some reason the Babylonian astronomers decided that adjusting the solar velocity by incorporating differences that themselves lay on a linear zigzag function was not sufficiently exact for this procedure, so they created a second order difference series in which the successive differences, rather than the values of the function itself, fall on a linear zigzag curve. J, then, gives the correction to G in large hours. J for month n is found by taking J of month $n-1$ and adding H for month n until J_{max} is reached, then H of n is subtracted until J_{min} is reached, where $|J_{min}|=|J_{max}|= 0; 32, 28$ H. From H, one can see that H of month $5=0$; 16, 15, and J for month $5=$J of month $4+$H of month $5= -0; 30$, 16, 30+0; 16, 15=**−0; 14, 1, 30** (see Figure 5.4b).

Column K then gives the corrected time between actual conjunctions where K(5)=G(5)+J(5)=3; 55, 20−0; 14, 1, 30=**3; 41, 18, 30 H** in excess of 29 days.

Now that we have the time between actual conjunctions, we want to know just when during the day the next conjunction will take place. Column L gives this in large hours after midnight of the 29th day; so L(n)=L(n–1)+K (n), and L(5)=3; 54, 53+3; 41, 18, 30=7; 36, 11, 30. But 6H is one full day, so the Babylonian astronomer records L(5) as **1; 36,11, 30,** and remembers that we are now talking about hours after midnight in addition to 30 days from the last conjunction, rather than 29 days.

In order to know the time interval between the beginning of the day and the conjunction (the Babylonian day begins at sunset, rather than at midnight). one must add D (½ the night) to L to get the time of the conjunction. So, in column M, M(5)=L(5)+D(5). In our case, 1; 36, 11, 30+1; 24=**3; 0, 11, 30H.**

The moment of first visibility of the new moon will depend on the expected time interval between the conjunction and first visibility at sunset, because the longer that time interval, the greater the separation between Sun and Moon by the time of first visibility. That time interval is given in Column N where N(n)=C(n)+D(n)−L(n). But if N is too small, for reasons to be discussed shortly, the Moon will not be seen, and if N is too large, the Moon will have been seen the previous evening, so the Babylonian astronomer chose to Make N=C+D−L+(0, or 6H, or 12H) so that N(n) always lay between 5H and 14H. In our case, C+D−L=3; 12,+1; 24−1; 36, 11, 30=2; 59, 48, 30. This value is much less than 5, so we add 6H, making N(5)=**8; 59, 48, 30H.**

There are two crucial parameters that determine when the new moon will first be visible. The first is the distance between the Sun and Moon along the path of the Sun (this path is called the *ecliptic*), for this determines the thickness of the sickle and hence the amount of illumination available. Column O deals with this issue. It multiplies the time from conjunction to first visibility given in Column N by the difference between the lunar velocity from F and the solar velocity which it approximates by 0; 10 degrees per second; so O(5)=N(5)(F(5)−0; 10), or 8; 59, 48, 30(13;10, 10−0; 10)=~ 9; (13;0, 10)=**1, 57; 1; 30.**

The second crucial parameter is the vertical distance of the Moon above the horizon when the Sun sets. If the Moon is enough below the horizon, it will not be seen, but if it is far above the horizon, it will be largely out of the atmospheric glow produced by the setting Sun. One factor that affects the lunar height above the ecliptic is the tilt of the ecliptic relative to the horizon. At summer solstice in Mesopotamia, the ecliptic is steeply tilted, whereas at the winter solstice it is more nearly parallel to the horizon. Column Q accounts for this phenomenon by multiplying the distance between Sun and Moon measured by O by a factor, q, which fluctuates as in Figure 5.4c. In our case, $Q(5)=O(5) \times q=-0; 12 (1, 57; 1, 30)=-18; 24, 18$.

The height above the horizon will also depend upon the lunar latitude. Column R accounts for this by taking the lunar latitude, given by E and multiplying it by a factor, r, which begins at zero at the summer solstice, increases linearly to one at the summer solstice, and then decreases to zero at the next summer solstice. At 14; 58, 17° Virgo, $r=0; 54$, so $R(5)=0; 54 (-3; 12)=-2; 52, 48$.

Finally, in Column P, we get a measure of the total height of the Moon above the horizon by adding the values of O, Q, and R. $P(5)=1, 57; 1, 30-18; 24, 18-2; 52, 48=1, 35; 44, 24$.

Now we are finally in a position to decide when the new moon will be visible. If it occurred immediately after the mean conjunction, the month would have had 30 days (because the conjunction occurs on day one rather than day zero), so the first visibility would be on the 31st night, but in step N, we added a full day, so we are considering visibility on the 32nd night. The Babylonian astronomers seemed to use the following rule: if $P+O>20$, the Moon will be visible; but if $P+O>30$, it must have been visible the previous night. In our case, $P(5)+O(5)=1, 35; 44, 24+1, 57; 1, 30=3, 32; 45, 54$, which is much greater than 30. So, we must go back a day and assume that visibility occurred on the 31st night after the conjunction for month 5. But if the previous month began on the first night after its conjunction, then this visibility occurred on the 30th night after the beginning of the previous month. so the Babylonian scribe wrote down 30 in the "answer" column, meaning that month 5 had actually had only 29 days (because what would have been the 30th day is now the first day of the next month).

GEOMETRY ENTERS ASTRONOMY AT ALEXANDRIA

Even though the *Arithmetic Classic of the Chou Gnomon* assumed a geometry of the heavens in order to offer a way to determine the heaven-earth distance and the size of the Sun, these considerations played no role in calendrical astronomy. Nor, in spite of the fact that modern interpretations of ancient calendars appeal to a three-dimensional, spatial model of the motion of celestial objects in closed orbits, did any ancient calendar discussed to this point depend openly on any assumptions about three-dimensional motions. Only one, out of the thousands of astronomical tablets excavated in ancient Mesopotamia, suggests that celestial objects might have been conceived as traveling in circular paths centered on the earth.

It was not until the rise of Hellenistic Greek culture at Alexandria that astronomers developed a way of predicting the positions of celestial objects grounded explicitly in a three-dimensional model of the universe. When they did so, they drew from many sources, including the period relationships and the apparent variable velocities of celestial objects established by earlier Mesopotamian astronomers, mathematical techniques developed at Alexandria, and a tradition of speculation about the character and causes of celestial motions developed by earlier Greek natural philosophers. The Alexandrian astronomers were not, however, completely constrained by speculative systems of natural philosophy. They developed an understanding of the nature of astronomy that allowed them significant freedom in their self-imposed task of predicting the positions of celestial objects without regard for the nature of the objects or causes of their motions. The relationship between Greek astronomy and Greek natural philosophy was particularly well articulated by Simplicius, a Greek mathematician who lived around 500 C.E. and who wrote commentaries on the work of earlier mathematicians and astronomers:

The astronomer, when he proves facts from external conditions, is not qualified to judge of the cause, as when, for instance, he declares the earth or the stars to be spherical; sometimes he does not even desire to ascertain the cause, as when he discourses about an eclipse; at other times he invents by way of hypothesis, and states certain expedients by the assumption of which the phenomena will be saved. For example, why do the sun, the moon, and the planets appear to move irregularly? We may answer that, if we assume that their orbits are eccentric circles [circles not centered on the earth] or that the stars describe an epicycle [a circle whose center moves evenly along another circle which is called a deferent], their apparent irregularity will be saved . . . It is no part of the business of an astronomer to know what is by nature suited to a position of rest, and what kind of bodies are apt to move, but he introduces hypotheses under which some bodies remain fixed, while others move, and then considers to which hypothesis the phenomena actually observed in the heaven will correspond. But he must go to the [natural philosopher] for his first principles, namely, that the movements of the stars are simple, uniform, and ordered, and by means of these principles he will then prove that the rhythmic motion of all alike is in circles, some being turned in parallel circles, others in oblique circles. (Cohen and Drabkin 1966, 90–91)

We will return in chapter 7 to discuss how and why Greek natural philosophers argued that the apparently irregular motions of the celestial bodies must be accounted for using simple uniform circular motions. Here, we will explore how Greek astronomers both used and gradually modified the principles of Greek natural philosophers to account not only for the apparent irregularities in the motions of some celestial bodies, but also their apparent variations in size. In doing so, we will focus on the *Almagest* of Claudius Ptolemy, a mathematician and astronomical observer of unknown background who worked at Alexandria at least from 127–141 C.E. The *Almagest* was unquestionably the most influential astronomical work in the Western world from its composition around 140 C.E., through the Middle Ages and at least until the publication of *De Revolutionibus* by Nicolas Copernicus in 1543.

Before turning to the technical content of the *Almagest,* however, I would like briefly to discuss the motives behind Ptolemy's work. Though Ptolemy's calculations of the positions of Sun, Moon, and planets could be and were used for calendrical purposes, he was neither authorized nor asked to develop astronomy for this purpose by any governmental or religious organization. Ptolemy was an advocate of theoretical science in the tradition of Aristotle's *Metaphysics*, discussed in chapter 1, and in the preface to the *Almagest* he argued that astronomy was a theoretical science that should be studied with no end in view other than the knowledge itself. In an epigram, he presents this view poetically:

Well do I know that I am mortal, a creature of one day.
But if my mind follows the winding paths of the stars
Then my feet no longer rest on the earth, but standing by
Zeus himself I take my fill of ambrosia, the divine dish.

—(Taub 1993, vii).

But Ptolemy was also the author of the most widely used practical manual of horoscopic astrology produced in antiquity, the *Tetrabiblos*, which was understood to be the second part of a comprehensive treatment of astronomy for which the *Almagest* was the first. Ptolemy's view of astrology was based on an Aristotelian notion that celestial bodies could influence sublunar events, but unlike the late Mesopotamian astral priests or the Stoa, Ptolemy thought that astrology was an art (*techne*) like medicine, rather than a science (*episteme*) like astronomy because the astronomical influences were modified by so many factors, including geography, race, personality, and so on that certainty was impossible. Even if we suppose that Ptolemy personally held that astronomy was more important for its own sake than as a foundation for astrology, there is little doubt that much of his audience in antiquity and in the Islamic Middle Ages viewed his astronomy as important primarily as the foundation for astrological practices.

As in connection with Mesopotamian astronomy, I will provide only a brief outline of relevant issues here. For more detailed treatments, one should go to Ptolemy, 1998 and Evans, 1998.

The first two books of the *Almagest* lay out the basic assumptions of Ptolemaic astronomy, that is: (1) The heavens are spherical and they rotate as a sphere, (2) the Earth is also a sphere situated in the middle of the heavens, (3) the Earth is so small that it can be considered as a point relative to its distance from the heavens, and (4) the Earth is at rest. The introductory books go on to demonstrate that several general features of the motions of the Sun, Moon, and planets might be accounted for by using epicycles (circles whose centers move constantly along a circular path, called the *deferent*) and other mathematical techniques drawn from Pappus and others. Finally, in book 2, Ptolemy goes on to develop new mathematical methods, roughly equivalent to modern trigonometric methods, to make calculations simpler than they would otherwise be. The remaining books then apply these methods to producing precise predictions of the position of the Sun (chapter 3), Moon (chapters 4 and 5), eclipses (chapter 6), the fixed stars (chapters 7 and 8) and the planets (chapters 9–14).

The kind of uniform cyclical appearances of celestial phenomena assumed in all of the early calendrical theories discussed above, except those from Mesopotamia, would have followed if each celestial object moved with constant angular velocity on a circle centered on the earth, as in Figure 5.5a Hipparcchus (c. 190–120 B.C.E.) had already used observations of the equinoxes and solstices to assert that it took 94 ½ days for the sun to move from the spring equinox to summer solstice, 92-½ days from summer solstice to autumnal equinox, 88 and ⅝ days from autumnal equinox to winter solstice, and 89 and ⅝ days from winter solstice to vernal equinox. Furthermore, he showed that those phenomena would follow if the Sun moved with constant velocity on a circle centered, not on the Earth, but on some point, C, displaced from the earth by a distance EC, as in Figure 5.5b. Such a circle was said to be an eccentric circle.

Equally importantly, Hipparchus had shown that an eccentric circle could be produced by making the Sun move with constant angular velocity, α, on a small circle (the epicycle) whose center moved with an equal but opposite constant angular velocity, $-\alpha$, along a larger circle centered on the earth (the deferent), as in Figure 5.5c

By appropriately adjusting the relative radii of the epicycle and deferent, the starting positions of the Sun on the epicycle and the center of the epicycle on the deferent, and the angular velocity, Hipparchus was able to use the epicyclic model to produce the observed position of the Sun at any point in time for many cycles. For future purposes, it is important to note that, when the motion of a celestial body is generated by an epicycle and deferent model, there will be a line that goes through the Earth and the points of maximum and minimum distance of the body from the Earth. This line is called the line of *apsides*, and it will become important later in connection with Ptolemy's lunar theory.

In book 3 of the *Almagest*, Ptolemy took over Hipparchus's model for lunar motion. But combining his own observations with those of Hipparchus, which had been made more than two centuries earlier, and those of Meton, which had been made in 432 B.C.E., Ptolemy argued that the period of solar motion from vernal equinox to vernal equinox (called a solar year) had to be revised to make it 1/300 of a day less than the 365.25 days used by Hipparchus. Furthermore, the initial positions of the Sun on the epicycle and the center of the epicycle on the deferent had to be adjusted to account for the errors that had accumulated by the time of his observations. The current best value of the solar year is very close to 1/128 of a day less than 365.25, and Ptolemy should have been able to get a much better value than he did, so there is some question about why he came up with the value he did (Britton 1992).

In book 4, Ptolemy gives Hipparchus's theory of lunar motion, which starts from recognizing, as the Mesopotamians had, that the lunar motion involves three different periods. The period taken for the Moon to return to the same position relative to the vernal equinox along its path (i.e., its longitude), the period to return to its initial velocity, and the period for its return to its initial latitude. The first two of these establish the time between successive oppositions or conjunctions, which is called the synodic month. Adding in the latter

Figure 5.5
Geocentric and Eccentric Circular Models for Heavenly Motions. Nick Livingston.

(a) Simplest Possible Geometrical Model of a Planetary Orbit.

(b) Eccentric Circle Model for Solar Motion.

(c) Production of an Eccentric Circle Using a Deferent and Epicycle.

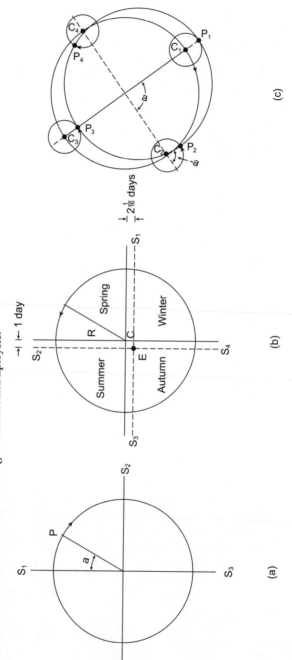

Figure 5.6
More Complex Models of Heavenly Motions Using Epicycles and Deferents.
Nick Livingston.

(a) Ellipse Produced by Deferent and Epicycle.
(b) Typical Ptolemaic Model for a Planetary Orbit.

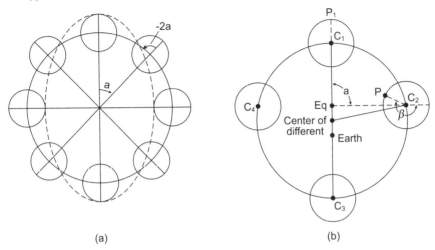

(a)   (b)

will, as we have already seen, establish when eclipses can occur by telling us
when the path of the Moon is close enough to the path of the Sun (i.e., near the
nodes or points of intersection between the lunar latitude path and the ecliptic). Hipparchus had tried to offer a simple epicycle model for the motions of
the moon, using the basic notion that the longitude and velocity periods can
be reproduced by a motion that varies only slightly from that of Figure 5.6a,
which produces constant motion along an ellipse. This motion will be seen
as slower when the Moon is more distant from the Earth and faster when it
is closer.

Hipparchus could not get this model to produce the exact values of lunar
position even when he made the line of *apsides* rotate very slowly so that the
difference between the anomalous month and the solar month could be accounted for, so in book 5 of the *Almagest*, Ptolemy improved Hipparchus's
theory by having the center of the deferent move with constant angular velocity on a small circle centered on the Earth. The effect was not simply to
slowly move the line of *apsides*, but also to simultaneously increase and decrease the distance of the center of the deferent from the earth, creating a
lunar theory that correctly predicted observed longitudinal positions of the
Moon for several centuries.

Combined with the results of book 5, a simple epicyclic model for latitudinal motion produced predictions for both lunar and solar eclipses in book 6.
Then, in books 7 and 8, Ptolemy discussed the motion of the sphere of the

fixed stars, including the observation, already made by Hipparchus, that the position of the vernal equinox appears to move, or "precess" through the stars (which really seemed to be fixed relative to one another) at a rate of approximately 50 seconds per year or one degree every 72 years along the ecliptic. These two chapters also contained Ptolemy's star catalog of over 1,000 stars with magnitudes (apparent sizes, based largely on brightness) judged from one (the brightest) to six (those barely visible to the naked eye).

The final five chapters of the *Almagest* presented models for the motions of the five planets. No combination of the techniques used so far could adequately reproduce the positions of the planets. Epicyclic motions using eccentric deferents consistently produced observed angular velocities that were too small near the Earth and too large far from the Earth. To resolve this problem, Ptolemy incorporated an additional point twice the eccentricity from the Earth and on the same side relative to the Earth as the center of the deferent. Equi-angular motion along the deferent was then measured about this point, called the *equant,* as in Figure 5.6b. Given this model, Ptolemy had seven parameters to adjust in order to produce a scheme that successfully predicted planetary longitudinal positions: (1) The ratio between epicycle radius and deferent radius, (2) the ratio between the radius of the deferent and the Earth-center of the deferent-distance, (3) the angular velocity of the center of the epicycle along the deferent as seen from the *equant,* (4) the angular velocity of the planet moving on the epicycle, as measured from the center of the epicycle, (5) the direction of the line of *apsides,* (6) and (7) the starting angles, α and β at some initial time in Figure 5.6b.

For all planets except Mars, this combination of parameters could be chosen so as to match prior observed positions and effectively predict future ones. For Mars, Ptolemy had to add a second epicycle moving on the first in order to establish a model that seemed viable during the rest of antiquity and into the Middle Ages.

CONCLUSION

The most complex and mathematically sophisticated science in almost every early civilization was associated with calendrical astronomy. Although the earliest ritual and agricultural calendars in several early civilizations did not incorporate astronomical phenomena in any obvious ways, two conditions led to the incorporation of astronomical elements in the calendars of all ancient civilizations. One was the fact that the timing of agricultural events was clearly related to the intensity of solar radiation and the varying length of daylight through the year. Second was the presence in many civilizations of astronomically based divination which had led to predictions of lunar eclipse phenomena and, in Mesopotamia, China, and Mayan civilization, to the prediction of Venus phenomena. Information gained in predicting eclipses made it possible to incorporate the timing of lunar phenomena into theoretical calendars. In all early cultures other than that of Mesopotamia, the observed angular velocity of each heavenly body was assumed to be constant through each cycle, limiting the precision with which predicted positions could be made to correspond to observed positions. Mesopotamian calendrical astronomers incorporated variable velocities in their calendrical work, allowing for much greater predictive success. The luni-solar calendars developed near Babylon form the foundations of Jewish and Islamic calendars into the present.

Greek theorists produced three-dimensional models in which the Babylonian-observed variations in velocity and brightness could be accounted for by using combinations of constant velocity motions along multiple circles. These geometrical theories were eventually modified by Copernicus, Kepler, and Isaac Newton to establish the modern Western calendar.

Six

Empirical and Religious
Medical Practices

Within every ancient civilization for which we have substantial evidence, at least two and sometimes three traditions coexisted to promote health and deal with problems of disease and injury. We shall call all of these traditions medical, though their techniques for prognostication and therapy varied widely and their understanding of and attitude toward the causes of illness and disability were often quite different. First, every ancient civilization had a priestly medical tradition, or a magico-religious tradition. Some of these traditions used dream interpretation for prognosis; others consulted omens or read the symptoms of a patient's condition by interrogation and visual, auditory, and tactile examination. Still others used shamanic ecstatic practices to communicate more directly with the gods about their patients' conditions. But all priestly traditions saw the fundamental cause of the illnesses that they treated as offense to the gods or ancestors or as the result of black magic practiced against their patients. Furthermore, all included rituals of cleansing, exorcism, prayer, and sacrifice among their therapeutic procedures.

Second, all ancient civilizations had an empirical-secular medical tradition that probably derived from the folk medicines of pre-civilized peoples. Recipes that had been successfully used to treat certain patterns of symptoms and had been handed down orally from generation to generation were now written down in the form of pharmacological texts. In many civilizations, the practice of secular medicine by family members or local wise men and women was augmented and sometimes succeeded by practice by a professional cadre of educated persons whose place in the social hierarchy varied from civilization to civilization. In early India, the priestly physician stood high in the social hierarchy, even above the local military and political leaders (Sigerist 1961), but in most civilizations the position of secular physician was comparable to that of other skilled artisans.

A chief feature of the empirically grounded medical traditions is that practitioners seldom if ever speculated about the causes of the conditions that they were able to identify and sometimes cure. Their focus was on prognoses (i.e., on identifying the patterns of symptoms and predicting the course of illnesses) and on therapies. These secular therapies usually involved the use of drugs, ointments, poultices, or suppositories concocted from combinations of organic materials and minerals, modifying the patient's diet or environment, or physical manipulation of the patient's body, as in setting broken bones or massaging sore muscles.

Finally, in most ancient civilizations, for example, in China, India, Mesoamerica, and Greece, and to a lesser extent in Egypt, a third medical tradition that based its prognoses and treatments on general theories of disease emerged. These theories tended to draw their assumptions from broader philosophical understandings of cosmic processes and natural laws. They might, therefore, be identified as philosophical, as opposed to religious or empirical traditions, though they appropriated much information from the empirical traditions and often shared important attitudes and sometimes, personnel, with the priestly traditions.

In some cultures—in Mesopotamia, Egypt, China, India, and Mesoamerica, for example—the different traditions interpenetrated in a variety of ways. Empirically discovered treatments were, for example, interpreted as serving to drive out demons or ghosts, or as acting according to some theoretical account. In some cultures, priests, shamans, or magician-sorcerers also served as physicians. That is, they were trained to use the prevailing secular therapies as well as magico-religious rites. In classical Greece, however, as in other cultural domains, there was also open competition, not only among practitioners within each tradition, but also between the different traditions. Greek medical empirics openly denigrated the notion that there were sacred diseases or that the speculative philosophical practitioners, who they labeled dogmatists, were competent physicians, while the philosophical physicians belittled the ignorance of mere empirics (Lloyd 1966).

If one accepted the positivist notion that in every domain religious understandings give way to philosophical understandings, which in turn give way to positive, or scientific, understandings that finally give up the notion of causality, then one would expect to see a temporal development in each civilization in which priestly medicine dominated early, followed by philosophical medicine, and eventually by empirical medicine, each one driving out its predecessor. As we shall see, however, the evidence suggests otherwise. Two or three medical traditions coexisted in every early civilization, usually, but not always, in open cooperation with one another. Where we can identify patterns of temporal change in the ancient civilizations, as in Mesopotamia, Mesoamerica, China, and in Greece, priestly and empirical medicine coexisted from the earliest periods, and philosophical medicine gradually grew in importance. However, for different reasons in different places, after an initial period of the ascendance of philosophical medicine, priestly medicine tended to increase in importance relative to empirical and philosophical medicine over time, and philosophical medicine increased in importance relative to empirical medicine (Oppenheim 1977; Sigerist 1951). Thus, positivist expectations are clearly not borne out.

EGYPTIAN EMPIRICAL MEDICINE

The earliest medical texts appear almost simultaneously in Egypt and in Mesopotamia, and there is evidence to suggest that in both places these texts reflect practices that go back much further. The Kahun papyrus from Egypt, which can be dated to around 1800 B.C.E., contains only secular medical discussions. It deals exclusively with gynecological and obstetrical issues and contains several tests for fertility and pregnancy, the efficacies of which were evaluated by a group of physicians in 1963 (Shafik and Elseesy 2003). To test whether a woman was fertile, a bulb of onion or garlic was placed in her vagina overnight. In the morning, the physician smelled her breath, and if he could detect the onion or garlic smell, she was deemed fertile. We now explain this test by saying that the volatile oils from the onion or garlic pass into the uterus and through the fallopian tubes if they are clear. From there, because there is no tight seal between the ovaries and the fallopian tubes, they enter the peritoneal cavity where they are absorbed by the blood. Reaching the lungs, the volatile oils are excreted into the respiratory tract to provide the odor of the breath. If there is a blockage at any point in the path, most likely the fallopian tubes, the breath will not smell, nor will the woman be fertile.

To test for pregnancy, a woman urinated on small bags containing emmer wheat and barley. If neither sprouted, the woman was not pregnant; if the barley sprouted, she was expected to give birth to a boy, and if the wheat grew she was expected to give birth to a girl. Though the sex determination feature of this procedure did not seem to work when tested, when male or nonpregnant female urine was used to moisten the grains, neither sprouted, but when pregnant female urine was used, in 28 out of 40 cases one or both of the grains sprouted. Modern doctors assume that hormones associated with pregnancy encourage seed germination.

The Kahun papyrus also offers several techniques for contraception. A wad of fibrous material was saturated or smeared with either a mixture of ground acacia spikes, dates, and honey or with crocodile dung, a strong source of sodium compounds, or natron (sodium carbonate) and placed at the entrance to the uterus. The fibrous pad blocked the sperm, and the lactic acid produced from the acacia spikes dissolved in honey or the sodium compounds acted as a spermicide (Hawass 2000).

A second, very fragmentary, papyrus found with the Kahun gynecological papyrus is on veterinary medicine. This suggests that, in Egypt, as was the case in India and Mesopotamia, veterinary medicine and human medicine developed in parallel and probably with the same initial practitioners.

Most of what we know of Egyptian empirical medicine comes from two papyri, the Ebers Medical papyrus and the Edwin Smith Surgical papyrus, both written around 1500 B.C.E., but almost certainly copies of older writings. Though both of these papyri contain some priestly medicine, they are primarily secular. The Smith papyrus describes 48 cases of wounds, starting with head wounds and moving down through the throat and neck, the collarbone, the thoracic cavity, and the spinal column. Each case has a title, an examination section, a diagnosis section, and a verdict, which might be: "An ailment which I will treat," "An ailment with which I will contend," or, "An ailment not to be treated" (Sigerist 1951, 306). In almost all cases with favorable or uncertain verdicts, a treatment section follows, but cases not to be treated are all presumed to be terminal, and the choice not to treat seems to have been a way to avoid liability on the part of the physician.

Egyptians performed no major surgery except for trephining—perforating the skull with a hammer and chisel—which is evidenced in mummies, but which still has no agreed upon justification. They did, however, remove surface tumors, set broken bones, suture severe wounds, and bandage less severe ones. In order to lessen the pain of the minor operations they performed, they numbed the region by pouring vinegar over crushed marble stone to produce an endothermic reaction that cooled the local area. When wounds were bleeding slowly, physicians covered them with animal flesh, and when they were infected, they treated them with medications such as green pigment (probably malachite, which contains copper salts that have an antibacterial effect) or they packed the wound with fermented pulp of bread (which probably included some penicillin mold). Set bones were splinted with wood padded in linen or encased in casts that were made from clay or from linen soaked in egg whites (Shafik and Elseesy 2003).

The Ebers medical papyrus is a 20.3-meter-long compendium of Egyptian medical lore that includes some elements of priestly medicine as well as the earliest known physiological theory, which we will discuss in the next chapter. About 80 of the more than 100 cases that it discusses, however, cover empirical medicine directed at treatment of internal diseases, eye diseases, diseases of the skin, problems of the hands and feet, women's diseases, and home hygiene, as well as a few miscellaneous prescriptions and a short section on surgery. Most cases involve drug therapy. Of the more than 300 plants, animals, and minerals used, only about 20 percent can now be identified.

Of the approximately 60 identifiable recipes, most have no currently known pharmacological effects, and many were probably suggested by a kind of rough notion of what is called sympathetic magic, which assumes that some characteristic of an object can be communicated to another object. For example, consider the following ingredients of a recipe for curing graying hair and baldness from the Ebers papyrus: "backbone of raven, blood of a she cat, raven's egg, blood from the horn of a black ox, burned hoof of an ass, fat of a black snake, and burned quills of a hedgehog" (Sigerist 1951, 342). Each item is connected either with blackness, with hairiness, or with both and might be expected to communicate that characteristic to a scalp into which it has been rubbed.

Several materials, however, do have well known medical effects and are used into the present for much the same purposes discovered by the ancient Egyptians. For example, here is a description of the virtues of the ricinus plant:

> If its peel is brayed in water and applied to a head that suffers, it will be cured immediately as though it had never suffered.

If a few of its seeds are chewed with beer by a person who is constipated, it will expel the feces from the body of that person.

The hair of a woman will be made to grow by means of its seeds. Bray [i.e., crush in a mortar with a pestle], mix into one mass, and apply with grease. Let the woman anoint her head with it.

Its oil is made from its seeds. For anointing sores with a foul discharge (the trouble will depart as though nothing had occurred). It will disappear by anointing thus for ten days. Anoint very early in the morning in order to expel them (the sores). A true remedy (proved) millions of times. (Sigerist 1951, 340–341)

Castor oil, which is made from the seeds of this plant, is still used in ointments for treating bedsores, as a laxative, and in preparations for treating the scalp.

MESOPOTAMIAN EMPIRICAL MEDICINE

The earliest Mesopotamian texts dealing with a medical issue are a pair of letters written around 1780 B.C.E. In a letter to his wife back home, the King of Mari provides the first known discussion of the isolation of persons with contagious diseases:

I have heard that the Lady Nanna, although afflicted with a purulent skin ailment [literally, "a wound with discharge"] frequents the Palace and is in contact with many women. Strictly forbid anyone to sit in her chair or sleep in her bed. She must no longer mingle with all those women; for her illness is contagious [literally, "is taken."] (Bottéro 2001, 176)

In a second letter, the king insists that she be quarantined: "as so many because of her, risk catching the same purulent illness in question, she must be isolated in a room apart" (Bottéro 2001, 176).

As is the case for Egypt, most of what we know of Mesopotamian medicine comes from two major sources, a 40-tablet *Treatise on Medical Diagnoses and Prognoses,* and a three-tablet listing of medical recipes using herbal, animal, and mineral materials. The first text exists in two versions from about 1500 and 600 B.C.E., but these are quite certainly copies of a text that dates to roughly the time of the letter on contagious diseases. The second was also found in a cache datable to around 600 B.C.E., but it, too, purports to be copied from an Old Babylonian (c. 1800 B.C.E.) original (Oppenheim 1977). The text on medications suggests that the drugs available to the Mesopotamian physician were very similar to those known in Egypt and that they were discovered in much the same way. For example, graying and thinning hair was treated with remedies including the gall of a black ox and the head of a black raven, suggesting the same origin in sympathetic magic as those used in Egypt (Sigerist 1951). Most drug treatments probably had little pharmacological effect, but others were at least moderately effective, as is exemplified in the following treatment for what seems to be bronchitis:

If the patient suffers from hissing cough, if his wind-pipe is full of murmurs, if he coughs, if he has coughing fits, if he has phlegm: bray together roses and mustard, in purified oil drop it on his tongue, fill, moreover, a tube with it and blow it into his nostrils. . . . Thus shall he recover. (Sigerist 1951, 481)

Well into the 20th century, powdered mustard was used in volatile substances to treat bronchitis. Even more effective were the use of such substances as ricinus seed oil in skin salves and opium to control pain (Sigerist 1951).

There is no discussion of surgery in the Mesopotamian medical literature, but sections from the law code of Hammurabi (c. 1800 B.C.E.) that give both a payment schedule for successful operations and a schedule of penalties for unsuccessful ones suggest that at least minor surgery was done from very early times. Moreover, because similar schedules were provided for veterinary surgery, it is likely that in Mesopotamia, as in Egypt, veterinary and human medicine developed in parallel.

GREEK EMPIRICAL MEDICINE

Homeric Greeks conceived illness and wounds as caused by the gods, and most treatment involved religious medicine, but both the *Iliad* and the *Odyssey*, which were written down in the eight century B.C.E. from oral sources that probably date from around 1200 B.C.E., describe warriors' self-treatment of wounds in ways that imply an empirical foundation. Thus, for example, when Eurypylus receives a thigh wound, he asks Patroclus to treat him: "cut the arrow out of my thigh, and wash away the black blood from it with warm water, and sprinkle thereon kindly simples of healing power, whereof they say that thou hast learned from Achilles" (Sigerist 1961, 27). Little is known about the drugs used during Homeric times, although some were described as powders and others as roots. Some warriors were particularly famous for their healing abilities. Chief among these were the two sons of a tribal chief named Asclepias. The sons, Podaleirios and Machaon, are described as "leeches," which seems to have been the title of itinerant Greek physicians in the archaic period before the growth of philosophical medicine in the sixth and fifth centuries. When Machaon receives a minor wound, his fellow warriors insist that he be moved far from the battle, "For a leech is of the worth of many other men/ For the cutting out of arrows and the spreading of soothing simples" (Sigerist 1961, 29–30). Asclepias, the tribal chief in the *Iliad*, was subsequently deified to become the primary god of healing in Greece and the focus of a tremendously powerful medical cult that we will discuss later (Sigerist 1961).

Evidence for a substantially changed attitude toward medicine appears in Greece around the mid-sixth century, with the greatest amount of evidence coming in the form of a series of medical treatises attributed to Hippocrates, a single physician of the late fifth century who lived on the island of Cos. Though there is evidence from the Platonic dialogs *Protagoras* and *Phaedrus* that there was a famous Asclepiad physician named Hippocrates who taught medicine on Cos, the 60 to 130 treatises that were eventually collected under his name (the number depends on the editor and what is counted as a treatise) represent multiple authors and multiple approaches to medicine. Nonetheless, they represent far and away the most extensive set of documents about virtually every aspect of medical practice in any ancient civilization.

Many of the Hippocratic treatises are deeply influenced by Pesocratic philosophies. In fact, what we learn of the historical Hippocrates from both Plato and Aristotle suggests that he was theoretically and philosophically oriented, but several texts clearly represent an openly antiphilosophical perspective, while many others, including the famous Hippocratic Oath, are neutral with respect to an empirical or philosophical perspective.

The most clearly antiphilosophical argument to be found in the Hippocratic texts comes in *On Ancient Medicine*, in which the author distinguishes sharply between the functions of the physician and those of the philosopher. He writes: "I am utterly at a loss to know how those who prefer hypothetical arguments and reduce the science to a simple matter of postulates ever cure anyone on the basis of their assumptions" (1978, 79). Then, he goes on to argue that hypotheses are, however, the appropriate subject matter for philosophers: "it is the province of those who, like Empedocles, have written on natural science, what man is from the beginning, how he came into being at the first, and from what elements he was originally constructed" (Jouanna 1999, 283).

Among those texts that were entirely or primarily empirical are a very small number dealing with anatomy. *On the Heart* is the only text sometimes identified as Hippocratic that clearly depended on detailed dissections (Sigerist 1961), though there are several surgical texts, including *On Wounds* and *On the Joints* that focus on anatomical knowledge that might have been gained in other ways. Some empirically oriented texts focus on descriptions and treatments of specific diseases or classes of medical conditions. Among these is the treatise on epilepsy titled *On the Sacred Disease*, which makes the point that epilepsy is no more sacred than any other disease and that all diseases have natural causes (Hippocrates 1978). Others include *On the Diseases of Women* and *On the Wounds of the Head*.

Among the most interesting empirical texts is *On Diet*, which is sometimes translated as *On Regimen*. This text, which emphasizes both diet and exercise, seems to have had its origins in the training regimes of the gymnasia, where Greek citizens were prepared for citizenship, including military duty, and for athletic contests. The professional trainers who were responsible for the physical conditioning of young men developed very little theory, but they had extensive knowledge of how to build health and strength. This knowledge, which had been growing at least since the period of the origin of the Olympic games in the eighth century B.C.E., was incorporated into Hippocratic medical practice and helps to explain the general emphasis on dietetic treatments relative to the use of drugs (Sigerist 1961).

A second interesting set of empirically oriented texts are *Prognostics I & II*, which not only discuss particular cases, but also explain the very practical importance of prognostication for the physician, who was likely to be un-known to the patient:

It seems to be highly desirable that a physician should pay much attention to progno-sis. If he is able to tell his patients when he visits them not only about their past and present symptoms, but also to tell them what is going to happen, as well as to fill in the details they have omitted, he will increase his reputation as a medical practitioner and people will have no qualms in putting themselves under his care. Moreover, he will the better be able to effect a cure if he can foretell, from the present symptoms, the future course of the disease. (Hippocrates 1978, 170)

Equally important and fascinating are the seven books on *Epidemics,* which seem to be case notes describing epidemic diseases and the environmental conditions under which they occur.

MESOAMERICAN MEDICINE

In classical Greece, though some physicians had been trained as Ascle-piad priests, most emphasized purely secular approaches to health. In Me-soamerica, on the other hand, though spiritual and physical medicine were distinguished from one another, both were practiced by *titici,* a cadre of professional healers who followed the profession of their parents. Both men and women could be *titici,* but there was some division of labor, with males treating wounds and fractures, doing suturing, and doing ear and nose plas-tic surgery. Women, on the other hand, were usually in charge of midwifery, ulcer treatment, ocular surgery, massage, and the application of salves, poul-tices, and other topical treatments (Viesca 2003).

Surgery, even some major surgery, was done in Mesoamerica. Trephina-tion was practiced from no later than 200 B.C.E., plastic surgery on the nose and ears was sutured using tiny stitches made from the tips of maguey leaves, and we know that a broken femur that did not heal initially was stabilized by inserting a wooden rod into the medular channel. Infection control was ac-complished by using wet corn tortillas that had been allowed to grow molds, which have antibiotic properties (Viesca 2003).

Nearly 2,500 plants were identified as having medicinal properties in Me-soamerica, in comparison with about 300 in Egypt or Mesopotamia. Once again, many of these cannot now be identified and many of those that can have no known pharmacological effect. Some medications were fairly clearly suggested initially through sympathetic magic, and some of those turned out to have pharmacological effects. Yolloxóchitl (*Talamuma mexicana*), for example, was prescribed for heart weakness because its flowers' shape was similar to a cross-section of the heart, but it turns out to be a useful cardio-tonic and diuretic. Similarly, ipecacuana roots, from which the modern ip-ecac is made, seems to have been first used to cure dysentery and other diarrhea-producing illnesses because its root color and consistency are like that of human excrement. In other cases, we simply have no way of guessing how treatments were discovered, although we now know how many of them work. Persons with arthritis, for example, were treated by allowing them to be bitten by ants, which expel formic acid, a known anti-inflammatory, when they bite (Viesca 2003).

INDIAN MEDICINE

We know virtually nothing of the medicine of the Harappan civilization of the Indus valley, though a few substances used in later Indian medicine have been found at Harappan sites. Moreover, the Harappan interest in sanitation, suggested by the construction of private and public baths as well as covered sewers, may have been motivated by interests in health. The problem of dating the Vedic material is severe because, though Vedic culture probably began around 1500 B.C.E., there is no telling how much change occurred by around 600 B.C.E., when the Vedas were written down. Most information regarding early Indian medicine, which came to be called Ayurveda (wisdom of life), comes from the *Atharvaveda,* which contains 731 hymns, prayers, and incantations, mostly associated with health, from the *Suśruta-Samhitā,* which deals primarily with surgery; and from the *Caruka-Samhitā,* which is primarily a series of glosses on the *Atharvaveda.* According to the *Suśruta-Samhitā,* Ayurveda included eight specialties:

1. Surgery; 2. Diseases above the clavicle; 3. Medications; 4. Spiritual possession; 5. Pediatrics; 6. Toxicology; 7. Preventive measures; and 8. Aphrodisiacs. (Chopra 2003, 80)

In Indian literature, many drugs are justified in terms of their effectiveness for driving out demons and are accompanied by prayers regarding their virtues. Here, for example, is a portion of the *Atharvaveda's* praise of a special mountain plant, *kushtha,* which was used for treating fevers:

Thou art born upon the mountains, as the most potent of plants, come hither, O *Kushtha,* destroyer of the Takman [a demon], to drive out from here the Takman!

Thou art born of the gods, thou art Soma's good friend. Be thou propitious to my in-breathing and my out-breathing, and to the eyes of mine! . . .

Pain in the head, affliction in the eye, and ailment of the body, all that shall the *Kushtha* heal—a divinely powerful remedy forsooth! (Sigerist 1961, 157–158)

Indian medicines also show evidence of being motivated by the same kind of belief in sympathetic magic that we have seen in Egypt, Mesopotamia, and Mesoamerica. For example, to treat jaundice, the vedic physician prescribed drinking water mixed with the hair of a red bull in order to bring redness to his patient to replace the yellow color associated with the disease (Sigerist 1961).

Finally, Indian physicians developed compound drugs that were understood to be universal remedies. Here, for example, is one recipe based on the plumbago-root:

Take eight handfulls of Danti (*Baliospermum Montanum*) and plumbago-root, twenty choice chebulic myrobalans, six pala of deodar, also six pala each of the larger and smaller kinds of Kadhamba (*Anthrocephalus Cadamba*), Varana (*Crataeva religiosa*), Rājavrisha (*Euphorbia neriflia*), Punarnavā (*Boerhaavia diffusa*) and rind of Chirivila (*Pongamia glabra*) . . . Then boil the whole in one drona of tank-water over a gentle fire, till it is reduced to one-fourth of the original quantity. Now boil the decoction once more in one ādhaka of clarified butter, throwing in also one Karsha each of the following drugs: long pepper, root of long pepper, Chavya (*Piper Chaba*), black pepper and the five salts. This preparation of clarified butter called the Dhānvantara is a remedy for all diseases. It cures the five kinds of abdominal tumors, the eight kinds of enlargements of the abdomen, swellings, consumption, piles, and the twenty-one kinds of morbid secretion of urine. It also relieves chronic diarrhoea and dyspepsia, and cures the many kinds of skin diseases. It counteracts the venom of snakes and mice, also every sort of artificial poisoning . . . Whoever makes suitable use of it will attain the highest prosperity. (Mukhopadhyaya 1922–1929, II, 319–320)

CHINESE EMPIRICAL MEDICINE

Chinese medicine, like that of India, was understood almost exclusively in spiritual terms until the beginning of the Han dynasty, though there is literary evidence that sometime during the spring-and-autumn period (722–480 B.C.E.) a distinction was being made between shamans, who were responsible for magico-religious medicine, and physicians, who were responsible for corporeal medicine (Ho and Lisowski 1993). The *Historical Memoirs* of the Han Grand Historian Sima Qian offers stories about the physician Bian Que (who worked around 501 B.C.E.), who developed the four main diagnostic techniques of classical Chinese medicine: (1) Visual observation, especially of signs in the face, eyes, nose, mouth, tongue, and throat; (2) Listening to coughing, breathing, and wheezing; (3) Asking the patient about his symptoms and medical history; and (4) Palpitating, including feeling the pulse (Ho and Lisowski 1993). Bian Que is also said to have used acupuncture, but a substantial collection of medical writings found in 1974 in a grave that can be dated to 168 B.C.E. suggests that acupuncture may have been a later Han creation, for it is not referred to in the collection and the first treatise devoted to its use is from around 90 B.C.E. (Unschuld 1985).

The first Chinese medical treatise of substantial scope is the *Huang-di Nei-Jinging* (*The Yellow Emperor's Manual of Corporeal Medicine*), which was written toward the end of the second century B.C.E., though portions were probably composed as early as the Warring States Period (480–221 B.C.E.). The first treatise focusing on herbal medicines, the *Huainan Zi*, comes from the same time. The latter refers to the mythical divine husbandman, Shen-nong, attributing to him the discovery of many drugs:

In ancient times the people subsisted on herbs and drank water. They collected the fruits from the trees and ate the flesh of [worms] and the clams. They frequently suffered from illnesses and poisonings. Then Shen-nunng taught the people for the first time to sow the five kinds of grain, . . . He tried the tastes of all the herbs and [investigated] the water sources to see if they were sweet or bitter. In this way he taught the people what they should avoid and where they should seek help. At that time [Shen-nong] found on a single day 70 [herbs and waters] that were medically effective. (Unschuld 1985, 113)

A more extensive herbal, the *Shen-nong ben cao jing* (*Shen-nong's Classic of Materia Medica*), listing the virtues of 365 substances appeared during the second century C.E. Few of these substances, other than such standards as ginger and ginseng among plants and oyster shell and deer antler among animal products, can now be identified, but they do seem to break into two categories. One includes materials used for external application to wounds, lesions, or burns in the form of ointments; the other, substances ingested orally for internal problems.

Simple minor surgical procedures including the lancing of boils, the excision of small external tumors using stone knives, and the setting of broken bones are attested from very early in China (Unschuld 1985), but more complicated procedures, including eye operations, were not attempted until after the Han Dynasty (Ho and Lisowski 1993). Though acupuncture will be discussed later, it seems that moxibustion, or moxacauterization—the burning of powdered mugwort to cauterize minor wounds—was used before it was modified for incorporation into more theoretical medicine (Unschuld, 1985).

THE TRAINING OF MEDICAL PRACTITIONERS
AND RELATIONS AMONG PRACTITIONERS

It is likely that the earliest training of physicians in all ancient civilizations was through an apprenticeship with a family member or a well-known master. This pattern seems to have continued as the dominant way of training physicians throughout the history of ancient civilization in Mesoamerica (Viesca 2003), in China (Lloyd 1996), and probably in India, but in Egypt, Mesopotamia, and Greece, more formal education in medical schools seems to have become the norm. Mesopotamian correspondence from as early as 1700 B.C.E., for example, suggests that the most capable physicians came from the city of Isin, which was a center of medical learning (Oppenheim 1977), and Egyptian sources suggest that there were at least two important "houses of life" associated with temple complexes where many physicians were trained (Sigerist 1951). In Greece, centers of secular medical education developed on the island of Cos, off the present Turkish coast, and at Cnidos, on a peninsula near Cos, sometime before the sixth century B.C.E. and before they became centers of Aesclepiad religious healing. The presence of multiple masters in these locations offered students exposure to a variety of approaches to healing. It is certainly the case that physicians who could claim to be trained at these centers were preferred by wealthy patients who could afford their services.

The Hippocratic Oath, portions of which follow, raises several interesting issues regarding Greek medical practices and practitioners:

I will fulfill according to my ability and judgment this oath and this covenant:
To hold him who has taught me this art as equal to my parents and to live my life in partnership with him, and if he is need of money to give him a share of mine, and

to regard his offspring as equal toy brothers in male lineage and to teach them this art—if they desire to learn it,—without fee and covenant; to give a share of precepts and oral instruction and all the other learning to my sons and to the sons of him who has instructed me and to pupils who have signed a covenant and have taken an oath according to medical law, but to no one else.

I will apply dietetic measures for the benefit of the sick according to my ability and judgment; I will keep them from harm and injustice.

I will neither give a deadly drug to anybody if asked for it, nor will I make a suggestion to this effect.

Similarly, I will not give to a woman an abortive remedy.

In purity and holiness I will guard my life and my art.

I will not use the knife, not even on sufferers from the stone, but will withdraw in favor of such men as are engaged in this work. . . .

What I may see or hear in the course of the treatment or even outside of the treatment in regard to the life of men, which on no account one must spread abroad, I will keep to myself, holding such things shameful to be spoken about.

If I fulfil [sic] this oath and do not violate it, may it be granted to me to enjoy life and art, being honored with fame among all men for all time to come; if I transgress it and swear falsely, may the opposite of all this be my lot. (Sigerist 1961, 301–302)

The first section of the covenant lays out the kind of rules that guide apprenticeship in virtually all crafts (*techne*) and confirms the notion that physicians held roughly the same status as other craftsmen in Greece. The second and third confirms much other evidence that Hippocratic treatments were much more often focused on diet and much less often focused on drug therapy than those of any other ancient civilization. The fourth and sixth suggest that this oath was intended to be used only by a small, and probably religiously oriented, segment of the medical community, because abortion was widely practiced within Greek society, some of the gynecological treatises recommend abortifacients, and many of the Hippocratic treatises (e.g., *On Fractures, On Joints, On Wounds in the Head, on Hemorrhoids,* and *In the Surgery*) were on surgical topics. It is, however, true that some surgeries were beginning to done by barbers in classical Greece, and this feature of the Hippocratic Oath, was particularly appealing to Christian clergy later on. The last section forms the basis for subsequent Western traditions of doctor-patient confidentiality.

Though there were clearly alternative therapies for illnesses within the traditions of medicine almost everywhere, in most early civilizations, empirical, magico-religious, and philosophical medicine coexisted and complemented one another, and within each tradition there was little evidence of open disagreement. Only in the Chinese and Classical Greek traditions do we find evidence of substantial conflicts among physicians regarding the treatment of particular cases or regarding general approaches to medicine. In China, Sima Qian's *Historical Memoirs,* for example, discusses the physician Chunyu Yi, who offers a series of case histories in which his diagnoses differ from those of other physicians because he uses the pulse in making his diagnoses, while the others do not (Lloyd 1996).

In Greece, for reasons already discussed in chapter 2, there were bitter disagreements among philosophical schools of medicine, but there were equally deep disagreements between empirical approaches to medicine and both magico-religious approaches and philosophical approaches. Thus, for example, in *On the Sacred Disease,* a treatise on epilepsy from within the Hippocratic corpus, the author denies that any diseases are sacred and insists that all have natural causes. Moreover, in *On Ancient Medicine,* another Hippocratic text, the author insists that medicine is an art rather than a science—one in which skill, judgment, and above all, direct experience with patients, are supremely important. Furthermore, he insists that those philosophical physicians who try to reduce medicine to a small number of principles inevitably oversimplify the situation (Lloyd 1996).

TRADITIONS OF PRIESTLY MEDICINE

Though empirical and magico-religious medical traditions were almost certainly coterminous in most civilizations, the magico-religious traditions left larger traces in the early stages of all civilizations other than that of Egypt. Discussions of the diagnostic and treatment practices of the *Āšipu* (conjurers) of Mesopotamia from the Sumerian and Old Babylonian periods offer some of the earliest and most complete accounts of magico-religious medicine. Most illnesses in Mesopotamia were understood as caused by one of four sources: (1) the capricious actions of demons (the primary cause in Sumerian texts); (2) some insult to one of the major gods who pursued revenge against the sinner or one of her relatives, usually by setting a demon or demons against her (the primary cause in most Old Babylonian and Assyrian texts); (3) the practice of witchcraft by a patient's enemy; or (4) the anger of a ghost of someone who was not properly cared for by his family (Sigerist 1951). Some combination of two or more of these four causes accounted for most diseases in each of the magico-religious medical traditions of the early civilizations.

In Sumer, as in Egypt, China, and Mesoamerica, amulets were often worn to ward off demons, and prayers were said to keep demons away from a house. Here, for example, is a prayer to keep the demons away:

Man may enter the house—thou shalt not enter it.

Man may approach the house—thou shalt not approach it!

If something enters, thou shalt not enter.

With an entering man, thou shalt not enter!

With an outgoing man thou shalt not enter. (Sigerist 1951, 443)

Once a demon had entered a man, one form of exorcism involved telling the demon that there was no sustenance to be had there:

Until thou art removed, until thou departest from the man, the son of his god,

Thou shall have no food to eat, Thou shalt have no water to drink.

Thou shall not stretch forward thy hand unto the table of thy father, Enlil, thy creator. (Sigerist 1951, 443)

Another involved prayer to one's guardian spirit to remove or forgive the sin that brought on the illness:

Loosen my disgrace, the guilt of my wickedness; remove my disease; drive away my sickness; a sin I know (or) know not I have committed; on account of a sin of my father (or) of my grandfather, a sin of my mother (or) my grandmother, on account of a sin of an older brother (or) an older sister, on account of a sin of my family, of my kinfolk (or) of my clan . . . the wrath of god and goddess have pressed upon me. (Sigerist 1951, 445)

When the sickness was caused by witchcraft, an exorcism like the following might be used:

O witch, whosoever thou art, whose heart conceiveth my misfortune, whose tongue uttereth spells against me, whose lips poison me, and in whose footsteps death standeth, I ban thy mouth, I ban thy tongue, I ban thy glittering eyes, I ban thy swift feet, I ban thy toiling knees, I ban thy laden hands, I bind thy hands behind. And may the Moon-god destroy thy body, and may he cast thee into the Lake of Water and Fire. (Sigerist 1951, 1945–46)

Similarly, when a ghost was the purported cause of the sickness, the ghost was first identified as one who was uncared for and then sent away (Sigerist 1951).

In most of the cases discussed in the extensive Old Babylonian *Treatise on Medical Diagnoses and Prognoses,* some form of ritual procedure to remove the disease and displace it accompanies an oral incantation. Thus, for example, the treatment recommended for an unidentified disease called *dimîtu,* includes both a plea to the healing god, Gula, to make the patient whole again and the following ritual:

You must take seven small loaves made of coarse flower, and join them by means of bronze fastener. Then you must rub the man with them, and make him spit on the remains that fall from them, uttering over him a "Formula from Eridu" after taking him to the steppe, in an isolated place, at the foot of the wild acacia. Then you will pass on the malady that struck him [through the mass of bread used to rub him and the crumbs that fell as a result] to Ninedinne [the patron -goddess of the steppe], so that Ninkilim, [the patron-god of small wild rodents] may cause these animals to take on his illness [by giving them the edible remains of the bread to nibble]. (Bottéro 2001, 170–171)

Mesopotamian religious diagnoses depended in part on the kind of analysis of symptoms that was done by the secular physicians, and in part on all of the kinds of divination carried out by a third type of priest, the *bârû,* or diviner. Dream interpretation was especially important for medical purposes in Sumer and in the Old Babylonian period, but as was the case with all divination in Mesopotamia, astral omens increased in importance for medicine over time, and as that happened, magico-religious medicine increased in importance relative to secular medicine.

In Vedic India, as in Mesopotamia, most illness and injury were understood within the magico-religious tradition as a consequence of sin (i.e., of the violation of some social norm that displeased the gods), especially Varuna, the guardian of law and order. A second frequent cause being witchcraft (Sigerist 1961, 159). Moreover, as in Mesopotamia, a patient might be the locus of divine vengeance for the sins of family members as well as for her own. Finally, as in Mesopotamia, the primary religious treatments for illness were prayer to keep demons away, exorcism, and sacrifice, with magical displacement rites sometimes accompanying incantations (Sigerist 1961).

In India, however, magico-religious medicine and empirical medicine were more closely integrated than in Mesopotamia because Vedic priests and physicians were usually the same persons, and they could move easily from one role to another. Thus the *Suśruta-Samhitā* directs the priest who has unsuccessfully attempted to cure his patient by spells and offerings to turn to drugs (Chopra 2003). The other major difference between Vedic medicine and Near Eastern medicine has to do with the status of the medical practitioner. Since medicine was a major responsibility of the Vedic priest, and since the Vedic priest held highest position in the developing caste system of ancient India, medicine was a very high status profession in India.

The Buddhist reform of traditional Hindu religion in the mid-sixth century B.C.E. was inspired primarily by the Buddha's experience of illness, old age, and death among the poor. Buddhism turned away from the rituals, prayers, and sacrifices of the Vedic tradition in favor of a dual emphasis on withdrawing from the cravings of the physical world and living a highly moral life, but Buddhism continued the longstanding Indian interest in medical issues, turning away from the ritualistic approach that had dominated the Ayurvedic tradition to focus on philosophical dimensions that we will discuss in the next chapter. Indeed, the Buddhist version of Ayurvedic medicine spread throughout Asia along with Buddhism to become the foundation for the Ayurveda, which persists into the 21st century C.E.

Egyptian medical texts, like those of Mesopotamia, distinguish between three kinds of practitioners—physicians, sorcerers, and Priests of Sekhmet—the latter two dealing with magico-religious medicine (Sigerist 1951). The earliest texts have far less religious emphasis than those of any other ancient civilization, but as in Mesopotamia and Greece, New Kingdom texts tend to have greater religious content than Old Kingdom texts (Sigerist 1951). As elsewhere, priests were principally involved in incantations and sacrifices to Gods who had been offended, though surgical procedures including male circumcision were done by Egyptian priests as early as circa 2300 B.C.E. (Shafik and Elseesy 2003). Finally, as in Mesopotamia, amulets were prepared to discourage or drive out demons, and physical rituals, including the laying-on-of hands or drawing a circle around the house to be protected, accompanied incantations (Sigerist 1951).

Early Mesoamerican magico-religious medicine shared many features with those medical traditions mentioned so far. Illnesses were most often caused by gods who wanted to punish humans for some kind of transgression, and as in the Egyptian case, particular gods were related to particular medical conditions, though more often as the senders of illness, rather than as protectors. The Mayan gods Ahalganà and Xiriquipat, for example, were responsible for bleeding and hemorrhages, Ahulph was responsible for swollen and ulcerated legs and jaundice, and Ahalmez and Ahaltogob were responsible for accidents and injuries (Viesca, 2003). As was the case in India, China, and Greece, Mesoamerican magico-religious medical practices often had a complex theoretical justification, which will be discussed later.

The evidence from oracle bones suggests that three causes of illness were recognized in Shang China: the curse of an offended ancestor, injury caused by the evil actions of a third party, or illness caused by spirits associated with natural entities, especially evil winds (Unschuld 1985). There is no indication of drug treatment; rather, all treatments seem to involve preventive rites, incantations, exorcisms, or, most often, sacrifices. By providing a proper burial site and by cleaning and rearranging the bones of an ancestor appropriately after the corpse had decayed, one could get the ancestor to guarantee prosperity and health; however, if one ignored the ancestor, then he might take revenge by causing an illness or injury (Unschuld 1985). If an ancestor did, for some reason, cause an illness, one could regain her favor by providing a suitable sacrifice. A typical oracle bone text, for example, reads: "Severe tooth illness. Should a dog be offered to the departed father Keng, and a sheep be ritually slaughtered?" (Unschuld 1985, 21). In cases of illness produced by nature spirits, such as evil winds, one called upon a shaman to perform rites either to stop the evil wind or to counter its effects by calling up a good wind (Unschuld 1985).

During the late Zhou period and through the Warring States Period, demonic possession largely replaced ancestral causes for disease, and the shamans became increasingly important. Following approved social conventions no longer virtually guaranteed health, just as following social conventions no longer guaranteed social success or even survival during a period of constant military and political upheaval. As Paul Unschuld argues, "Demonic medicine thus reflects certain central aspects of the political process during the decline of Zhou feudalism, including general uncertainty and the existential *angst* that seems to have marked the relationship among states as well as among individuals" (1985, 37). Medical rituals often even mimicked chaotic military actions:

Several times a year, and also during special occasions, such as the funeral of a prince, hordes of exorcists would race shrieking through the city streets, enter the courtyards and homes, thrusting their spears into the air, in attempt to expel the evil creatures. Prisoners were dismembered outside the gates to the city, to serve both as a deterrent to the demons and as an indication of their fate should they be captured. (1985, 37)

He continues, "It may well be the case that the ancient writing of the character for 'healer' and 'healing' was formed at that time. Its lower half consists of the character wu 'shaman'; the upper half combines a quiver with an arrow on the left and a spear or lance on the right. The entire character thus depicts exactly they type of practitioner active in the rituals described" (1985, 37).

The first drugs mentioned in Chinese medical literature appear during the Zhou period as pills to deal with demonic possession. The following description of such a drug, which comes from circa 600 B.C.E., also suggests the initial Chinese connection between alchemy and medicine, which became very important later:

Pills for the five kinds of possession . . . pills worth a thousand times their weight in gold; pills that bring about a turning point in suffering caused by possession; pills that control fate; pills that kill demons. . . .

Cinnabar—pulverize

Arsenopyrite—burned for half a day

Realgar—pulverize

Croton seed—discard the skins, roast

Hellebone—roast

Aconite root—subject to dry heat

Use 2 *fen* of each of the above ingredients

Centipede—broil, remove the feet

Press these seven ingredients trough a sieve and combine with honey to form pills the size of small beans. The correct dose is one pill daily. This will result in a cure. If the suffering is not relieved, an additional pill should be taken at midnight. This will certainly end all complaints. (Unschuld 1985, 41–42)

Cinnabar, the only nontoxic mercury compound, became a favorite material for medical alchemists, first in China, and later in the Islamic and early modern European worlds.

With the unification of the empire, beginning with the Qin and Han Dynasties, and with the rising importance of Confucian philosophy, Chinese medicine took a new philosophical turn to be discussed in the next chapter, but as revolts began within the Han Dynasty starting around 184 C.E., religiously based medicine that again saw evil spirits and demons as the principal cause of disease made a comeback, though now there was a sense that, if one led a moral life, one would be protected against demonic attack.

Asclepiad medicine developed in Greece rather differently than priestly medicine elsewhere in the ancient world. Unlike the case elsewhere, patients typically had to travel to an Asclepiad temple to be treated, though eventually this did not imply much of a trip, for over 320 Asclepiad temples have been identified throughout the eastern Mediterranean. The cult spread from Epidarus, reaching Cos and Cnidos, where centers of secular medicine already existed around 430 B.C.E., and coming to Athens about the same time. Asclepiad healing had remarkable staying power and widespread appeal outside of Greece, expanding into the Roman Empire and persisting through early Christian times. Many Asclepiad priests, including Hippocrates, the most famous of Greek physicians, were trained in secular medicine, and some Asclepiad cures involved the use of ordinary drugs, or massage, and so on, though having them prescribed by the god probably provided an additional psychological benefit.

Thus, for example one patient wrote:

There is, I think, a compound of Philo's. This I was not even able to smell previously, but when the god gave me a sign to use it and also signified the time at which it was necessary to do this, not only did I drink it easily, but even as I drank it I was at once happier and better. Moreover, it would be possible to relate ten thousand other things concerning drugs—some of which he himself compounded, others belonging to the common ordinary varieties which he prescribed as a cure of the body, as it were appropriate in each particular case. (Edelstein 1998, 207)

Rituals of purification played some role in most priestly medical traditions, but purification was essential to virtually all Asclepiad healing. When a patient arrived at the temple she spent several days bathing in warm mineral waters, abstaining from alcoholic drink, and eating a special bland diet. No doubt, this period of purification alone played a major role in many cures. After being purified, the patient spent a night sleeping in the *Abaton,* a special room within the temple. There, the patient would be expected to have a dream related to her cure, after which she sacrificed an animal, paid her fee to the temple, and, sometimes, if she was wealthy enough and well satisfied, she erected a stone votive tablet attesting to her cure. We have learned much of what we know about Asclepiad treatments from these tablets and from other literary testimonies.

Many cures involved only a dream. For example one of the tablets reads:

A man whose fingers, with the exception of one, were paralyzed, came as a suppliant to the God. While looking at the tablets in the temple, he expressed incredulity regarding the cures and scoffed at the inscriptions. But in his sleep, he saw a vision. It seemed to him that, as he was playing at dice below the Temple and was about to cast the dice, the god appeared, sprang upon his hand, and stretched out his fingers. When the god had stepped aside it seemed to him [the patient] that he bent his hand and stretched out his fingers one by one . . . When day dawned, he walked out sound. (Edelstein 1998, 230)

Some modern physicians have suggested that a disproportionate number of dream cures relate to forms of paralysis, including muteness, paralysis in the limbs, and blindness, that may have been symptoms of hysteria, and that the psychological relief gained through the temple rituals may have effected the cures.

Aesclepiad medicine seems to have increased in importance relative to secular medicine throughout the period from around 400 B.C.E. to nearly 400 C.E. Even from a purely secular perspective, it is fairly easy to understand why this happened. Asclepiad medicine incorporated almost all of the techniques of secular medicine, but the psychological force of divine advice probably made patients more likely to follow the advice they received carefully. This interpretation was already offered in antiquity by the physician, Galen of Pergamum, who tells us:

We see that those who are being treated by the god obey him when on many occasions he bids them not to drink at all for fifteen days, while they obey none of the physicians who give this prescription. For it has great influence on the patient's doing all which is prescribed if he has been firmly persuaded that a remarkable benefit to himself will ensue. (Edelstein 1998, 202)

Asclepiad medicine had the additional advantages of emphasizing purification rituals that improved diet and increased sobriety as well as the psychological techniques of faith healing associated with dreams.

Seven

Philosophical Medicine, Cosmology, and Natural Philosophy

With a few minor exceptions, it was possible to understand technical developments in mathematics and astronomy in ancient civilizations without knowing much detail regarding any broader understanding of natural and cosmic processes. Moreover, it has been possible to learn much about both the priestly medical traditions and the empirical medical traditions in many places while understanding very little about broader issues regarding nature and how the human body, human society, and human artifice relate to the natural world. When we come to try understand what became at least temporarily the dominant medical traditions in ancient India, China, Greece, Egypt, and Mesoamerica, however, we must stand back and explore some general features of cosmology and natural philosophy. This is so because, in all of these civilizations, the most fundamental assumption of philosophical medicine was that the human body was composed in the image of and functioned like the natural world as a whole. It was a microcosm that reflected the relationships that pertained in the great macrocosm of the world. Furthermore, as Plato argued, that world was assumed to be a cosmos (i.e., an ordered and lawfully behaving entity), rather than a chaos that could not be understood. The ancestors, demons, gods and other capricious and willful agents that dominated magico-religious medical traditions played no role in philosophical or theoretical medicine.

As we saw in chapters 4 and 5, early Mesopotamian cultures were relatively uninterested in the spatial structure of the universe, and they developed no theoretical understanding of the natural world that was independent of their astral theology. There was a clear sense from the beginning of the second millennium that the events of the political and social worlds were controlled by the cosmic astral world. Furthermore, by the late fifth century B.C.E., astrological horoscopes even presumed that the events of an individual's life might be controlled by the stars. However, the links between the astral world and the terrestrial and personal worlds were generally presumed to be causal rather than analogical. It was not presumed, for example, that the human body resembles the cosmos structurally. Instead, it was assumed that the body could be influenced directly by the stars. Indeed, the whole notion of influence—literally "flowing inward"—derives from the idea that the heavens act on the sublunar world through the in-flowing of special substances or spiritual entities which act to direct the behavior of terrestrial objects, including the human body. As a consequence, we have no early Mesopotamian texts suggesting special analogical relationships between particular heavenly bodies and particular human bodily structures, as was the case in other ancient civilizations. Indeed, Mesopotamia saw no theoretical medicine outside the magico-religious tradition.

EGYPTIAN THEORETICAL MEDICINE

Egypt, too, lacked a tradition of naturalistic cosmological speculation, and most Egyptian medical materials are descriptive and are focused on treating the symptoms of disease as the disease itself, but there are several short texts, one from the Ebers Papyrus, one from the Edwin Smith Surgical Papyrus, one from the Berlin Papyrus, and one from the Hearst Papyrus, that have significant theoretical content. All of these papyri date from between 1700 and 1500 B.C.E. The theoretical section of the Edwin Smith papyrus begins with the claim that vessels connect the heart to all parts of the body and that, "If you want to know how the heart is, put your hand on any organ because the heart speaks through its vessels" (Shafik and Elseesy 2003, 37), a claim that justifies using the strength and rapidity of the pulse as a diagnostic tool. It then goes on to list 46 different vessels and gives the presumed physiological function of roughly half of them. Here are some of the most significant:

> There are 4 vessels in the nostrils; 2 give mucous and 2 give blood.
>
> There are 4 vessels in the interior of his temples which then give blood to the eyes; all diseases of the eyes arise through them, because there is an opening to the eyes.
>
> There are 4 vessels to his 2 ears together with the ear canal, 2 on the right side and 2 to his left side. The breath of life enters into the right ear and the breath of life enters into the left ear . . .
>
> There are 4 vessels to the Liver; it is they which give to it humor and air, which afterward cause all diseases to arise in it by overfilling with blood . . .
>
> There are 2 vessels to the bladder; it is they which give urine.
>
> There are 4 vessels that open to the anus; it is they which cause humor and air to be produced for it. Now the anus opens to every vessel to the right side and to the left side in arms and legs when it is overfilled with excrements (Sigerist 1951, 350).

Given this speculative physiology, almost all illnesses were attributed to the state and functioning of the vessels from the heart.

A primary cause of many diseases was theorized to be the overflow of excrement from the anus into other parts of the body through the system of vessels. Thus, for example, mental diseases were attributed to the carrying of feces to the heart (Sigerist 1951). The principle that appears in these early

Egyptian medical theories with respect to blood in the liver or feces in the anus can be generalized to assert that disease stems from the excess of some substance in a place that has some normal amount in the healthy body or to the presence of a substance in a place where it does not belong. This general claim is one that is central to ancient medical theorizing in all civilizations that engaged in theorizing.

Egyptian medical theory also seemed to have a major impact on the structure of the Egyptian medical profession. Ancient Egyptian physicians were famous for their degree of specialization, and one of the most important specialists was the physician of the anus, which undoubtedly reflects the importance of the anus in theoretical medicine.

Many other diseases were thought to be caused by pathological conditions of the vessels themselves. Here, for example is a description of an aneurism:

If you examine as swelling of a vessel in an extremity, and this swelling is hemispherical and dilates under your hand, but if you isolate it from the body, it does not pulsate, and so it does not dilate or shrink, say: it is a swelling of a vessel, and I will cure this disease.

Treatment involved tying off the vessel feeding the aneurism (Shafik and Elseesy 2003, 37). The Hearst Papyrus emphasizes drug treatments to sooth the vessels when they are irritated, to soften them when they are stiff, and to cool them when they are hot (Sigerist 1951). This constitutes the full extent of the record of what might be called philosophical medicine in Egypt until the arrival of Greek medicine after 320 B.C.E.

INDIAN THEORETICAL MEDICINE

The second-oldest textual material that incorporates theory into medical discussions probably comes from the Vedic literature of India, much of which might be as old as the seventh century B.C.E. It is in this material that we begin to see an explicit emphasis on the correspondence between the human and the cosmic that is at the core of most ancient philosophical medicine. It is worth noting that, at its base, this philosophical medicine is built on the explicit recognition of a kind of magical thinking in which connections are made via correspondence rather than causality.

There were several philosophical systems of medicine associated with different Indian philosophies, but that associated with a philosophy called *Dharmashastra* (roughly "science of mortality") became dominant very rapidly (Trawick 1995). For the Vedic cosmologist or natural philosopher associated with *Dharmashastra,* the entire phenomenal world is composed of five elements: earth, water, fire, air, and space. Likewise, the human body is composed of these same five elements. Consider now the composition of sweet foods, which are made up primarily of earth and water. Similarly, fatty tissue in the body is composed primarily of earth and water, so when the body ingests too many sweet foods, it produces fatty tissue in the body

(Chopra 2003). Generally speaking, the composition of any substance can be known by its qualities, of which Vedic cosmology and Ayurvedic medicine recognized 20, divided into 10 sets of opposites:

heavy	light
cold	hot
wet	dry
dull	sharp
stable	moveable
soft	hard
non-slimy	slimy
smooth	coarse
small	large
viscous	liquid

A general principle of Ayurvedic medicine was that one should avoid excess, so this list of 20 qualities was used to guide dietetics in particular. If the body seemed to have an excess of any of these qualities, dietetic treatment involved eating foods with opposite qualities to bring back a balance (Chopra 2003, 75–76).

The most important theoretical element within Ayurvedic medicine was the theory of three *dosas,* which is often translated as the theory of three humors because of certain similarities with Greek theories to be discussed later. This theory incorporates the doctrine of 20 qualities, but sees them as being carried by three substances (the *dosas*), which are identified as *vāta* (wind), *pitta* (bile), and *kapha* (phlegm) (Chopra 2003). The *dosas* are responsible for all bodily processes. The wind especially embodies the quality of mobility, but like wind in the greater world, it is also responsible for drying and cooling. Bile provides heat and luminosity, while phlegm provides moisture and cohesiveness (Trawick 1995). Each of the *dosas* has its own channels extending from the heart—likened to the veins in a leaf extending from the stem—in which to flow. As in the case of the Egyptian theory of the vessels, in the Ayurvedic system,

Disease is caused by the blockage and overflowing of channels; if one substance overflows into the channels of another, then the "invaded" channels become diseased. Every disease, ultimately, is caused by an excess or deficiency of some substance flowing in channels. When a substance is excessive it overflows its own channels and makes troubles in other channels; when a substance is deficient, its channels dry up, provoking other substances to enter and make trouble there (Trawick 1995, 286).

It is highly likely that the system of *dosas* depended not only on a cosmological system involving elements and qualities, but also that it drew heavily from two other metaphors that were widely used in other ancient medical theories. One was the metaphor of a well-ordered society in which all authority derives from a single central king, pharaoh, or emperor, and in which each person follows the path appropriate to him without trying to take on the jobs of others. Thus, the heart was the central governor of the entire system and each vessel was responsible for carrying only its proper material. The other was the metaphor of an irrigation system, "in which the flow must be carefully monitored so that each field gets its proper share of water, no field gets too much or too little, and no farmer breaks the irrigation ditch and steals another farmer's share of the water" (Trawick 1995, 287). In each metaphor, the goal was to achieve the appropriate balance in the system so that each element functioned as intended. To see how this theoretical structure functioned in connection with the diagnosis and treatment of a particular illness, we will look at the case of epilepsy as it appeared in the *Caraka-samhitā*. I choose to focus on a small selection from the text, which Francis Zimmerman has translated in full, and I have reordered the sequence of passages to make them easier to follow:

Epilepsy is defined as an entrance into unconsciousness, an episode accompanied with loathsome gestures [vomiting of froth, convulsions] due to the ruin of memory, intellect and *sattva* [the purity component of mind] . . . There are four types of epilepsy respectively caused by wind, bile, phlegm or the conjunction of the three.

Specific Features of Each Type of Epilepsy

Signs of Epilepsy Due to Wind:

Repeated fits, instantly regaining consciousness, protruded eyes, violent vociferations, froth from the mouth, neck excessively swollen, . . . hands and feet constantly moving, the nails, eyes, face and skin are red, rough, and blackish, vision of unstable, fickle, coarse and dry objects, indisposition to windy substances and disposition to their contraries.

Signs of Epilepsy Due to Bile:

Repeated fits, instantly regaining consciousness, groaning sounds, one strikes the ground, the nails, eyes, face and skin are green, yellow, and coppery, vision of things wet with blood and bodies agitated, fierce, in flames, irritated, indisposition to bilious substances and disposition to their contraries.

Signs of Epilepsy Due to Phlegm:

Delayed fits, delayed recovery of consciousness, falling down, gestures not so abnormal, saliva from the mouth, the nails, eyes, face, and skin are white, vision of white heavy, unctuous objects, indisposition to phlegmy substances, disposition to their contraries

The One Due to the Conjunction of All Three Humors Combines All These Signs; Incurable . . .

Wise physicians treat the curable ones cautiously, with acrid substances, evacuants, or calmatives according to the humoral condition (Zimmerman 1995, 300–302).

In each case, the symptoms exemplify those qualities of the causative *dosa,* and the treatment involves use of a drug with the opposite qualities, thus bringing the body back into equilibrium. The form of epilepsy that exhibits all qualities, and for which there are therefore no appropriate contraries, is deemed incurable.

THEORETICAL MEDICINE IN MESOAMERICA

There was no single cosmological model utilized by all Mesoamerican peoples for whom common elements of culture were accompanied by many local variants. Just among the Maya, who occupied an area no greater than Greece and the Peloponnesus, for example, there were some 20 languages and 100 dialects. Most Mesoamericans, however, agreed on certain basic issues. They thought of the cosmos as a large plant or tree with multiple "floors" organized into three basic categories: a large heavenly part, which housed the Sun, Moon, planets, and stars, a very small middle part on the surface of the Earth, which was the abode of man, and another large underworld (Viesca 2003). Similarly, the human body was composed of three regions, each corresponding to one of the cosmic regions, with the diaphragm representing the Earth. Above that, the heart was like the Sun, the lungs like the airy region above the Earth, and the top of the head like the outer heavens with the fixed stars. Below the diaphragm, the liver, abdominal cavity, reproductive organs, and legs were likened to parts of the underworld, with which they communicated through the perineal holes, the vagina, and the soles of the feet (Viesca 2003). From each of the astral regions came a "soul." From the heavens came *tonalli*, which above all provided the heat that was essential to life, but which, in excess, could cause illness. This soul was situated in the top of the head and also governed mental functions. The *teyolía*, which came from the middle part of the cosmos, resided in the heart, and provided energy. Influences were transmitted to it through the senses. Finally the *ihíyotl*, which came from the underworld, carried the cold, which moderated the heat brought by the *tonalli* in the healthy person, but which, in excess, could also cause illness. Imbalances of heat and cold played a role in other theoretical medicines, but it seems to have been the only causative principle in Mesoamerican medical theory, so fever and chills became the central indicators of illness.

Each part of the body had its appropriate level of heat or cold. The upper part of the body—especially the heart and head—were naturally hotter than the lower part of the body, including the liver and reproductive organs, because the former was governed primarily by the *tonalli*, while the latter was governed primarily by the *ihíyotl*. Treatments in Mesoamerica were primarily magical, but some drugs were identified as hot and cold, and treatment involved inducing opposites, so hot diseases were treated with cold medicines and vice versa.

CHINESE THEORETICAL MEDICINE

In part because we have the greatest amount of evidence regarding ancient Greek and Chinese medical theories and cosmological speculation, they both seem to be vastly more complex than the cosmologies and theo-retical, or philosophical, medicines of other ancient civilizations. The rise of secular philosophies was roughly coterminous in the two civilizations, as were the lives of the two most famous Chinese philosophers, Confucius (551–479 B.C.E.) and Zhuang Zhou (369–286 B.C.E.), who was the chief early spokesman for the *daoist* philosophy of the probably mythical Lao-tzu, and those of the most prominent Greek philosophers, Plato (427–348 B.C.E.) and Aristotle (384–322 B.C.E.), but some of the most important features of al-most all subsequent Chinese cosmological and medical theories already appear in the *Book of Changes,* or *I Jing,* whose origins are traditionally dated to the beginnings of the Zhou Dynasty around 1150 B.C.E., nearly 500 years before the beginnings of Greek philosophy. Much of the *I Jing* was certainly composed well before the time of Confucius, since he wrote commentaries on the text, so we explore Chinese cosmology and medicine first.

The *Book of Changes,* which is the oldest Chinese book to have been con-tinuously transmitted into the present, is an anonymous and probably col-lective compilation of fragments regarding divination without any fully coherent theoretical component. Nonetheless, several key elements of later systematic thought are found there. Here are several relevant passages:

What cannot be measured by *yin* and *yang* is called spirit. . . .

The Changes is equivalent to heaven and earth, that is to say, with nature. Nature is transformation, and this transformation arises out of the two *qi* of *yin* and *yang.* . . .

The situation in which a balance of the two *qi* is maintained is the ideal for human beings.

One *yin* and one *yang* [that is, their alteration] is called the Way [*Dao*]. What makes the process continue to completion is the original moral nature of mankind. (Yosida 1973, 73–74)

The first implication of these passages is that yin and yang are natural principles rather than theological or spiritual ones. In particular, they are not subject to willful whim, but are absolutely regular in their action. Fur-thermore, these two principles drive all natural phenomena, the central feature of which is change. All subsequent Chinese natural philosophies con-tinued to see nature as fundamentally dynamic rather than static, and all that have left a significant trace appealed to the alternation of yin and yang as the underlying process that produces change. Finally, as one might expect in a book on divination regarding human activities, these passages integrate humans into the natural order. Moreover, they do so in two interesting ways. On the one hand, humans, like nature in general, are governed by yin and yang. In a pattern that reflects the theories we have seen elsewhere, it is an appropriate balance of the two principles that is good for humans.

This integration of the human into the natural order continued to be a central focus of Chinese philosophical thought, especially of *daoist* thought associated with Lao-zu and Zhuang Zhou. According to Zhuang Zhou,

To recognize the ways of nature, and to understand how they must relate to the ac-tions of man: that is the goal. Understanding the ways of nature is brought about by nature itself, and the understanding of the [natural] action of man is attained by recognizing that which is knowable, and thankfully enjoying that which is inaccessible to man. To complete the years of life and not suffer an early death half-way along: these are the fruits of knowledge. (Unschuld 1985, 105)

The last of the passages cited from *The Book of Changes* suggests that, in some important sense, human morality is responsible for natural events. While other ancient civilizations may well have used basic metaphors from human social and economic activities in understanding the natural order, their members tended to turn this notion around when they thought explicitly about the relationship between the cosmic and the human. That is, humans were viewed as reflecting the cosmic order, rather than vice versa, so when there was a discussion of influences coming from one domain into another, other civilizations thought of those influences flowing from the cosmos into man. In Mesopotamia, for example, humans were subject to astral influences, and in Mesoamerica, the three human souls came into the body from the heavens, the earth, and the underworld. In China, on the other hand, at least for many purposes, the effects flowed the other way as we have already seen in the case of astral omens that reflected corruption in the court.

Before going much further we should discuss the meanings of some key terms, including the way (*dao*), yin, yang, and qi. In modern Western science, great effort is made to keep the meaning of every term univocal (having a single denotation and no connotations), but in ancient Chinese philosophy the emphasis seems to have been the reverse. That is, the goal was often to use terms to evoke awareness of a number of relationships in a pattern that reflects the early development of early Chinese writing. Here, for example, is one of Lao-tzu's discussions of what he called the way:

There is a thing confusedly formed,
Born before heaven and earth.
Silent and void
It stands alone and does not change
Goes round and does not weary,
It is capable of being mother of the world
I know not its name
So I style it "the way."

—(1963, 82)

In this passage, multiple and even contradictory images characterize the way as the progenitor of the cosmos. It is at once changeless and cyclically changing. It is born and gives birth, yet it is empty. But the way is also a process characterized by the alternation of yin and yang, as we have seen. Equally, it is the appropriate path to be followed by each entity in the cosmos. Above all, the way was a context dependent concept that usually implied nature or something natural as well as regular. For Lao-zu, humans followed the way when they submitted to the natural morality which distinguishes man from other creatures. Failing to act morally (i.e., failing to follow the *dao,* brought on both social and personal disaster in the form of disease).

Yin and yang began by referring to the shady and sunny sides of a hill or banks of a river, with no suggestion of a broader cosmological meaning, and those seem to be their principle meanings until the late fourth century B.C.E. (Lloyd 1996). Used in the *Book of Changes* and later, by Lao-zu and other *daoists,* however,

the relationship between *yin* and *yang* is one of mutual interdependence and reciprocity. Even when *yang* is at its strongest, *yin* begins to reassert itself: conversely, at the moment of maximum *yin, yang* already starts to reemerge. *Yin* and *yang* are opposites, for sure, but they are correlatives defined in terms of one another. They are aspectual and relational: what is *yin* in one regard may be *yang* in another. So far from mutually excluding one another; neither exists in isolation from the other. (Lloyd 1996, 121)

Among the best illustrations of this notion is the famous yin-yang symbol applied to the seasons (see Figure 7.1). At the winter solstice, which is in

Figure 7.1
Yin and Yang Applied to the Seasons. Nick Livingston.

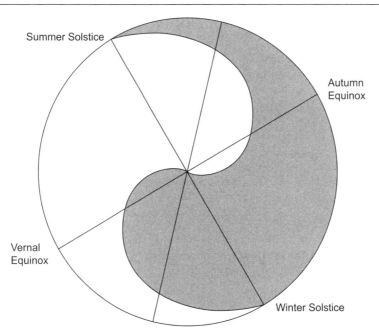

the shortest day of the year and the day in which dark lasts the longest, the day length begins to increase, and dark begins to retreat. Similarly at the summer solstice, which is in the longest day of the year and that in which light lasts the longest, the day length begins to decrease, and light begins to retreat.

From very early times, yin and yang became associated with many other pairs of corresponding notions. Thus, in a folk song that may go back to the very early first millennium, yin is identified with cold, clouds, rain, femininity, inside, and darkness. Yang then becomes associated with heat, sunshine, spring, summer, and masculinity. According to Paul Unschuld, when yin and yang enter philosophical discourse, "they no longer retain any specific meaning themselves; they function merely as categorizing symbols to characterize the two lines of correspondence" (1985, 56).

The term qi (sometimes written as ch'i) seems to have begun by meaning something like basic principle, without regard to whether the principle was immaterial or material. Thus, the *Zuo Zhuan*, an early Han text, identifies six qi as yin and yang, wind and rain, and dark and light (Yosida 1973). Up to around 300 B.C.E., qi was also used to designate almost anything which was what we might call vaporous, such as mist, fog, smoke, cloud forms, and even air and breath (Lloyd and Sivin 2002). In later Han, texts it is sometimes translated as breath, but, more generally, it seems to be the carrier of various qualities from place to place, still without clear identification as a material substance (Lloyd 1996).

In addition to *dao*, yin, yang, and qi there was one additional set of concepts associated with the term *wuxing* (the five phases), that became central to the dominant Han cosmological and medical thought. Though until recently the *wuxing* ideas were thought to be much older, evidence from tombs dated to 168 B.C.E. suggests that their full development came between that date and about 100 B.C.E. In *daoist* cosmology, the five phases, metal, wood, water, fire, and earth, are born out of the six qi, and from these the five flavors [sour, salty, acrid, bitter, and sweet] the five colors [green, yellow, crimson, white, and black], the five modes of music, and the five materials [metal, wood, water, fire, and earth—to confuse things, the same ideograms were used to designate both the five phases and the five materials] develop (Yosida 1973). Indeed, as in the case of yin and yang, the five phases came to stand, not for particular things or processes, but as symbols to signify lines of correspondence. So, for example, in the major Han medical text collection, the *Huang-di Nei-jing* texts from around 90 B.C.E., wood, fire, earth, metal and water correspond respectively to the liver, heart, spleen, lungs, and kidneys (Unschuld 1985).

Some Basic *Wuxing* Correspondences

Wood	Fire	Earth	Metal	Water
Spring	Summer	Late Summer	Autumn	Winter
East	South	Center	West	North

Liver	Heart	Spleen	Lungs	Kidney
Turquoise	Red	Yellow	White	Black
Jupiter	Mars	Saturn	Venus	Mercury
Sour	Bitter	Sweet	Acrid	Salty

Just as important as the five phases themselves was the idea that they were related to one another in several cycles, the two most important of which were the cycle of destruction and the cycle of generation (see Figure 7.2). In the cycle of destruction, "water overcomes fire, fire melts metal, metal—in the form of a knife, for instance,—overcomes wood; wood, in the form of a spade—overcomes soil [earth]; soil, as in a dike—subdues water" (Unschuld, 1985, 59). In the cycle of generation, on the other hand, "water produces plants and trees, that is, wood; wood brings forth fire; fire produces ash, that is, soil; soil brings forth metal; when heated metals produce steam, that is, water" (Unschuld, 1985, 59).

Figure 7.2
The *Wuxing* Cycles of Destruction and Generation. Nick Livingston.

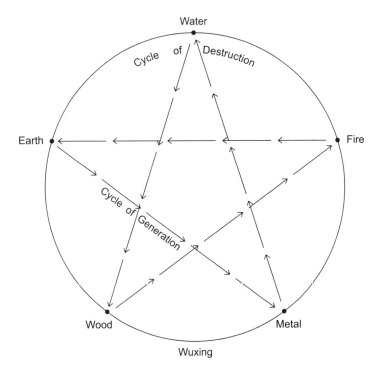

One final basic element completed the foundation for traditional Chinese theoretical medicine, that which posited the existence of vessels through which qi flows in the body. This notion did not play a significant role in broader cosmological discourse, but it did pre-date the *Huang di Nei-jing* texts (Unschuld, 1985) from which the following passage comes:

The Emperor asked: "I should like to hear which influence (*qi*) causes mans depots [i.e., organs] to suffer from sudden pain." *Qi Bo* replied: "the flow in the conduit vessels never stops; [it moves] in an annular circuit without a break. When influences of cold enter the conduits, [this flow] is retarded. [The contents of the conduits] congeal and do not move . . . As a result there is sudden pain." (Unschuld 1985, 75)

Although there is no evidence of systematic dissection being done in ancient China, the conduit vessels mentioned in this passage, through which qi flows in a circuit, may have been suggested by the blood vessels, lymphatic system, or nerves. It is, however, very clear that at least the most important set of 12 vessels was not identical with any of the physical vessels identified in Western medicine.

Up to this point, everything that I have considered regarding the cosmological foundation for Chinese medicine has been derived from *daoist* ideas, which focused on individuals and ignored society, but Confucianism, which focused on the conditions that would provide stability to the family and the state, was the favored philosophy in Han China, and the *Huang-ti nei-ching* texts incorporated Confucian ideas as well. Thus, in addition to the correlations between the organs and the five phases and yin and yang, the *Huang-ti nei-ching* texts posited a set of correlations between the organs and governmental offices:

The heart is the ruler, Spirit and enlightenment have their origin here. The lung is the minister; the order of life's rhythm has its origin here. The liver is the general; planning and deliberation have their origin here. The gall is the official [whose duty it is to maintain the golden] mean and what is proper; decisions and judgments have their origin here. The heart-enclosing network is the emissary; good fortune and happiness have their origin here. The spleen and stomach are officials in charge of storing provisions; the distribution of food has its origin here. The small intestine is the official charged with collecting surpluses; the reformation of all things has its origins here. The kidneys are officials for employment and forced labor; technical skills and expertise have their origin here. The triple burner[?] is the official in charge of transportation conduits; water channels have their origin here. The urinary bladder is the provincial magistrate and stores body fluids; once the influences [of the latter are exhausted through] transformation; they may leave [the bladder]. (Unschuld 1985, 100)

The *daoist* admonition to follow the way of natural morality fit well with the Confucian argument that the moral life conduces to the stability of family and state as well, so the syncretism of Confucianism and *daoism* has been amazingly stable. In no domain has this stability been greater than in connection with medicine. Individual Chinese philosophers in virtually every age have offered alternatives to this Confucian-*daoist* fusion, but in medicine, at least, the basic ideas have proven highly resilient and changes over time have involved details rather than challenges to the basic concepts.

Given all of the systematic correspondences mentioned above, several systems of treatment emerged. Suppose that a patient describes his condition as one involving the heart. The heart is associated with fire and heat, so an illness of the heart may be caused by an excess or a deficit of heat. If a deficit, it may be because the liver, which corresponds to wood, and which influences the heart in the generation cycle, is not supplying enough heat. In this case, the patient would be diagnosed as having a depletion evil, and a drug associated with wood and heat, or something correlated with wood and heat, would be prescribed. If, on the other hand, the heart was getting too much heat, that could be because the kidneys, associated with water and next to the heart in the cycle of destruction, was not providing enough cooling. In that case, the patient might be diagnosed as having a repletion evil, and a drug associated with water, or something corresponding to water, would be prescribed.

Alternatively, the illness might be caused by a blockage in the qi circulation system of 12 vessels, some of which were yin vessels, and some yang. In this case, a treatment that seems to have been newly developed after 168 B.C.E., though probably based on older empirical medicine, might be employed. This treatment was acupuncture or acumoxibustion, which involved either inserting thin needles at certain points in the body to eliminate the blockages in the system of conduit vessels (acupuncture) or the burning of an appropriate combustible material at the acupoint (acumoxibustion). Finally, the disease might be caused by external environmental influences, in which case the physician might choose among therapeutic options.

To decide which type of disease the patient had, the Chinese physician would use a combination of pulse diagnosis, visual inspection to determine color, interrogation of the patient, and so on. Just from the strength and rapidity of the pulse taken at the right (yang) wrist or the left (yin) and with different degrees of pressure, the Chinese physician, using another set of correspondences, believed that he could determine whether the illness was a depletion illness, a repletion illness, a yin illness or a yang illness, an illness caused by environmental factors, or an illness caused by qi blockage. Indeed, the pulse alone offered 30 different possible combinations (Jingfeng and Yan 2003) that could be expanded or refined using other signs.

Finally, the Chinese physician, like physicians almost everywhere else, suggested dietary advice to both prevent illness by providing an appropriate balance of yin and yang foods, hot and cold, sweet and sour foods, and foods associated with each of the five phases.

CLASSICAL GREEK PHILOSOPHY

Prior to the Christian era, when Platonic cosmology as represented in the *Timaeus* came to dominate Western thought, there was no single cosmological theory or medical theory that could be said to dominate in ancient Greece, probably in part because there was no central authority like the Chinese emperor or Egyptian pharaoh, capable of imposing his personal preference on intellectuals through the awarding or withholding of patronage. Moreover, as we saw in connection with mathematics in chapter 2, Greek philosophers sought to distinguish themselves as teachers of youth by differentiating their theories from those of their competitors. Because each major Greek philosophical perspective both drew from medical knowledge and shaped medical theory, here we briefly characterize the major philosophical schools from about 600 to 300 B.C.E. before turning to medical theories.

One of the topics discussed by the earliest Greek philosophers, the Milesians (600–550 B.C.E.), was what material the universe was composed of. According to the evidence that we have, Thales (whose career peaked around 585 B.C.E.), the first of the Milesians that we know of, argued that water was the first elemental principle, probably because water seemed necessary for the growth of plants and the survival of animals.

Anaximenes (first half of sixth century B.C.E.), one of Thales' students, argued that the first principle was air, and that by "felting" (i.e., compressing) with air, one could make a liquid, water; by compressing it more, one could make a solid, earth; and by expanding it, one could make fire. Anaximenes thus introduced into philosophical discourse, what seems to have been the set of four traditionally accepted basic substances: earth, water, air, and fire, and gave an account of how they came from a single first kind which justified qualitative change in terms of quantification.

Anaximander (first half of sixth century B.C.E.), who supposedly learned from both Thales and Anaximenes, insisted that the most primary substance was a kind of formless and limitless *Aperon,* out of which pairs of opposites emerged and into which they returned by mutual annihilation after they had played out their roles according to some kind of natural law that he likened to justice (Kirk and Raven 1963). In making this claim, he appealed to what we now call the principle of sufficient reason: since there is no reason for Anaximenes' decision to choose one element as more primary than another if they can be transformed into one another. He used this same reasoning to argue that the earth is suspended at the center of a spherical universe because it has no reason to go any particular direction if the universe is equally extensive in all directions.

Even at the end of the most creative period of Greek philosophical development in fourth century Athens, at least four major philosophical schools vied for prestige and authority. There was Plato's Academy, which promoted a cosmology that drew heavily from an earlier Pythagorean emphasis on mathematics and on the logical principles developed by Parmenides and his followers. According to Plato and his followers, the physical world was a kind of imperfect copy of a more perfect world of eternal and unchanging ideas created by a god whose goodness mandated that he create the world to reflect his own goodness as much as the imperfect materials that he had to work with (i.e., earth, water, fire, and air) would allow. It is important to note that Plato's god is anything but willful. Indeed, its sole function is to create an orderly cosmos in which everything takes place according to what would later be called natural law.

Plato's student, Aristotle, who came from a medical family, grounded his philosophy more empirically. For him and students in his school, the Lyceum, the most fundamental objects in the universe were the particular objects of our experience. We recognize similarities among classes of objects and create universal terms which stand for those classes. Thus, for Aristotle, we have experiences of many specific objects that have four feet, that bark, that are domesticated, and so on, and we create the term "dog" to include them all. For Plato, on the other hand, there is an ideal dog that has no physical existence (much as there is an ideal circle that has no physical existence), and the dogs of our experience are imperfect physical manifestations of this ideal. Like Plato, Aristotle argued that there is a small number of primary elements—earth, air, fire, and water—plus a special fifth essence or aether. We recognize the initial four primary categories because we experience two sets of opposed qualities that are capable of communicating themselves to objects that they contact. These are hot and cold (both hot bodies and cold ones are capable of making other objects take on their character) and wet and dry (both wet and dry objects can communicate their qualities by contact). Since our universal categories reflect the characteristics of experience, the two pairs of opposites can result in only four different kinds of things: hot-dry ones, which we call fire; cold-dry ones, which we call earth, hot-wet ones which we call air; and cold-wet ones, which we call water.

By imposing a change of one of the pairs of opposites on any one of these elements we can transform it into another. The world beneath the Moon is created out of the four fundamental elements, each of which has its natural place: earth nearest the center, water in a spherical shell beyond that, air outside of that, and fire outside of that. If the elements could not be transformed into one another, the sublunar world would be completely static. It is true that, generally speaking, earth is below water, which is below air, which is below fire, but because each element can be transformed into the others by appropriate changes of quality, physical processes take place. The creation of water in air, for example, leads to the falling of rain, or the creation of fire out of earthy materials such as wood, leads to the attempt of flames to rise upward to reach their natural place.

Because the heavenly bodies—the Sun, Moon, Planets, and stars move eternally and changelessly in their orbits, they must be made of a nontransformable element—the aether. When we ask why these heavenly substances move, we cannot appeal to a natural place theory, because they are already where they belong. As the result of a complex logical argument Aristotle argues that the heavenly bodies are moved by an unmoved mover outside the sphere of the fixed stars. Later Christians appropriated the characteristics of the unmoved mover for God.

In contrast with the cosmologies of Plato and Aristotle, each of which at least allowed for the possibilities of gods, the school of Epicurus

(341–270 B.C.E.), called the Garden, was openly hostile to religion. Indeed, for the Epicureans, the primary reason for studying the natural world was to avoid the fear created when humans thought that capricious gods rather than natural causes were responsible for events. Epicurus drew heavily from the earlier ideas of the atomist Democritus (b. 460 B.C.E.). For the early atomists, the world was made up of a huge number of unbreakable particles of various shapes and sizes that existed from the beginning. These particles were so small that they were individually invisible, and they moved in random directions in the void; but they tangled together into relatively stable configurations to create the objects of ordinary experience, including the heavenly bodies and inanimate and animate bodies on the Earth. Epicurus added the notion that the atoms move naturally downward and that they occasionally swerve very gently to create collisions which cascade into the same nearly randomized condition superimposed over the initial downward motion.

Epicurus and the early atomists and were deeply interested in the processes of sensation. They argued that bodies sloughed off surface layers of different kinds of atoms that traveled outward from the body. Some were shaped so that they fit into receptacles in the eye, creating vision, others produced sound, while others produced the sense of smell and of taste, with rounder atoms producing sweet tastes and sharper atoms producing bitter tastes.

The final major school in late fourth century Athens was that of the Stoics, whose place of assembly was called the Porch. For the Stoics, physical objects were composed of combinations of earth and water suspended in a gelatin-like substance called the *pneuma,* made of air and fire. Vibrations in the *pneuma* produced motion in the objects of the world much as waves in the sea created motion in the boats that rested upon it. Both sound and light were propagated as vibrations in the *pneuma.* These vibrations struck the ears and eyes, which were, in a sense, tuned to the appropriate frequencies. Furthermore, according to the later stoic philosopher Posidonius (135–51 B.C.E.), the tides were produced by tensions in the *pneuma* generated by the Sun and Moon.

GREEK PHILOSOPHICAL MEDICINE

Many of the Greek philosophers of the classical world were independently wealthy or they earned their living as teachers, but some of them turned their philosophizing to medical topics. Though we do not have copies of the texts, a list of the works of Democritus, for example, includes *On Flesh, On Diet, Medical Knowledge,* and *On Fever and Those Who are Made to Cough by Illness* (Jouanna 1999). Anaxagoras (500–428 B.C.E.), who was exiled from Athens for suggesting that the Sun was nothing but a burning mass about the size of the Peloponnesus, suggested that the basic seeds of all things were flesh, bone, and so on, which were mixed together in foods so that they could be separated out by the digestive system and sent to their appropriate places in the body (Kirk and Raven 1963).

A few philosophers were even trained as physicians, and they naturally turned some of their attention to medical topics. Empedocles (492–452 B.C.E.), for example, wrote on the process of respiration, arguing that we breathe in and out through the pores of the skin (Kirk and Raven 1963,). Hippon of Samos (who lived in the second half of the fifth century B.C.E.) resurrected Thales's theory that water was the primal substance and argued that illness is a consequence of an excess or deficit of moistness in the body, with death a consequence of extreme dehydration (Jouanna, 1999), and Diogenes of Apollonia (who lived during the first half of the fifth century B.C.E.), embraced the argument of his teacher, Anaximenes, that the primal element was air. He also explored the topic of human generation, claiming that the seed responsible for human reproduction was blood infused with air to create a warm, foamy material (Jouanna, 1999).

Much more important among the Presocratic philosophers (i.e., those who wrote before the time of Socrates, 469–399 B.C.E.) for the development of medical theory were two Pythagorean physicians, Alcmaeon and Philolaus of Croton (both of the late fifth century B.C.E.). Alcmaeon introduced to Greek medicine the idea that we have seen in connection with early medical theorizing elsewhere that health is a consequence of the proper balancing of opposed qualities—hot and cold, wet and dry, bitter and sweet, and so on (Jouanna 1999). Philolaus, on the other hand, introduced a theory that resembled the *Ayurvedic* notion that diseases are caused by the three *dosas.* For him, as for the *Ayurvedic* physicians, bile and phlegm were two of the humors whose imbalance in particular parts of the body were responsible for disease. But while the Indian theorists identified wind or breath as the third humor, Philolaus identified blood as his third (Jouanna 1999).

The similarities between the humoral theory of Philolaus and the theory of *dosas* among *Ayurvedic* physicians clearly suggests the possibility of interactions between the Greek and Indic traditions, and this suggestion is supported by a tradition that claims that Pythagoras, or Pythagoreans, visited India and drew some of their doctrines from Indian philosophy. However, several considerations stand in the way of taking this theory very seriously. First, there is no direct evidence of Pythagorean contact with India. Second, the doctrine of metempsychosis (the rebirth of souls up and down the hierarchy of organisms based on the morality of one's life in the present cycle), which has been used to support the notion of Indian sources for Pythagorean ideas, comes much more plausibly from Zoroastrian influences in Mesopotamia, from which the Pythagoreans also got their emphasis on music and the Pythagorean theorem, than from Indian sources. Third, there is a significant difference between the emphasis on blood in Philolaus and that on wind in the Indian theories. Finally, given the great difficulty of dating the Indian ideas and the relatively early date for Philolaus, if there was contact, the direction of influence is uncertain.

Regardless of the origins of the theoretical perspectives Alcmaeon and Philolaus offered, they were fused and modified by the late fifth-century Hippocratic author of *On the Nature of Man,* into a doctrine of four humors that would become the basis of something approaching an orthodoxy within Greek and subsequent Western theoretical medicine well into the early modern period. After an introductory critique of all medical theories that assert that there is a single primary substance, the author of *On the Nature of Man* puts forth his own theory:

The human body contains blood, phlegm, yellow bile, and black bile. These are the things that make up its constitution and cause its pains and health. Health is primarily that state in which these constituent substances are in the correct proportion to one another, both in strength and quantity, and are well mixed. Pain occurs when one of the substances presents either a deficiency or an excess, or is separated in the body and not mixed with the others. It is inevitable that when one of these is separated from the rest and stands by itself, not only the part from which it has come, but also that where it collects and is present in excess, should become diseased, and because it contains too much of the particular substance, cause pain and distress. Whenever there is more than slight discharge of one of these humors outside the body, then its loss is accompanied by pain. If, however, the loss, change, or separation from the other humors is internal, then it inevitably causes twice as much pain, as I said, for pain is produced both in the part whence it is derived and the part where it accumulates. (Hippocrates 1978, 262)

It may be that the doctrine of deficit and excess was derived from the Greek contact with Egyptian theoretical medicine, which is well established, or from India, but given the ubiquity of such theories of balance in independent traditions, that is not certain.

It is clear that the choice of four humors is at least justified in *On the Nature of Man* on the basis of empirical evidence. These are the four kinds of material evacuated from wounded or diseased persons in all seasons and by persons of every age, though diseases associated with the different humors are more common at different seasons and in different places. The seasonal and geographical differences probably suggested the qualitative characteristics of the four humors, which "are dissimilar in their qualities of heat, cold, dryness and moisture" (Hippocrates 1978, 263), because the seasons vary in temperature and rainfall as do different places. Phlegm is natural to winter because it is cold and damp; blood to spring because it is warm and wet; yellow bile is natural to summer, which is hot and dry; and black bile (cold and dry) is natural to autumn because it is the season during which coldness is increasing, but also during which the rains have not yet made the season wet (Hippocrates 1978). It follows from this notion that different diseases will be more common in different seasons and in places with differing climates.

Before going further in discussing theoretical medicine, I would like to point out a probable but unusual application of the microcosm-macrocosm analogy that we have seen in virtually all other civilizations. Aristotle, who was trained as a physician and well acquainted with the writings attributed to Hippocrates, who preceded him by about a century, almost certainly appropriated the theory of four fundamental humors defined by the four basic qualities of heat, cold, dryness, and wetness from the microcosm of human beings in formulating his macrocosmic theory of the nature of the sublunar world, for there, too, he posited four basic elements defined by the four possible combinations of hot, cold, wet, and dry.

As was the case in Egypt, Mesoamerica, China, and India, treatments for illnesses in Greece generally involved prescribing opposites. Thus:

Diseases caused by over-eating are cured by fasting; those caused by starvation are cured by feeding up. Diseases caused by exertion are caused by rest; those caused by indolence are cured by exertion. To put it briefly: the physician should treat disease by the principle of opposition to the cause of the disease according to its form, its seasonal and age incidence, countering tenseness by relaxation and vice versa. This will bring the patient most relief and seems to me to be the principle of healing. (Hippocrates 1978, 266)

The emphasis on diet and exercise in this passage is once again reflective of the gymnastic background of Hippocratic medicine mentioned in the discussion of Greek empirical medicine in chapter 6. Other treatments included the use of drugs and venesection, or bloodletting from a vein that serves the area in which the pain is found (Hippocrates 1978). Bloodletting was a common form of treatment in Greco-Roman antiquity and persisted in Western medicine well into the 20th century in spite of early modern attacks on its theoretical justification.

We have also mentioned that there was an important empirical element involved in the choice of the four humors discussed in *On the Nature of Man,* but there is evidence of many more extended and controlled observations—including observations on other animals and applied to humans—in other Hippocratic writings. Just as the early Presocratic philosophers seem to have been particularly fascinated with the origins of the universe, Greek physicians seem to have had a special interest in the origins of humans. One of the most extensive and detailed treatises among the Hippocratic writings is thus *On the Seed* (or *On Generation*) *and the Nature of the Child.* This work contains an extensive discussion of human embryology, but when it comes at last to provide a discussion of the evidence for its views, it provides the following discussion:

(If you accept the evidence which I am about to give) you will find the growth of the infant is, from the beginning to end exactly as I have described it in my discourse. If you take twenty or more eggs and place them to hatch under two or more fowls, and on each day, starting from the second right up to the day on which the egg is hatched, you take one egg, break it open, and examine it, you will find that everything is as I have described—making allowance of course for the degree to which one can compare the growth of a chicken with that of a human being. You will find, for instance, that there are membranes extending from the umbilicus—in fact, that in every point all the phenomena I have described in the human child are to be found in a chicken's egg also. (Hippocrates 1978, 341)

Aristotle took up the notion that one might learn about humans by studying other animals in a number of works on comparative anatomy and reproduction, and Galen (129–210 C.E.), working at Alexandria, based many of his claims about human anatomy on the dissection of the Barbary ape.

There is a second surprise in *On the Seed and the Nature of the Child* for anyone who has been exposed primarily to Aristotle's later and more often-discussed theory that the male sperm provides the form of the child, while the female egg provides only the passive matter. In the Hippocratic treatise, male and female seeds are given equal roles in determining the character of the child, and this claim is justified in terms of the observed characteristics of the children:

Sperm is a product which comes from the whole body of each parent, weak sperm coming from the weak parts and strong sperm from the strong parts. The child must necessarily correspond. If from any part of the fathers [*sic*] body a greater quantity of sperm is derived than from the corresponding part of the mother's body the child will, in that part, bear a closer resemblance to its father; and vice versa. The following cases however are impossible: (a) The child resembles its mother in all respects, and its father in none; (b) the child resembles its father in all respects, and its mother in none; (c) the child resembles neither parent in any respect. No: it must inevitably resemble each parent in some respect, since it is from both parents that the sperm comes to form the child. The child will resemble in the majority of its characteristics that parent who has contributed the greater quantity of sperm to the resemblance, and from a greater number of bodily parts. And so it sometimes happens that although the child is a girl she will bear a closer resemblance in the majority of her characteristics to her father than to her mother, while sometimes a boy will more closely resemble his mother. All these facts too may be regarded as evidence for my contention above, that both man and woman have male and female sperm. (Hippocrates 1978, 321–322)

Classical Greek medicine was certainly refined and given increasingly extensive evidentiary foundations through the works of comparative anatomy and physiology done by Aristotle, through the anatomical studies of Erasistratus and Herophilus (mid-third century B.C.E.) at Alexandria, and through the physiological speculations of Galen of Pergamon, who worked at Alexandria and later at Rome. The basic character of Greek philosophical medicine, however, was already formed in the Hippocratic corpus during the late fifth century B.C.E.

Eight

Construction Technologies:
Materials, Tools, and Fixed Structures

In this chapter, we will consider the technologies involved in building fixed structures—dwellings, water-control and delivery systems, roads, and monumental structures, including temples, funerary monuments, and public buildings. Since materials, tools, society, the environment, and design elements interact in complex ways to produce such structures, there is no single simple organizational structure that will allow this discussion to proceed without some temporal backing and filling, but an organization based on materials used seems to offer the greatest coherence and natural opportunities for comparisons.

BUILDING IN VEGETABLE MATERIALS:
WOODS, REEDS, AND FIBERS

Evidence from nearly all civilizations suggests that dwellings, at least, were first constructed out of wood or other vegetable materials, sometimes with flooring of packed earth, walls covered with mud daubed on a vegetable frame or with woven mats, and roofs of daub or thatch. Unlike the earlier moveable dwellings associated with pre-civilized groups, the earliest fixed dwellings of civilized peoples show little evidence of the use of animal hides, bone, or hide lashings.

Because organic materials decay relatively quickly except under extremely dry circumstances or under water where oxygen supplies are scarce, archeological evidence of wood and fiber construction is spotty. As a consequence, the reconstruction of vegetable based structures depends heavily on pictorial representations, on records that record the purchase or sale of materials, on unusual climatic conditions, and on the presumed continuation of ancient local building traditions into the present. Thus, we are generally less certain about aspects of building done primarily in fibers and wood than we are about building in less perishable materials. In fact, because of the hot-moist conditions prevailing in the territory inhabited by the Maya, we have virtually no knowledge of any vegetable material they might have used in construction.

Unsurprisingly, because climate was most favorable and artistic representation and record-keeping were most extensive in the Near East, we know the most about early vegetable–based construction in Egypt and Mesopotamia. In both places there is evidence of early structures made of bundled reeds. The evidence is primarily pictorial in Egypt and archeological in southern Mesopotamia, where the flooding of previously marshy areas has helped in preserving remains. In southern Iraq, 20th-century building patterns in marshy regions remained consistent with the evidence for the earliest reed structures. In both places, evidence of reed hut and larger-scale building goes back into the early fourth millennium B.C.E., prior to the development of writing and the development of metal tools.

In Mesopotamia, flooring was made of woven reed mats, and walls and ceilings were framed with bundles of reeds, which might have a diameter of 15–30 centimeters for a small dwelling and up to a meter for public structures, some of which spanned up to six meters and reached a height of five meters or more. Bundles were tied with fibers of vegetable material, woven to provide strength, and they were fashioned in an arch-like shape. In their modern incarnations, the arched framing elements are placed about two meters from one another and are connected with smaller (about 10–20 centimeters in diameter) horizontal bundles of reeds lashed to the arches with fiber. Then, the whole framework is covered in reed matting that can be rolled up from the bottom for ventilation. This construction allows for building structures of almost any length. Buildings' fronts and rears were usually flanked by tall reed columns that probably helped support the horizontal bundles that constituted the framing for the front and rear walls, but which also formed a kind of ornamentation. For long structures with intermediate partitions, columns were also provided on which to hang cross members to frame the partitions.

In Egypt, similar reed structures are suggested by the shapes of later temple architecture in other materials, which seems to mimic the forms of an original structure made of reeds. In addition, the existence of round reed- or palm branch-framed huts is depicted in wall paintings from around 3500 B.C.E. (Bradford 1954) to roughly 150 C.E. (Wright 2000), so the earliest known form of construction continued for building small light structures for over three millennia. In Egypt, the walls of reed- or palm-framed buildings were sometimes made of wattle (i.e., of a woven reed or small branch element lashed to the frame and then covered with mud), which was a common wall and roof structure in many places.

Elsewhere, such as in parts of China where reeds were not as easily available in large quantities, early building in wood usually involved round huts with slightly sunken, rammed earth floors up to about 16 meters in diameter. Four central posts surrounding a hearth supported a conical roof made of smaller poles, whose eaves came close to the ground, where they rested on short posts set close to one another. The roof was probably made of wattle tied to the rafter-like poles, a guess based on the clay residue scattered on the floor of excavated structures (Watson 1961). By the beginning of the Shang period, this round house structure had given way to a pattern in which relatively nar-

Figure 8.1
Wooden Post and Beam Construction Common for Dwellings in China, Greece, and Rome. Nick Livingston.

row (2–3 meters) and long (up to 10–20 meters) segments were built along three sides of a courtyard. Floors continued to be rammed earth, but now supporting posts, placed at a few meter intervals, were given stone footings. Beams supported by these posts, in turn, supported the rafters of a steep pitched roof, probably covered in thatch or wattle (Watson 1961) (see Figure 8.1). Evidence suggests that the same type of post and beam structure was used in Greece and Rome as well (Wright 2000), while lighter wattle structures were predominant in India between the Harappan period and the second rise of cities, beginning around 600–400 B.C.E., when brick became common for urban houses (Allchin 1995).

Throughout the Near East, India, and Mesoamerica, when the use of mud brick became common for the construction of bearing walls, wood continued to be used to support the flat roofs of almost all dwellings (see Figure 8.2). Unshaped logs on the order of 10–20 centimeters in diameter and set on approximately 30-centimeter centers spanned up to 5 meter spaces in Egypt, with smaller spans of less than 3 meters in Mesopotamia. (As a general rule, the dwellings of ordinary Egyptian workers' homes were substantially larger than those of their Mesopotamian counterparts.) These were either laid on the top of the brick walls or set into notches, probably depending on the wealth of those for whom the structure was built. On top of these beams, a layer of small sticks placed very close to one another was laid at right angles to the beams, and on top of the sticks, a layer of reeds or palm fronds was placed to provide an almost watertight layer. Finally, a top dressing of 10–25 centi-meters of mud was added, though this was replaced in Mesoamerica by a thin-ner layer of cement made from burnt, crushed shells and sand after around 200 B.C.E. (Wright 2005b). Wooden ladders gave access to the roof, where fami-lies spent much of their time except during the hottest parts of summer days. In Egypt, India, and Mesoamerica, one usually entered the dwelling through a door at ground level, but in the large Mesopotamian cities, roof holes often provided the only entry. Windows or additional ventilation openings in ordi-nary people's dwellings were a rarity.

Unshaped poles have continued to be used to support the roofs of small houses throughout the Near East and Central America into the present, but as soon as metal tools became available, wrought timber and plank construction began almost everywhere for more substantial structures. We will wait until chapter 10 to discuss the development of metal mining, smelting, and form-ing, which made metal tools possible. Here, we focus on evidence for their pres-ence and use. The earliest evidence for timber squared off with the use of tools comes from a model house found in late pre-dynastic Egypt (c. 3400 B.C.E.). This model includes the representation of a squared off timber door frame. Dynasty I royal tombs (c. 3200 B.C.E.) included squared timber roof beams spanning up to six meters and wall planks 7–10 centimeters thick and up to a meter wide. Moreover, plank construction was used for some housing as well. Vertical planks between 1.8 and 2.5 meters long, approximately 30 centi-meters wide, and 3–5 centimeters thick, were overlapped and lashed to one another. As was the case with reed structures, these plank structures were soon imitated in other materials, including mud brick.

Pictures from Egyptian tombs as early as the third dynasty (c. 2600 B.C.E.) show wood cutters felling trees by notching them with copper axes, and sixth dynasty (c. 2400 B.C.E.) drawings depict Egyptian carpenters creating planks by splitting trimmed logs along the grain with a wedge and lever (Wright 2005b). Local wood resources were rapidly depleted in the Nile Valley, and wood frame construction soon gave way to mud brick construction for ordinary dwellings, but the flat roofs of dwellings in which mud brick formed the bearing walls continued to be supported by wooden beams because wood has far greater strength under shearing stress than other building materials (excluding metal). The latter was not used for massive structural purposes until the 19th cen-tury C.E., though it was used in Classical Greece to reinforce wood, brick, and stone lintels over window and door openings and to support cantilevered stone cornices (Wright 2005a).

By early dynastic times, most timber had to be imported into Egypt from Lebanon, Macedonia, Corsica, and the Alpine regions, and records of quanti-ties delivered and held in stock in early Pharaohnic timber yards have also been found (Wright 2005a). Large timbers were also transported into Mesopotamia for supporting roofs and for reinforcing brick structures. For Mesopotamia, we not only have records of transactions, but we also have pictorial evidence of the water transport of timber both as deck cargo and as logs floated behind ships (Wright 2005b).

Figure 8.2
Brick Flat-Roofed Dwelling Common in Mesopotamia, Egypt, Harappan
Civilization, and Mesoamerica. Nick Livingston.

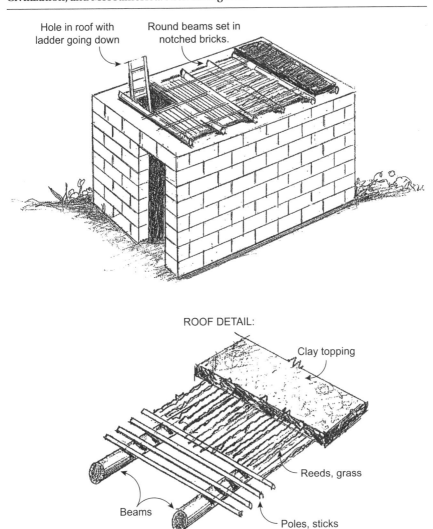

Soon after shaped timber began to be used in construction, lashing was replaced by a variety of methods for joining, including simple notching of crossed
pieces, mortices and tenons for corners and longitudinal joints, and pegs or
dowels for securing many joints. Nails were not used until Roman times, when
wood was widely used for constructing temporary forms for concrete. All of

Figure 8.3
Methods of Spporting Greek Temple Roofs. Nick Livingston.

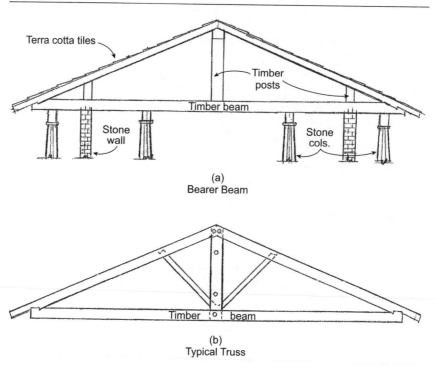

(a)
Bearer Beam

(b)
Typical Truss

the joins used in pre-Roman antiquity demanded the use of increasingly spe-cialized tools. Pictorial evidence for saws and drills applied to wood appears in early New Kingdom Egypt (c. 1300 B.C.E.), but evidence for the use of saws in quarrying soft stone(e.g., limestone and sandstone) dates back to around 2500 B.C.E., as does the use of drills. Collections of woodworking tools includ-ing bronze-headed axes, saws, adzes, chisels, augers, and bow-drills also come from the New Kingdom's 18th Dynasty (c. 1300 B.C.E.) (Wright 2005b). By this time, all of the handheld woodworking tools available to early modern Euro-pean carpenters and cabinetmakers were present except for the plane, which Romans created to replace the multipurpose adze for leveling wood surfaces.

The final major use of wood for building fixed structures in ancient civiliza-tions was developed in the construction of monumental temples in Greece, starting around 600 B.C.E.. There, as we shall see, stone was used for bearing walls and in columns that served both as weight-bearing elements and for or-namentation. However, the ceilings and low pitched roofs of the temples were supported by wooden frames. Initially, massive beams spanned the temple width, and short vertical posts rose from these beams to support the rafters and horizontal wood framing, which in turn supported the roofing material (usually terra cotta tiles). Around 400 B.C.E., this bearer beam system was supplemented with and replaced by a system of trusses, which took advantage of the rigidity of triangles, allowing the weight of the roof to be distributed across all elements of the truss, including the rafters and posts as well the horizontal beams (see Figure 8.3). This system allowed for the use of beams with smaller cross sections to provide the same strength.

BUILDING IRRIGATION SYSTEMS IN UNMODIFIED EARTH AND RUBBLE

Though we have said that the earliest cities, especially in Mesopotamia, Egypt, and, probably, India and China, were associated with floodplain agriculture and with irrigation practices, virtually nothing is known about the construction of the earliest irrigation systems from archeological evidence. The dikes, dams, and canals that constituted them were almost certainly created by piling up or digging out the local natural soil, which was earth mixed with occasional deposits of gravel or stones (rubble). When it was time to let water in or out of a canal or field, the irrigation manager simply ordered some worker or workers to dig a ditch through the dike or canal wall, or the water was lifted out of the canal using a *shaduf.*

Shown on Mesopotamian cylinder seals from as early as 2400 B.C.E., *shadufs* were used throughout the ancient world by around 1500 B.C.E. They involved a leather or woven fiber bucket suspended by a rope from one end of a pole. The pole, which had a counterweight on the opposite end, was balanced over a horizontal member supported by wood or brick posts. A worker dipped the bucket into a canal, lifted it over the bank with the help of the counterweight, and dumped it into the field or garden being irrigated. In this manner, a single worker might move up to 600 gallons of water per day.

Over time, the earthen structures of ancient irrigation systems filled in with silt or washed away in floods, leaving very little trace. Evidence for the early existence and importance of irrigation systems thus comes largely from written records, including law codes, administrative records, from pictorial representations including local maps (Drower 1954), and from the titles of government officials, who were responsible for building and/or maintaining the irrigation systems. The principal government officers in each Egyptian Nome, for instance, included an "inspector of the dykes," and a "chief of the canal workmen." (Smith 1975, 11). Letters from Hammurabi, king of Babylonia (c. 1780 B.C.E.) include commands to the governors at Larsa and Erech to clear canals to allow for boat traffic, and the code of Hammurabi contains the following passages regarding the care of irrigation works:

If a man neglect to strengthen his dyke and do not strengthen it, and a break be made in his dyke and the water carry away the farm-land, the man in whose dyke the break has been made shall restore the grain which he has damaged.

If he be not able to restore the grain, they shall sell him and his goods and the farmers whose grain the water has carried away shall share (in the proceeds from the sale).

If a man open his canal for irrigation and neglect it and the water shall carry away an adjacent field, he shall measure out grain on the basis of the adjacent fields.

If a man open up the water and the water carry away the improvements of an adjacent field, he shall measure out ten GUR of grain per GAN. (Smith 1975, 10)

However, the most important evidence regarding irrigation comes indirectly from the rapid increases in crop yields produced on irrigated land and the attendant growth of population densities (Drower 1954).

Only after irrigation systems had been in use for two millennia or more in Egypt and Mesopotamia were earthen dams and canals faced with water resistant materials to prevent erosion. We read, for example, from the Babylonian King Nebuchadrezzar I (who reigned c. 1146–1123 B.C.E.):

I had a mighty dyke of earth thrown up, . . . from the bank of the Tigris to that of the Euphrates 5 *beru* [26.6 kilometers] long, and I surrounded the city with a great expanse of water, with waves on it like the sea, for an extent of 20 *beru*. That the pressure of water should not damage this dyke of earth I fashioned its slope with bitumen and brick. (Drower 1954, 555)

Assyrian King Sennacherib (c. 690 B.C.E.) built a canal nearly 12 meters wide and 60 kilometers long lined with limestone. Portions of this canal, including a 300-meter-long aqueduct bridge supported by five corbelled arches, still survive (Smith 1975).

Nebuchadrezzar's dikes and waterworks were intended more to provide a defensive barrier than to conduct water from one place to another, and the use of huge earthwork ramparts fronted by ditches, whether water-filled or dry, is attested at numerous sites in India as well from around 1400–600 B.C.E. (Allchin 1995).

THE USE OF UNMODIFIED EARTH AND RUBBLE IN DWELLINGS AND MONUMENTAL STRUCTURES

In both Egypt and Mesopotamia, earth was used from before around 5000 B.C.E. in the form of rammed earth walls for dwellings and storage structures. Temporary wooden forms were constructed, and wet earth was compacted within them. Typically, this procedure was done in courses less than 50 centimeters high so that a lower course was allowed to dry before another course was added. Early structures in China also used rammed earth for foundations and for the lower portions of walls.

Earth and rubble were also used in two additional ways in connection with monumental architecture. In Egypt, Mesopotamia, and Mesoamerica, power and permanence seem to have been represented by size. In Mesopotamia during Sumerian times (to around 2000 B.C.E.), temple compounds were sited at the tops of artificial mountains called ziggurats. The bases of these structures were huge—one constructed at Ur around 2000 B.C.E. has a base of 72 by 52 meters (Lloyd 1954,), a little larger in area than an American football field. Up to seven levels of earth and rubble, each around 10 meters high and faced with

Figure 8.4
Block & Tackle. Nick Livingston.

(a) Double Mechanical Advantage, Half Speed.
(b) Triple Mechanical Advantage, One-Third Speed.

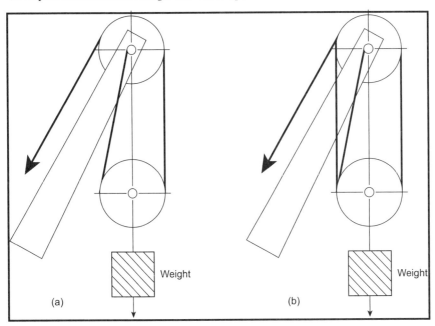

retaining walls of other materials (discussed below), were stepped upward to provide the place for the temple or temple compound, which was reached by massive ramp-like stairways filled with earth and rubble and faced with brick or stone. Because earth and rubble transmit lateral stresses that can cause high retaining walls to bow when the fill becomes wet and plastic, the Sumerian ziggurat builders incorporated drains that carried water out of the fill through holes in the walls, and they created large, woven reed cables running through the fill at several levels to bind opposite walls to one another in a way that reminds one of the way that metal cables are used to stress concrete in modern structures (Lloyd 1954).

In Greece and Mesoamerica, temples and collections of monumental structures were sited on raised platforms of earth and rubble, sometimes several meters high and faced and paved with brick or stone. In early Pharaohnic Egypt, before the construction of pyramids began around 2650 B.C.E., massive funerary structures (*mastabas*) were created by imbedding tombs in brick or stone-faced platforms several meters high. Sometimes *mastabas* were carved out of rock, but often, as at Saqqara, they were made primarily of earth and rubble fill. When pyramid building began, earth and rubble continued to be used as fill, stabilized by the use of compartments to reduce horizontal stresses.

Finally, the construction of monumental buildings faced with stone was made possible by the use of earthen ramps that provided the ways along which massive stones were skidded to raise them to the level at which they were needed. The ramps were then removed when the buildings were completed. This method of raising large stone blocks lasted from when stone became a favored material for monumental construction around 2600 B.C.E. in Egypt to around 600 B.C.E., when the block and tackle using pulleys (see Figure 8.4) was invented in Greece.

BUILDING IN BRICK AND CONCRETE

Though tamped earth (*piste*) remained in use for some time for rough and small buildings, it was soon overtaken by the most ubiquitous building material in the ancient world—mud brick. Initially hand formed, by around 5200 B.C.E. bricks of earth mixed with binding materials such as straw were made in Mesopotamia by packing the wet material into molds and letting them dry in the sun (Wright 2000). The size and shape of bricks varied from place to place—in Egypt, most were square and relatively flat (about 30 cm square and 8 cm thick), while in both Mesopotamia and the Harappan civilizations they tended to be rectangular, with the length twice the width and the thickness about one half of the width, but brick became the standard material for constructing load-bearing walls or for facing walls constructed of earth and rubble (and later, in Rome, of cement) in almost every ancient civilization—Mesopotamian, Egyptian, Harappan, Greek, Roman, and Mesoamerican.

In some civilizations, such as in Egypt, Greece, Rome, and among the Maya, monumental public building was done in dressed stone after a period of wood or brick construction, but even in these civilizations, private dwellings, including those of the most wealthy people, were always or often done in brick. Moreover, in the Mesopotamian and Indian civilizations even the largest and most sacred buildings continued to be made primarily of brick until foreign building technologies partially supplanted indigenous ones around 650 B.C.E. in Mesopotamia and around 300 C.E. in India. Similarly, brick remained the almost universal material for constructing city walls and other fortifications virtually everywhere once its use began. In these structures, walls might be up to 10 meters thick. In China, brick was sometimes used to fill in walls between weight-bearing posts in dwellings and was the load-bearing material in such massive structures as the Great Wall, which was begun before the beginning of the Han Dynasty.

In early mud brick construction, bricks were either simply placed on one another without mortar, or the mortar between bricks was made of the same mud as the bricks, but in a plastic (wet) condition. Even where mud mortar was used, it tended to lose strength and crumble over time, so to help stabilize mud brick walls against either vertical or horizontal slippage, builders occasionally embedded long horizontal and vertical timbers in the wall. Most free-standing defensive walls were made very thick, in part to keep them from tipping over; however, a unique way of stabilizing relatively thin brick walls was developed in Middle Kingdom Egypt, where walls about a meter thick and with roughly sinusoidal (i.e., wavy) footprints were used (Dumas 1969).

By around 3000 B.C.E., a soft pulverized limestone called *huwwar* and featuring very strong adhesive characteristics was used along with sand to produce mortar in Mesopotamia, and by 2500 B.C.E., crushed limestone was being burnt to produce quick-lime, which was combined with water and sand to create what we call cement mortar. At roughly the same time, gypsum was being burnt to create the basis for what we call plaster-based mortars. Both lime and gypsum had been crushed and heated since late Neolithic times (c. 8000 B.C.E.), for use in floors, for plastering walls, and for sculpting. These uses continued, but after 3000 B.C.E. their use in mortar for construction became increasingly frequent. Since gypsum deposits are relatively common in Mesopotamia, and because gypsum can be chemically modified at below 752° Farenheit while limestone must reach nearly 1,652° F, gypsum-based mortar was used in Mesopotamia before limestone-based mortar was used elsewhere. In Mesoamerica, lime was produced beginning around 250 B.C.E. by burning marine shells. Mixed with sand, it was used as mortar to hold together both bricks and small stones as well as to stucco the exposed surfaces of both brick and small stone walls (Dumas 1969).

Unburned gypsum and limestone also have moderate adhesive qualities, and they were used with rubble to form a weak concrete-like material in Mesopotamia and Egypt. Only during the Roman period did concrete made with burnt lime become common for use in walls, roofs, and other structures, and then it was almost always faced with stone in public buildings. Roman cement construction allowed wealthy Romans to construct large blocks of residential apartments, sometimes up to five stories high, for occupancy by the working poor of Rome. Built with private capital amassed from imperial activities, these buildings were usually faced with burnt brick. They were often shoddily constructed, creating the first modern slums and slumlords.

Doorways and other openings in brick walls were initially spanned by timber or stone lintels because brick has virtually no resistance to shear, but the use of corbelled arches and vaults in which a small portion of one brick extends beyond those of the course below, moving outward from each side of the opening to meet in the middle, was well established in both Egypt and Mesopotamia by around 3000 B.C.E., and arches using wedge-shaped brick followed shortly except in Mesoamerica, where corbelled arches were never superseded during Pre-Columbian times. True arches, as opposed to corbelled arches, offered greater flexibility in size and shape, but had to have a temporary framework centering until the topmost brick, corresponding to the keystone in stone arches, was in place. Alternatively, arches were produced by wedge-shaped bricks laid on one another at some angle between the horizontal and the vertical to create barrel-like vaults without the need for temporary supports. Multilayered vaults in which a tilted-arch vault was used to center vertical-arched vaults were used to roof tombs as early as First Dynasty Egypt (c. 3000 B.C.E.).

In at least three civilizations, the Harappan, the Mesopotamian, and the Mesoamerican, ordinary, sun-dried brick, which became plastic and crumbled under damp conditions, was chemically transformed into a waterproof material beginning around 3000 B.C.E. in Mesopotamia, from the initial presence of Harappan culture around 2800 B.C.E., and in Mesoamerica from around 200 C.E. These bricks were made by baking ordinary mud bricks at temperatures from 1,112° F to 1,652° F. This burnt or baked brick was used wherever waterproofing was necessary (e.g., in foundations, in the lower courses of walls that were subject to occasional flooding, in the linings of canals and sewers, in baths, and in water storage structures). It was also frequently used in regular mud brick structures in the construction of arches and vaults, where its resistance to shearing stress and to crumbling under compression was advantageous (Wright 2005a). In Mesopotamia, burnt brick was usually associated with bitumen-based mortar because bitumen was plentiful, strongly adhesive, and waterproof. Because of the extra cost of producing burnt brick, especially where fuel for baking was scarce, it was rarely used anywhere except in special circumstances and was virtually unknown in Egypt before Roman times.

One striking application of burnt brick was made by the Assyrians in Mesopotamia. The walls of Assyrian monumental structures were frequently ornamented with reliefs of many kinds. The reliefs were carved in soft clay or mud, laying on the ground. Cuts were then made to separate the pictures into small blocks, and the blocks were then baked into burnt bricks and reassembled on the walls with mortar backing.

One special form of baked brick material, terra cotta, deserves mention because of its specialized uses almost everywhere. Terra cotta, or fine fired clay, was almost certainly used initially for pottery, but the fact that it could be fashioned into relatively strong, thin shapes and molded easily into specialized shapes made it especially valuable for flooring tiles, roofing tiles, window-like inserts in brick walls, covers for sewers, toilet seats, and eventually, in Roman times, for the construction of water mains and flues for carrying hot air in heating systems.

Terra cotta screens were used in lieu of windows for ventilation in the larger and wealthier dwellings in Mesopotamia as early as around 2000 B.C.E. Terra cotta drain pipes made of sections of tube about 52 centimeters long and about 15–20 centimeters in diameter, with slightly diminished radius at the downslope end to fit into a slightly larger radius on the up-slope end were already being used late in the third millennium B.C.E. in Mesopotamian septic systems. Moreover, terra cotta slabs with a central hole and shaped foot emplacements, much like the ceramic latrine floors still to be found in Europe, have been excavated in India (Allchin 1995). However, terra cotta became an important primary building material in Greece, India, and China only after 600 B.C.E., where its major use was in the form of roofing tiles on lightly pitched roofs.

Though shapes and sizes differed from place to place, the basic form used in Greece for roofing both dwellings and temples was a 60-centimeter square about 2–3 centimeters thick. This square had slightly raised edges on the sides

Figure 8.5
A Terra Cotta Tile Roofing System. Nick Livingston.

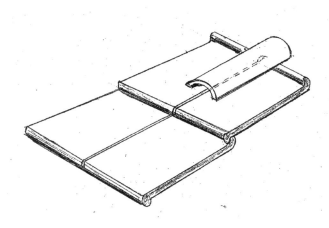

to send rainwater running downward through the center. Tiles were over-lapped, with the bottom edge of the higher course of tiles covering the top edge of the lower course. In order to avoid slipping, a groove was formed in the bottom of each tile parallel to the lower edge and a bead that fit into the groove was built into the top near the upper edge of each tile. Seams between tiles were covered with much narrower domed tiles (see Figure 8.5).

Terra cotta pipes began to be used in water distribution and waste disposal systems as early as 600 B.C.E. in Athens. They were carried throughout the Mediterranean Basin during the Hellenistic period and became central to the massive water distribution system in Rome, where they tended to be used for the large mains, while lead piping was used to deliver water to individual homes (Wright 2005b).

BUILDING IN STONE

Stone had been used by very early pre-civilized cultures for the construction of massive, mound-shaped structures covered with earth and for such monuments as Stonehenge, but the use of dressed stone obelisks and masonry was an Egyptian innovation around 2600 B.C.E.. Stone was apparently chosen for monumental funerary structures because of its extreme durability. These monuments were intended for eternity, and nothing less than stone would do if time and money were available.

Two different techniques of building in stone were developed in Egypt. The first, associated with the funerary *mastaba* and step pyramids of the third dynasty pharaoh Zozer (c. 2600 B.C.E.), used relatively small blocks of soft limestone, squared up and dressed to uniform size on one side only. These blocks,

which could be carried by an individual human, were basically used as a fa-
cade to cover the vertical, or nearly vertical, faces of the rock and rubble filled
mastabas, including the six *mastabas* of decreasing size that formed the step
pyramid. Behind the squared face, each block tapered inward so that, behind
the surface of finely dressed masonry, there was a thick layer of limestone rubble that filled in between the stones, acting like mortar because of the adhesive properties of crushed limestone. The blocks were quarried near Saqqara,
where they were used, and depictions indicate that metal (copper) picks,
adzes, and chisels were used in the quarrying and dressing processes. At times,
the very close fit of blocks was achieved by placing roughly dressed blocks on
one another and running a saw down the seam to remove protrusions on the
two facing sides (Wright 2000). This small block method of building in stone
spread throughout the Mediterranean Basin by 1500 B.C.E., probably by traveling Egyptian stone masons. Stone-based monumental architecture developed
in India with its own spectacularly ornate style, but this did not happen until
the period of the Maurian Empire, around 400–200 B.C.E., when contact with
Egypt was well established. Similarly, stone-based monumental building was
very rare in China until after the Han period.

Within less than a century after 2600 B.C.E., a new method of building in
stone had been developed in Egypt, one that incorporated massive monolithic
pillars, columns, and bearing walls as well as facades constructed of blocks up
to several meters long, weighing many tons, and faced on at least five sides.
Moreover, these blocks were often irregularly shaped, so dressing to make
them join precisely had to be done on site, rather than at the quarry. Typically
the quarries that produced these massive blocks, pillars, and columns were
at great distances from the construction sites. Blocks were often carried from
the quarry to the river, or more often to a canal dug toward the quarry from the
river, down earthen ramps on large wooden sledges, or they were slung from
the axles of huge wheels or the blocks themselves formed an axle to which
large wheels were affixed. For very large blocks, for columns, and for obelisks,
the wheels from which the stone piece was hung were often set wide enough
to span the canal. A boat loaded with ballast was floated under the stone object, and as the ballast was removed, the boat floated up until it was carrying
the load. At the riverside near the construction site, the process was simply
reversed, with the earthen ramp carrying the block to the level at which it was
needed.

The first stone dressed on several sides to be quarried for use in monumental construction was granite from deposits near Aswan. Among the hardest
and most difficult to prepare of all rocks used in monumental building, granite was quarried by first preparing a flat horizontal face in a bedrock deposit.
Next, the outline of the block to be removed was marked on the top of the bed.
Then, the marked channels were pounded out by crushing the granite with
harder, diorite balls about 15–20 centimeters in diameter. The block was then
removed by pounding out holes about 10 centimeters wide on 15-centimeter
centers at the appropriate depth along the horizontal face, inserting metal
wedges, and tapping them to separate the top block from its bed, or inserting

wooden wedges and wetting them so their expansion split the top block out. Square cross-sectioned needle-like obelisks up to 30 meters high and 2.5 meters on a side at the base, as well as large rectangular blocks, were quarried in this way and dressed using hard, stone-headed tools.

Though the irregular shapes of the blocks used in large-block construction certainly helped to limit lateral movement, techniques were developed almost immediately to make certain that the blocks did not move relative to one another. Sometimes holes were drilled at matching points in the upper surface of one block and in the lower surface of the block above and a dowel of appropriate length linked the two blocks. To restrict lateral motion, butterfly notches, narrow where they met at a joint and broadening out as they were cut into the blocks, were cut in the top surface of adjacent blocks in the same course, then wood or copper rods, or cramps, were laid in them, or molten lead was poured into the notches to clamp the blocks together (Wright 2005a). The great monuments for which Egypt is best known today, the temples at Thebes, Karnack, Edfu, and Denderech, for example, as well as the great pyramids at Giza, were all constructed using this large-block method, which lasted in Egypt until the period of Roman rule.

No other civilization appropriated the large-block construction technique in its entirety, but many of its features were adopted and adapted by the Greeks for their monumental temple construction around 600 B.C.E., and Greek techniques were sometimes appropriated and refined by the Romans. Like Egyptian large-block masonry, classical Greek masonry used stones dressed on all sides and doweled and cramped in the same way to provide stability. Furthermore, the Greeks adapted the Egyptian use of stone columns to create the colonnades that were a common feature of Greek temple architecture, but the Greeks used stone blocks of more moderate size than their Egyptian counterparts—usually less than a ton—and rather than forming their columns out of single blocks of stone, they stacked smaller stone drums on one another to produce columns. The smaller masses allowed the Greeks to raise their stone blocks into place with their newly invented block and tackle cranes, which used multiple pulleys to gain mechanical advantage. There are no surviving Greek block and tackles, nor are there known Greek depictions of their use. Instead, we infer their use from the notches in blocks that were almost certainly used to hold the ropes affixed to the block and tackle system and which correspond to the notches in Roman stones that were depicted as being lifted with multiple pulley cranes. Additionally, there is no evidence of the kind of earthwork ramps needed to move large-blocks, nor were Greek masonry blocks small enough to be lifted without some mechanical device.

Mesoamerica saw a unique tradition of construction in stone that paralleled the Egyptian small block tradition, with minor variants. The basic bearing walls of Mayan monumental architecture, including both temple and pyramidal structures, were built of small stones bonded with mud, occasionally interrupted with large but thin horizontal stone slabs to provide stability. These walls were either faced with cement composed of gravel and lime and then a layer of stucco using only sand and lime, or they were faced with dressed stone blocks larger than bricks, but small enough to be manipulated by a single strong person. Unlike the Egyptians, the Maya dressed all sides of their small stone blocks, but they did not make them all with square or rectangular faces. Many were trapezoidal, and some had other polygonal shapes that fit together to cover the wall (Dumas 1969).

ROMAN ROADS, AQUEDUCTS, AND HEATING SYSTEMS

Other civilizations, including those of the Babylonians, Chinese, and Assyrians, built roads and paved segments of them with flat stones. Other civilizations, including that of the Assyrians in Mesopotamia, built aqueducts to transport water over long distances. Still other civilizations, including the Harappan, constructed covered sanitation systems and public and private baths as well as systems to heat them. The Romans, however, were by all odds, the most outstanding engineers of antiquity. They borrowed techniques from almost everyone with whom they came into contact and produced new innovations as well, so their roads, water supply systems, public baths, and heating systems were more extensive and more complex than those of any other ancient civilization. Furthermore, they were better documented. In his *Ten Books on Architecture,* the Roman writer Vitruvius (c. 50–26 B.C.E.) provided the first general manual of civil engineering, explaining virtually all known construction technologies. Moreover, Sextus Julius Frontinus (c. 30–104 C.E.), the administrator of the Roman water supply around 97 C.E., furnished us with a detailed account of the construction, maintenance, monitoring, and financing of the Roman water supply system of his time in *On the Water Supply of Rome.*

In order to facilitate the rapid movement of troops to quell rebellions among their Latin neighbors and sometime allies, the Romans constructed the Appian Way in 312 B.C.E.. This was the first segment of what was eventually to become a network of more than 89,280 kilometers of major roadways between 5 and 10 meters wide and 200,000 kilometers of narrower, secondary roads throughout the Roman Empire (Dumas 1969). Main roads were slightly crowned and provided with drainage ditches on both sides. They were typically paved in several layers, beginning with a base layer of sand about 10 centimeters thick. This base was covered with a thin mortar layer and then by a layer of stone and brick rubble set in cement, followed by a layer of crushed rock in cement. Finally, all of this was topped by a layer of stone cobbles set in mortar. Bridges were constructed where necessary, and tunnels up to a kilometer long were dug through mountainous terrain to maintain a moderate slope and a relatively constant direction (Dumas 1969). Some of these roadways were so well constructed that they still carry traffic between small towns in Britain and in continental Europe.

Though Rome contained springs and wells adequate to supply water to its population in its early days, by 312 B.C.E. the population of over 100,000 needed additional water, especially because the Romans were probably the most profligate water users in history, with a per capita water use nearly 10 times that of a typical American urban dweller at the beginning of the 21st century. Romans around 300 C.E. used nearly 400 million liters of water per day in their 11 public baths, 1,352 public fountains, and 856 registered private fountains (Humphrey 2006). Already, by the time of Frontinus, with the population nearing 1 million persons, up to 200 million liters of water per day were supplied by 247 different holding tanks at high sites in Rome (Forbes 1955). These tanks were, in turn, supplied by 9 aqueducts between 12 and 86 kilometers in length.

Each aqueduct drew water from a spring, lake, or river source. Water from the source was allowed to enter a large settling tank or tanks in which the sediment it might carry was allowed to settle out. Near the top of the tank, a sluice was opened to allow water to enter the aqueduct when needed. With a few exceptions to be mentioned soon, the cross section of an aqueduct channel was a rectangle with an area between one and six square meters (over time, aqueducts generally became larger). The channel was made up of burned brick or stone set in and surfaced with mortar on the inner floor and two sides, and was covered with terra cotta or stone slabs that could be removed for maintenance. In order to keep the flow within the aqueducts at an acceptable rate, a nearly constant slope of one part in 2,000 was maintained. Part of the length of each aqueduct was below the level of the hills between the water source and Rome, and when this was the case the aqueduct was tunneled through the hill using the same techniques as those used to construct the ancient Near Eastern qanaats. Tunneling began from both sides of the hill and was guided either by line of sight from a ridge that had views of both ends or by using simple geometry to establish both the vertical and horizontal angles of attack, and access holes were cut up to the surface about every 75 meters (Humphrey, et al. 1998). Of the nearly 440 kilometers of aqueducts delivering water to Rome between 312 B.C.E. and 226 C.E., about 350 were underground, about 16 were on the surface, and about 74 were above the earth's surface (Smith 1975).

Where a relatively shallow valley up to about 50 meters deep had to be spanned, the aqueduct was usually supported by the multi-tiered stone arches that have become the visual signature of Roman engineering. When deep valleys—some as deep as 135 meters—could not be avoided by following natural contours, lead pipe inverted siphons carried the water from the high side to the opposite, slightly lower side through the deep dip between, where water pressures sometimes demanded that several smaller and stronger pipes be used rather than a single pipe of greater radius (Humphrey, et al. 1998). In a few aqueducts, the total gradient from the source to the Roman water tank was so great that the flow of water had to be interrupted in order to limit its velocity entering Rome. Water from the segment of the aqueduct nearer the source would be allowed to freefall into a pond or tank, from which it again was allowed to flow into another segment of the aqueduct, reducing the effective head of the water.

Once it had arrived in one of the Roman water tanks, the water was distributed through terra cotta or lead mains that left the tanks at three levels. The mains that left at the highest level delivered water to private parties whose water would be the first to be cut off in periods of short supply. The mains that left at the second level delivered water to the public baths and fountains that were used by ordinary citizens and to military garrisons. The lowest mains, which provided the most uninterrupted sources of water, were reserved to be used at the Emperor's discretion. Junction boxes existed in the mains at appropriate distances, and private residences drew from these boxes through lead pipes of standard diameters. Though Frontinus recognized that the amount of water delivered to any customer depended both on the size of the pipe and on the water pressure at the point of delivery, as well as on the duration of use, clients were charged for water based simply on the size of their delivery pipe (Humphrey, et al. 1998).

The major public baths, or *thermae,* as well as some private baths, required heating. The water itself was usually heated directly by a fire before it reached the bathing room, but the Romans wanted the room to be heated as well. This was accomplished by laying the floor of the bathing room on brick pillars one or two meters high and set about one meter apart. A large opening into this cellar-like space, called a *hypocaust,* connected to a room in which a fire was kept burning. The hot air warmed the floor of the bath, and terra cotta flues exhausted the hot smoky air through the walls, warming them as well.

Finally, when the used water left the fountains or baths, it was sometimes used for cleaning streets and public spaces. More often, it flowed through private or public latrines (there were 144 public latrines, some with up to 65 holes and slots cut into a marble bench, by around 300 C.E.) on its way to a covered sewer that emptied into the *Cloaca maxima,* a central covered drain that had been begun by the Etruscan inhabitants of Rome around 600 B.C.E. This drain emptied into the Tiber River just downstream from the center of Rome. Though Roman sanitation may seem very crude to a 21st century inhabitant of the industrialized world, the Roman system of flushing waste with massive amounts of water almost certainly made Rome the healthiest large city in the ancient world.

Nine

Producing and Processing
Food and Clothing

Among the necessities of human life, both food and some kind of personal protection from the elements precede even the need for artificial shelter. Early humans gathered wild plants, fished, and hunted for wild game, and they dressed primarily in animal skins. By the time civilizations emerged, however, some varieties of most of the major food crops and most of the domestic animals used today for food or food production had already been domesticated, and textiles had replaced animal skins for everything but footwear, foul weather protection, and protection against weapons. River bottom fishing, agriculture, and herding allowed virtually all to eat and clothe themselves adequately, and some to do so magnificently, except during extremes of wet or dryness or in the aftermath of other environmental disasters such as volcanic eruptions or earthquakes. In most early civilizations, dining and costuming became the primary venues for displaying wealth, status, and power. Relationships between food and status were well defined, and wealthy elites sought to experiment and expand the range of tastes, smells, and visual experiences available to themselves and their guests.

The wealthier a civilization became and the more hierarchical its social structure, the more extreme its food and raiment became, the more those extremes were recorded in both writing and pictures, and the more they were complained about by sober moralists. Thus, Seneca, writing at the time of Roman imperial excess, harkens back longingly to the time of the early republic:

[Then] men's bodies were still sound and strong; their food was light and unspoiled by art and luxury whereas when they began to seek dishes not for the sake of removing but of arousing an appetite and devising countless sauces to whet their gluttony, then what was nourishment to a hungry man became a burden to a full stomach. (Alcock 2006, 163)

And Mo Zi, writing during the late Zhou period (approximately 1100–200 B.C.E.) when a banquet for distinguished guests might have as many as 16 dishes involving exotic substances, offered the following advice:

Stop when hunger is satiated, breathing becomes strong, limbs are strengthened and ears and eyes become sharp. There is no need of combining the five tastes extremely well or harmonizing the different sweet odors. And efforts should not be made to procure rare delicacies from far countries. (Chang 1977, 49)

In this chapter, we will look first at what different groups of people ate and the technologies by which their food and drink was procured, processed, stored, distributed, and consumed. We will then consider the manufacture of textiles and the production of clothing.

WHAT PEOPLE ATE

The food traditions of each ancient civilization were based on two critical factors. One was the ensemble of available indigenous foodstuffs, and the other was the range of techniques available for preparing foods. Well before the end of antiquity in each civilization except for that of Mesoamerica, which remained isolated until the post-Columbian period, virtually all of the foodstuffs available in any civilization were available to the wealthy either because the plants or animals were now domesticated in new locations or because the edible materials were traded for. However, each food tradition remained distinctive in part because food preferences had been established early and were not easily changed, as when Greek and Roman preferences for olive oil lead them to reject the use of butter for both cooking and as a condiment. Other food preferences were reinforced by religious taboos, as in the Hebrew rejection of pork as human food. Still others were shaped by the character of local cooking technologies. Wheat, for example, had been used for making breads in the Near Eastern cultures from which it was appropriated, but when it arrived in China, the Chinese had not developed ovens for baking breads, mills for grinding flour, or a taste for baked breads and cakes, thus the new materials were adapted to local cooking techniques and turned into noodles, dumplings, and steamed buns, which reentered the West only during the Renaissance. Baking ovens were eventually imported from the West, but baked goods never became a central form of grain food in China as they were in the West.

The earliest civilizations were all characterized by dramatic increases in grain production made possible by river basin and irrigation agriculture. It should hardly be surprising, then, that grains became the primary source of calories in all ancient civilizations, though it is less obvious that fermented grains should become the major source of liquids in people's diets as well. Both cultivated and wild varieties of indigenous vegetables and fruits were also eaten in all civilizations. Dairy products were highly prized in some early civilizations, but they were completely absent from Chinese foods, and while the Greeks and Romans enjoyed cheese, they looked down on those who drank milk and used butter. Meat protein from fish, fowl, domesticated animals, and, to a lesser extent, from wild game and insects became a much less predominant form of nutrition than it had been in pre-literate societies. The poor in most early societies got most of their animal protein from fish, eating meat almost exclusively in connection with religious ceremonies during which sacrifices were made and then shared. Those who were wealthy continued to eat meat with most meals, but even for them, grains were the most important foods. Today, those of us who are not vegetarians are likely to see the reduced availability of meat in negative terms, but those in most early civilizations saw grain eating as superior to meat eating, characterizing the uncivilized people around them as people who wear the skins of animals, live in caves, and "do not eat grain-food" (Chang 1977, 42).

What follows are lists of the most common foodstuffs that have been established either archeologically or from literary sources for each major civilization during its early years, supplemented by lists of major items appropriated through cultural exchanges at a later period but before the end of antiquity for each civilization. These lists have been compiled from the food texts in the bibliography. Where I am aware of disputes about whether a foodstuff was available or not, I have generally not included it. In many cases, those foods listed as indigenous came originally from elsewhere but were in place by the time that writing began and/or large cities came into existence. In almost all cases, grains and vegetables were smaller, harder, differently colored, and, in the case of vegetables, more bitter, than present-day varieties. Classical Greece and Rome had access to almost all foodstuffs in use in Mesopotamia and Egypt, especially after Alexander the Great's conquests (by 323 B.C.E.) and the maximum extension of the Roman Empire (by 100 B.C.E.) respectively, so I have chosen to emphasize their indigenous foodstuffs and those that they consciously chose to adopt extensively.

Mesopotamia: *Original grains:* einkorn wheat, emmer wheat, barley. *Later additions:* durum wheat, spelt wheat, bread wheat, millet. *Original vegetables:* onions, lettuce, leeks, peas, beans (green, kidney), garlic, cabbage, cucumber, carrots, eggplant, radishes, beets, turnips, chickpeas, lentils. *Original fruits:* dates, apples, figs, pomegranates, apricots, cherries, pears, plums, quinces. *Later additions:* grapes. *Original meats:* sheep, goat, cattle, pig, ducks, geese, quail, fish (about 50 varieties), shellfish, locusts. *Later additions:* chicken. *Dairy products:* milk (lower class), butter, cheeses. *Original other:* salt, flax seed, eggs, anise, asafoetida, bay, capers, coriander, cress, cumin, dill, fennel, fenugreek, marjoram, mustard, mint, rue, saffron, sage, thyme. *Later additions:* sesame, olives, honey, pepper.

Egypt: *Original grains:* emmer wheat, barley. *Later additions:* bread wheat, spelt wheat. *Original vegetables:* onions, garlic, leeks, water melons, squashes, cos lettuces, celery, papyrus, lotus, radishes, turnips, mustard greens, lentils, peas, chickpeas, lupines, fenugreek. *Later additions:* fava beans. *Original fruits:* dates, grapes, pomegranates, figs, carobs. *Original meats:* pigs, sheep, goats, donkeys, cattle, ducks, pigeons, geese, game, freshwater fish, crocodiles. *Later additions:* chickens. *Dairy products:* none widely used. *Original other:* salt, duck and goose eggs, linseed, honey, aniseed, asafetida, basil, chervil, cumin, dill, juniper, marjoram, mint, rosemary, rue, sage. *Later additions:* hens' eggs, olives, safflower, black pepper, cinnamon, coriander.

China: *Original grains:* foxtail millet (*Setaria italica*), ordinary millet (*Panicum milaceum*), rice (only in the more rural south), hemp. *Later additions:* rice (in the north), bread wheat, barley. *Original vegetables:* artemesia, soybeans, velvet bean, broad bean, taro and yam (in the south), malva, musk melon, gourd, turnip, leek, lettuce, field sowthistle, cattail, lotus roots, various grasses, Chinese cabbage, mustard greens, garlic, spring onion, water chestnuts, bamboo shoots. *Later additions:* peas, cucumbers. *Original fruits:* apricot, pears, peaches, plums, strawberries, oranges. *Later additions:* jujube, lychee, oranges, grapes, pomegranate. *Original meats*: dogs, pigs, sheep, horses, cattle, water buffalo, game, chicken, pullet, goose, quail, partridge, pheasant, pigeon, quail, sparrow, peacock, crane, fish (mostly varieties of carp), turtles, shellfish, snakes, bees, snails, frogs. *Dairy products:* none widely used. *Original other:* salt, eggs of many fowl, fagara, cinnamon, honey, ginger root. *Later additions:* walnuts, sesame seeds, coriander, caraway seeds.

Harappan and Vedic India: *Original grains:* spelt wheat, rice, barley. *Later additions:* bread wheat, emmer wheat. *Original vegetables*: long peppers, lentils, beans, cucumber. *Original fruits:* jujube, banana, lemons, limes, dates. *Later additions:* pears. *Original meats*: chicken, sheep, humped cattle, pig, turtle, goat, water buffalo, fish. *Other:* manna (sweet insect secretion deposited on tamarisk bush), cane sugar, curry.

Classical Greece: *Grains:* barley, emmer wheat, bread wheat. *Vegetables:* lettuces, leafed cabbages, onions, asparagus, lupines, peas, beans, parsnips, mushrooms (for the poor). *Fruits:* grapes, figs, apples, cherries, pears, peaches, plums. *Meats:* chickens, pigs, sheep, goats, cattle, dogs, game, fish, shellfish. *Dairy products:* cheese. *Other:* olives and olive oil, honey, long peppers, silphium, sumac, local herbs, acorns.

Classical Rome: *Grains:* emmer wheat, bread wheat, spelt wheat, barley. *Vegetables:* lettuce, cabbage, beets, turnips, radishes, onions, carrots, parsnips, celery, asparagus, peas, beans. *Fruits:* grapes, berries, apricots, peaches, quince, citron. *Meats:* pigs, sheep, goats, cattle, chickens, dormice, rabbits, wild birds, fish, shellfish (including cultured oysters), grasshoppers. *Dairy products:* cheese, milk for cooking only. *Other:* olive oil, honey, mushrooms, cumin, coriander, lovage, black pepper.

Mesoamerica: *Grains:* maize. *Vegetables:* sweet potato, tomato, chilies, pumpkins, squashes, gourds, zucchini, kidney beans, lima beans, manioc. *Fruits:* prickly pear, lucuma (star apple), pacae, avocado, guava, papaya. *Meats:* dog, turkey, guinea pig, llama, alpaca, fish, shellfish, caterpillars, grasshoppers, bees, ants, termites. *Other:* honey, mushrooms, peanuts.

THE PRODUCTION AND STORAGE OF BEERS AND WINES

Humans in all civilizations undoubtedly drank water, either straight or mixed with something else, for every adult has to replace approximately 2.5 liters of water that are eliminated on average each day, but water was not the drink of choice in any ancient civilization. All civilizations produced beers and/or wines that were strongly favored because of their taste, their intoxicating effects, and possibly because the alcohol killed many bacteria, making beer and wine safer than water to drink. Furthermore, the fermentation process that produces beer and wine increases lysine levels, making the proteins in grain more useable by the body. It also increases the B vitamins and boosts the body's ability to absorb calcium and other minerals, so fermented grain is more nutritious than cooked or raw grain (Kaufman 2006).

Both beer and wine are produced by fermenting grains or fruits to create alcohol. In general, beers are produced when the ferment is heated enough to speed up the fermenting process but not enough to kill the yeast that converts the initial sugars to alcohol. This heat can be supplied either by exposure to fire or by exposure to the sun or even high ambient temperatures above about 85° Fahrenheit. Thus, beer was very easy to produce in the hot climates of Mesopotamia and Egypt, and beer became the primary drink of the common people. Sumerian documents indicate that eight different beers were made from barley, eight from emmer wheat, and three from mixtures well before 2000 B.C.E. Egyptian pyramid texts suggest that five beers were brewed there (Brothwell and Brothwell 1969).

Wines are produced when fermentation proceeds under relatively cool conditions. When the ferment is hot, the long organic molecules in the mature grains and fruits, such as the tannins in grapes, are broken down, leaving the characteristic bitter taste of beer. When the temperatures during the fermentation process remain low enough, the long chain molecules persist and the liquor retains more of the natural flavors of the initial fermenting stock. Wines were more difficult to produce in the semitropical climates of Egypt and Mesopotamia, and probably in Mesoamerica, so then, as now, wine became the preferred drink of those who could afford it. In Greece, Rome, and China wine was both easier to produce and the preferred drink of all classes. In the cases of both beer and wine, fermentation is a self-limiting process because the alcohol eventually kills the yeast that produces it. Because heat also destroys yeast, beers generally have a lower alcohol content than wines. Wines, however, were almost always diluted with water, so as they were usually drunk, wine and beer probably had roughly equivalent alcohol content. Some strong beers were produced in antiquity, however, by adding large amounts of yeast, and these were almost certainly the most potent drinks normally available.

There were two basic methods for producing beer in ancient Egypt, from which the greatest amount of archeological evidence is available. Both were in use before 3000 B.C.E., and both remained in use throughout antiquity. In what was probably initially the most common method, an appropriate amount of grain—usually barley in Egypt and Mesopotamia—was husked and ground into flour and then mixed with water and a yeast starter to leaven it. The dough was formed into a loaf and only partially baked, so as to leave the yeast alive. The partially baked dough was then crumbled into a fired clay container of water to create a mash. The container, which was usually flat-bottomed and conical in shape, was then placed in an oven with several others (at one of the oldest brewery sites dating from around 3500 B.C.E., each oven had 35 conical containers about 50 cm high and set into the ground about 15 cm deep) to ferment (Curtis 2001). The containers were coated with clay and mud bricks and then hot fuel embers were piled against them to provide heat. After about two days, the beer was decanted into amphorae (narrow necked fired clay vessels, usually with pointed bottoms) to be stored or transported to where it would be used. Beer made in this way contained a large amount of residual solid matter, and pictures suggest that it was drunk through a narrow straw to extract the liquid.

In what gradually became the predominant method of beer making, the barley or other grain was wetted and allowed to germinate, which produced enzymes that broke down the starches in the grain into sugars. The damp and barely germinated "malt" was dried and heated enough to stop the further growth of the rootlets; then it was usually roasted in an oven to cure it at over 176° Fahrenheit. The extent of roasting usually determined the taste and strength of the resulting beer. The cured malt was then ground and stored for later use. When the brewer was ready to brew the beer, the malt was ground into flour, mixed with unmalted grain, and then placed in hot water (to reactivate the enzymes). After several days, the mixture was strained to produce a liquid that contained relatively little solid matter. This liquid was then boiled and cooled. Finally, yeast was added so the sugars in the liquid could be converted to alcohol, probably by reheating.

Mesopotamian beer making probably began slightly earlier than that in Egypt, but we have fewer details about the process, though greater evidence of the amounts of materials used. As far as we can tell, brewing in Mesopotamia differed from that in Egypt largely because the Mesopotamians tended to add more fruit flavorings to the mash, which provided both a wider range of tastes and a slightly stronger beer. There is also no indication that Mesopotamian beers were artificially heated while they fermented, rather the jars of mash were allowed to stand in the sun to provide heat. Some fermenting jars were provided with small holes in the bottom and smaller jars were left under them to collect the clear beer, while the solid matter was left in the fermenting jar. Finally, up until the Old Babylonian period, around 1800 B.C.E., brewing was done primarily by women and was frequently associated with taverns run by women (Curtis 2001).

The Greeks and Romans considered Beer a barbarian drink, though Roman soldiers stationed in beer-producing regions often turned to it when wine was not available. There is no indication that the Chinese produced beer, rather than wine, and we simply do not know whether the fermented drinks of the Harappan or Mesoamerican civilizations were beers, wines, or both.

Evidence suggests that the first wines produced from grapes were imported into Egypt from the eastern Mediterranean around 3150 B.C.E., but within 200 years, Lower Egypt had a strong grape growing tradition and wine presses appear in tomb paintings. Yeasts are found naturally as white powdery deposits on grape skins, so fermenting begins only hours after grapes are picked if any are crushed. Wine making thus took place near the vineyards and almost immediately after the grapes were harvested. Some grapes were crushed by groups of workers treading on them with bare feet in large vats, while others were squeezed in a sack press as depicted in Figure 9.1.

Since treaded grape juice, or *must*, contains seeds and skins, or *marc*, which produces red wines when left in the fermenting liquid, and sack press-

Figure 9.1
An Egyptian Sack Press. Nick Livingston.

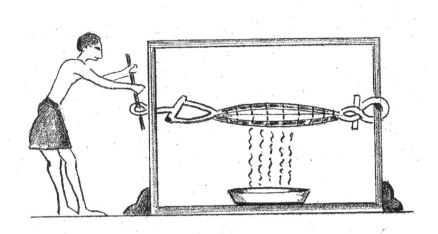

ing produces a nearly clear must that could result in a white wine, it seems likely that all red wines were produced by treading. It has, however, been suggested that sack presses were only used to squeeze the last must out of the marc left in the bottom of the crushing vats. If so, it produced the strongest and reddest wines available. New Kingdom drawings in Egypt show spouts on the vats in which grapes were crushed by treading. The spouts presumably drew off the clear top layer of must for making white or light red wines, wile the remainder of the juice, with skins and seeds, was dipped out into open-mouthed jars to allow further fermenting at temperatures below 80° Fahrenheit. When fermentation was nearly complete, the wine was filtered into closed vessels and sealed with stoppers that had very small holes in them so that any further fermentation, which produced carbon dioxide gas, would not crack the container or produce an explosion. Finally, the fully fermented wine was decanted into fully sealed amphorae or into sealed casks to age so that airborne organisms would not initiate the transformation of the wine into vinegar. Since amphorae were usually made of fired clay, which could slowly allow wine to seep out, they were often lined with resin that made them waterproof and also added a slightly resinous taste to the wine. Information about the wines in them was often inscribed into the amphorae, so we know that wines were often designated by the locale in which they were made, whether they were sweet or dry, whether they were good, very good, or very, very good, and whether they were made from fruits other than grapes, such as dates, pomegranates, or figs.

Though wealthy Mesopotamians consumed substantial amounts of wine from the mid-third millennium, beer remained the most important drink of all classes. There is little evidence of wine making in Mesopotamia until almost 800 B.C.E. Wines were imported primarily from Anatolia, where wine making probably began, and from the area that is now Syria and Lebanon.

In early China, three of the four types of wine were produced from grains, and only one from fruits. The process is not well understood, but it probably involved the production of malt from sprouted grain that was then allowed to ferment at low temperatures.

It was the Greeks and Romans who turned viticulture into a fine art and wine into the universally preferred drink of all classes. Wine making followed the basic pattern established in Egypt, but the Greeks placed large wicker baskets in some of their treading vats so that the must that flowed out contained no marc (Curtis 2001). These vats were presumably used to produce white wines, while those vats in which the must and marc were not separated produced red wines. There is no evidence of the use of mechanical presses in Greek or Roman wine production, although presses used to extract the oil from olives could have been used. Some must was sold directly to consumers who allowed it to ferment in wineskins made of goat's stomachs. These skins were slightly permeable, so evaporation from the moist exterior of the bag kept the inside temperature relatively low. Most must seems to have been dipped out of the treading vat directly into resin-lined amphorae that were initially stoppered with clay plugs that contained small holes to allow the carbon dioxide produced during fermentation to escape. When fermentation was complete the amphorae were permanently stoppered with cork or clay. Like the Egyptians, the Greeks and Romans often inscribed information about the wine inside on the amphorae, but unlike the Egyptians, the Greeks and Romans tended to age their superior wines for up to 10 years before drinking them.

OTHER CEREAL USES

There has been substantial debate about whether beer making or leavened bread baking came first in Egypt and Mesopotamia, but no one seems to doubt that a third use of grains preceded both. In every civilization, one of the first and most persistent ways to prepare grain for consumption was to create a gruel something like modern Cream-of-Wheat or oatmeal, which could be thinned to provide a slightly thickened soup stock. In doing so, the first step was to remove the husks from husked grains by parching (drying at a low heat under the sun, in pans over a low fire, or in a relatively cool oven) and pounding or rolling lightly in a saddle quern (see Figure 9.2) in order to separate the husk from the grain kernel without smashing the kernel into flour.

In this process, the lighter husks rose to the top and were blown off, or the smaller kernels were allowed to drop through a colander-like vessel with holes in the bottom. The grain was then soaked in water and boiled in a pot or cauldron to create a staple food that could be flavored and augmented in an almost indefinite number of ways—by adding herbs, spices, vegetables, fish, insects, or, in rare cases, meat from fowl or four-legged animals. Early in most civiliza-

Figure 9.2
Saddle Quern and Rubber. Nick Livingston.

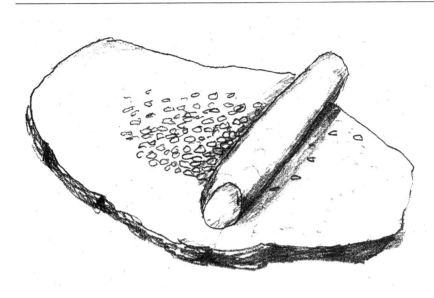

tions, the basic cooking pots were baked clay, but as time went on these were replaced in at least wealthy homes by bronze or, eventually, iron vessels.

In Egypt, Mesopotamia, Greece, and probably Harappan civilization as well as in Mesoamerica., cooking fires were at ground level or only slightly raised; cooking pots were rounded on the bottom, and they were set in free-standing rings supported by three legs or on four-legged grills above the cooking fire. In China, three legs were integral to most cauldrons and cooking pots so they could be set directly in the fire or coals. The Romans built their hearths almost at waist height, so cooks did not have to do as much bending or squatting, and they were supplied with a shallow lip so coals did not fall off when they were stirred.

In many cases lentils, chickpeas, peas, and some kinds of beans were used in much the same way as grains to produce porridge, soup stock, and even flour. In the following Roman recipe recorded by Apicius for a fancy porridge, note that the grain, along with chickpeas, lentils, and peas, provides the base stock to which other vegetables and a special sauce (to be discussed later) are added:

Soak chickpeas, lentils and peas. Boil crushed grain with these. Drain, then add oil and the following chopped greens: leeks, beets, and cabbage. Add dill, mallow, and coriander. Pound fennel seeds, oregano, asafoeteda, lovage, and blend these with *liquamen*. Pour this mixture over the vegetables and grain, heat, and stir. Put chopped cooked cabbage leaves on top. (Alcock 2006, 37)

In China, lentils, broadbeans, and fava beans were classified with grains as *fan* or "principle foods" to distinguish them from *cai*, or "dishes." The most common way of preparing *fan* was to steam the husked grain or other starch in a special steaming vessel, or *zeng*, which sat on top of the cauldron, or *fu*, containing a *cai* food. The process used the steam rising off the *fu* to cook the grain—usually millet, hemp seed, or barley during most of the Shang and early Zhou dynasties, and rice later on. Grains and other starches were also boiled in China, but they were almost never baked into breads. In part, this seems to be because the Chinese never developed querns or grinding wheels to produce flour, but even when flour was introduced from the West during Han times, it was almost always made into steamed buns or fried into pancakes rather than baked. Boiled grains and beans were often dried and roasted to produce an important travel food for persons of all classes because they were light and did not easily rot (Chang 1977).

All other civilizations seem to have used grains to produced baked breads—first flatbreads and then leavened breads, except in Mesoamerica, where leavened breads never became common. Husks were first removed from the grains by pounding in a mortar and pestle, possibly after parching. Then, the grain was ground into a flour using a saddle quern or metaté (in Egypt, Mesopotamia, Mesoamerica, and Greece) as in Figure 9.2 or using some kind of mill in which the grain was ground between a rotating surface or surfaces and a fixed base (in Rome). After these milling operations, bits of stone ground off the quern, small chunks of unground grain, and other solid contaminants usually remained in the flour, so the flour was sieved through a wicker surface to remove most of the grit.

Because model bakery-breweries have frequently been found in Egyptian tombs and because bread making was a frequent theme of tomb paintings, we have a better understanding of bread making in Egypt than in any other early civilization. After the flour had been prepared, water and salt were added and then the dough was kneaded either by hand or, in larger operations, by treading on it with the feet in a large vat. At this point, different treatments followed, depending on the intended use. For ordinary flatbread, the dough was simply formed into flat cakes to be baked in a pan, in embers, or, during the New Kingdom, in a special oven.

If special flatbreads or cakes were wanted, eggs, milk, spices, honey, dates, figs, or ground nuts might be added before placing or pouring dough into a mold. If raised bread or pastries were desired, either yeast or a starter of fermented dough from the previous day was added before placing the dough into a mold to be baked. Some 15 different kinds of bread were made in the Old Kingdom, while by the New Kingdom, that number had risen to somewhere between 30 and 50 (Curtis 2001).

The simplest and oldest way of baking bread, but one still used in Old Kingdom Egypt, was to place a flat, hand-formed loaf into the embers of a fire. When the bread was done, the ash was wiped off and the bread was eaten. The second way depicted in Old Kingdom paintings involved the use of an open-topped oven. A thin, flat stone was supported on three stones set on edge and a fire was built under the flat stone, which became a griddle on which the dough, typically formed into a flat circular shape and sometimes with a slightly thickened outer rim to form a shallow bowl, was cooked. More often, the dough was placed in thick terra cotta pan-like molds shaped in various ways, but with wider tops than bottoms. In locations identified as bakeries, several of these molds were placed in a shallow trench in the floor. Cone shaped, thick terra cotta lids that had been pre-heated were placed on them and then hot embers were placed in the trough, baking the bread inside.

During the Middle Kingdom, these thick, lidded molds were replaced by tall and narrow thin-walled conical molds. The molds were filled with dough, placed in the trench, and embers were piled up among them without using lids. Finally, during New Kingdom times, bread was baked in large, dome shaped ovens. A fire was built in the oven, which had a vent in the top. After the oven had been heated, the embers were raked, the vent was stopped up, and thin dough-filled molds, often imitating Old Kingdom shapes, were inserted on the oven floor; then the floor-level opening was stopped up and the bread baked in the retained heat. Given the number of broken molds at sites where the large ovens were used, it seems that the mold frequently had to be broken to remove the bread.

In the early Mesopotamian civilization, when temples still owned land and provided goods to the citizens, bread making was done on a massive scale. Records from Lagash, for example, indicate that a single milling house that prepared the flour for the temple bakers employed up to 950 workers—mostly women (Curtis 2001). The Mesopotamians also baked flatbreads in embers or on hot stones. In addition, from early in the third millennium, they used beehive-shaped ovens with a relatively large hole at the top. The baker leaned down through this hole and slapped moist pancake-shaped pieces of dough onto the inside surface of the oven, where it stuck. the fire was lit and tended until baking was complete. After the oven cooled, the breads were removed.

Leavened breads were baked in large (up to five meters in diameter) domed ovens like those used in New Kingdom Egypt, but the Mesopotamians used them from the early third millennium, and the Mesopotamian bread molds often had geometric and animal-shaped designs in the bottoms, giving the bread an extra decorative touch.

The classical Greeks were still making flatbreads directly in the embers of fires and on griddles, which were now usually made of metal, rather than flat stones, and their leavened breads were usually baked in pans rather than terra cotta molds. For small amounts of bread, a light dome-shaped cover was placed over embers until it got hot. The embers were removed, and the dome was placed over the pan of bread to be baked. These portable domes could also be used as field ovens to bake flatbreads. The dome was placed over a fire and when it was hot, pancake-shaped pieces of dough were slapped onto the outer surface. They were then turned to bake on the other side when one side was done. For bakeries that made many loaves of leavened bread, vaulted ovens were built so that their floors were above a firebox. At the rear of the oven, a slot was made in the floor so that the air heated by the fire filled the oven. Pans of dough were placed on the floor of the oven, and the fire was maintained until baking was completed, much as it is in modern ovens, though the fronts of these Greek ovens were depicted as open, rather than closed (Curtis 2001).

The greatest Roman innovation associated with bread making was the invention of rotary mills for grinding the grain into flour. A water-driven mill was described by Vitruvius in book 10, chapter 5, of his *Ten Books on Architecture*. A vertical water wheel caused a horizontal axle to turn; a large cogged wheel was attached to this axle., and as the cogged wheel turned, its teeth engaged a small horizontal wheel attached to a vertical axle that caused a slightly concave stone wheel to rotate over a slightly convex stone wheel through which the axle passed. A hopper of grain with a bottom opening into a small hole at the center of the top stone allowed grain to enter the mill near the top of the fixed convex stone. As the top stone turned, crushing the grain into flour, the flour gradually moved outward between the stones, becoming finer and finer, until it fell into a trough to be collected (see Figure 9.3) and

Figure 9.3
Vitruvian Water-driven Mill. Nick Livingston.

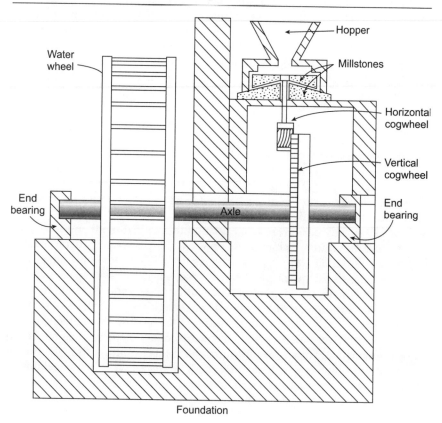

possibly re-run through the mill. Smaller, hand-driven mills were used in individuals' home kitchens.

Once the flour was made, it was sieved in wicker baskets, watered, salted, and kneaded, sometimes using an animal- or human-powered kneading machine in which teeth fixed to a vertical axle rotated between teeth fixed to the internal walls of a cylindrical vat. Once kneaded, the dough was formed into loaves without using pans and baked in ovens modeled on the Greek bakery ovens mentioned above, but with a smaller front opening for inserting and removing loaves of bread with a paddle. Home baking was often done simply by placing dough on a tile over the fire in the hearth and covering it with an inverted pot.

The maize-based flour used in Mesoamerica was made into gruels and stew stock and it was boiled in water with white lime to make a meal that was mixed with shortening, stuffed with meat, and steamed in a banana leaf to make tamales. Whether it was patted very thin and cooked on thin rock griddles in pre-Colombian times, much as corn tortillas are still made today, is debated.

VEGETABLES AND SAUCES

Except in India, where they were not highly valued, onions, leeks, and garlic were among the most important vegetables in early civilizations. In both Egypt and Mesopotamia, bread, onions and beer constituted the basic diet of working people. Onions were eaten raw with bread, incorporated into gruels and soups to provide flavoring, or, as in Rome, they were pickled in vinegar and brine and eaten without cooking. Both onion and garlic were used in preparing sauces to accompany meat, fish, and game; garlic was widely used in dressings for salads, especially in Greece. Radishes were another root crop that was much more widely used in the ancient world than at present. Their greens were used in salads, their seeds were pressed for oils, and radishes were boiled and usually eaten with some form of pungent sauce or spice.

The most famous of these sauces was called *liquamen* in Rome and *garos* in Greece. It was made by fermenting small fish and fish entrails in brine for up to three months, after which the liquid portion was used in many recipes instead of salt. When combined with herbs and spices, it was used as a table sauce and dressing for salad vegetables. The Chinese used a similar fermented fish sauce, and by the end of the Zhou period they also used soy sauce, a ferment made from crushed soybeans and lightly ground grains soaked with a microorganism from the *Aspergillus* family. This substance was then refermented with brine and yeasts. There is evidence in the Harappan civilization that the curry powders, which continue to characterize Indian food, were already in use at the earliest sites (Mackay and Mackay 1976).

Turnips were widely used in Mesopotamia, Egypt, Greece, and Rome, though they were usually a food for the poor or for emergency use when other vegetables were not available. Carrots were widely known but not extensively used, and parsnips were known to the Romans but were not widely used in the ancient world. Though regular potatoes were widely used in upland South

America, they did not grow in the lowland areas of Mesoamerica, where sweet potatoes and yams were common. In addition, many plant roots not now used for food were also used in antiquity. The Egyptians fried, roasted, or boiled the roots of the white lotus; Mesoamericans roasted the bulbs of the American aloe; the Chinese ate lily bulbs; and the Greeks and Romans ate a large number of bulbs, including squill, asphodel, and gladiolus.

Finally, gourds were eaten virtually everywhere. In Mesoamerica, it seems that they were virtually always picked while immature and eaten whole, while in most other civilizations they were allowed to mature and their cubed flesh was used in many recipes (Brothwell and Brothwell 1969).

FRUITS

Local varieties of wild berries were eaten in all civilizations, though none were domesticated, but orchards of tree-born fruits began to be tended sometime between 4000 B.C.E. and 3000 B.C.E. in Mesopotamia and slightly later elsewhere. Myths suggest that trees were cultivated at least in part to provide the shade needed to grow other vegetable crops, and it was natural to choose to grow trees that provided their own foods. Virtually all fruits were eaten fresh without being processed in any way, though some were preserved for storage and there are a few ancient recipes for fruit jams, compotes, and other dishes. Apples were among the first trees to be cared for in both Mesopotamia and Egypt. From there, domestic apples spread to Greece and Rome. Exactly when grafting was developed as a method of promoting the spread of selected varieties of fruit is uncertain, but the Roman writer on natural history, Pliny the Elder, discussed 36 different and well established varieties of apple, which were used in a variety of ways. Date palms were first cultivated in Mesopotamia, providing an important source of sweetening, food, and wine. They soon moved to Harappan civilization and to Egypt, which reciprocated by providing figs, which were used in many of the same ways. Dates did not do well in the cooler climates of Greece and Rome, but figs became a staple food of all classes in both classical civilizations.

Pears also began to be cultivated in Mesopotamia, though not until around 1000 B.C.E. They spread rapidly to China and Greece and were introduced to India from China in the first century of the Common Era. Like apples, pears were eaten fresh and dried for storage, but unlike apples, they were often stored in must and made into a conserve with boiled wine. Again, in Roman times the number of varieties of pear became so great that the first century Roman agricultural writer Columella said there were too many to catalog. Plums, which were also first domesticated in Mesopotamia, were initially sour enough that they were typically eaten with honey and butter and used as an ingredient in various sauces. Cherries seem to have been domesticated in Mesopotamia sometime before about 700 B.C.E., where they were pressed to produce a thick juice and the residue was formed into cakes.

Of all fruits, among the most important for Greece and Rome was the grape. Though cultivated earlier in Mesopotamia and Egypt both for table use and for making wine, grape wine became the favored drink of all classes in both Greece and Rome, so viticulture was widely practiced and many varieties of grapes were cultivated.

Perhaps as important in both Greece and Rome as grapes were olives. Though used in many places primarily for producing oil (see below), they were also eaten as food in Egypt, Mesopotamia, Greece, and Rome. In fact, olives, along with bread, became the staple diet of the Roman working classes and peasants. For the wealthy palate, olives were preserved in jars of brine, must, or vinegar, with layers of fennel on the top and bottom.

Peaches, apricots, and oranges were all first cultivated in China before 2000 B.C.E. The first two reached Mesopotamia by around 1800 B.C.E. Neither peaches nor apricots were widely used by the Greeks or Romans, although they feature in a couple of very expensive recipes provided by Apicus, the Roman writer on cuisine. Oranges did not reach the West until the early years of the Common Era. The citrus fruit that did arrive in Mesopotamia and Egypt relatively early seems to have been the citron, a thick-skinned, lemon-like fruit that came from the Harappan civilization. Lemons and limes were also grown near Mohenjo-Daro, but they did not arrive in the West until they were imported during the time of the Roman Empire. Finally, pomegranates seem to have originated in northern India, but they had become a favored fruit in Mesopotamia well before 1500 B.C.E. and they arrived in Egypt around 1300 B.C.E. They were used in many recipes and were preserved by soaking in hot sea water and then dried in the sun.

Almost all of the fruits eaten in Mesoamerica were first cultivated in Peru and then appropriated by other Central American groups. The prickly pear, lucuma, papaya, avocado, guava, and pineapple, as well as a relative of the plum, the pepino, were cultivated in pre-Columbian Mesoamerica.

MEAT AND FISH PREPARATION

Unlike fruits, which were often eaten raw, meats and fish were almost always cooked or processed in some way in ancient civilizations. Large animals, including sheep, goats, pigs, and cattle, were usually butchered before cooking, though for some ceremonial occasions and large feasts they might be roasted whole or without the viscera. Both spit and pit roasting were widely used in all civilizations. In the first case, small animals or cuts of meat were skewered and either held over the fire, usually by a servant in wealthy households, or the skewer was supported at both ends and someone turned the spit to assure even roasting. In the second case, the meat or fish was either wrapped in large leaves or encased in thin clay and surrounded by embers. Clay had the advantage that the hair and skin of roasted animals usually stuck to the clay, so when cooking was finished and the clay was broken open, only the edible meat remained. Romans fattened dormice and roasted them in clay as a special delicacy.

Roasting could also be done in clay or metal pans, in covered pots, or by placing the meat directly over a fire on a gridiron of some sort. The latter was a favorite method of roasting among the Romans, but the flare-ups when grease hit the open coals often caused fires, with two consequences. The emperor Augustus created a corps of watchmen-firefighters to patrol the city watching for kitchen fires, and Roman kitchens were usually placed in separate buildings, so if a fire did start, the principle structure would not burn down (Alcock 2006). Fires caused fewer problems in Egypt or Greece, where cooking was generally done outside or in a roofless courtyard.

Fish and thin cuts of meat were also occasionally fried on griddles or in pans and very rarely they were deep-fried. Much more commonly, meats and fish were boiled, fricasséed, or stewed (i.e., cooked in a pot, cauldron, or pan in some form of liquid) in water for boiling, some form of sauce for fricasséeing, or in a grain-based stock, usually with some vegetables added. Even the most exotic Chinese dishes were usually prepared as stews or fricassées, and almost everywhere when the poorer classes had meat or fish it was as part of a stew.

OILS

Animal fats were probably used instead of vegetable oils before civilizations began to extract oils from seeds or from the olive. In Italy, for example, there was no vegetable-based oil until olives were introduced about 600 B.C.E. (Brothwell and Brothwell 1969). Butter was produced from the milk of horses, goats, sheep, and cattle before the rise of civilizations, but in Egypt, Mesopotamia, Greece, and Rome, olive oil became the primary source of oil for both cooking and for use as a condiment. Prior to their use of olives, the Egyptians extracted oil largely from radishes, lettuce, and flax seed, and the Mesopotamians extracted it primarily from sesame seeds. Olive oil never reached ancient China, where hemp and flax seeds provided most oil until the introduction of sesame during the Han period.

Wild olives were probably native to Greece, Crete, Syria, and Palestine. During the fourth millennium B.C.E., they began to be cultivated and used for producing oil in Syria and Palestine. By around 2000 B.C.E., they were cultivated in northern Mesopotamia, though they never did well in the hotter, southern region. Throughout antiquity, most olive oil was imported into Mesopotamia from the eastern end of the Mediterranean, where an important technological innovation occurred around 1300 B.C.E. Up until that time, olives had been pressed with mortar and pestles, in querns, or by simply placing large flat rocks on top of the olives, but by around 650 B.C.E. in Israel, which was then an Assyrian client state, lever type presses such as that shown in Figure 9.4 were used to press most olives. One end of a beam was set in a wall, relatively close to the stone base on which the olives were placed. A flat-bottomed top stone was attached to the lever to lower onto the base, and weights were hung on the end of the beam to multiply the pressure exerted by on the olives by a factor of the hanging weight-to-wall distance divided by the wall-to-press distance. After it emerged from a small trough in the lower stone of the press, the liquid was allowed to separate in a special pot, with the oil floating to the top. The oil was then removed from the top or, more often, a

Figure 9.4
A Lever and Weight Olive Press. Nick Livingston.

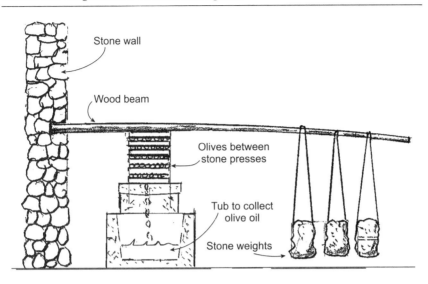

plug in the bottom was opened to allow the juice below the oil to be decanted. Ruins found at Tel-Miqne-Ekron, in southern Israel, indicate the scale of commercial olive-pressing operations in the ancient world. At that site, 105 double presses may have produced 290,000 gallons of oil per year and employed up to 2,000 persons (Curtis 2001).

A FEW ILLUSTRATIVE RECIPES

Meat sauce or "pickle" used widely in soups or other hot dishes from Zhou China:

To prepare boneless meat sauce and meat sauce with bones, it is necessary first to dry the meat and then cut it up, blend it with moldy millet, salt, and good wine, and place it in a jar. The sauce is ready in a hundred days. (Chang 1977, 34)

Preparation of "kippu" (a type of bird) from Mesopotamia around 1700 B.C.E.:

They are first split open, rinsed in cold water and placed in a cauldron [to braise or fry quickly to seal]. When the cauldron is removed from the flame [after the braising or sealing], a little cold water is added and a sprinkling of vinegar. Then mint and salt are pounded together and rubbed into the *kippu,* after which the liquid in the cauldron is strained and mint is added to this sauce, in which the *kippu* are replaced. Lastly, a little cold water is again added and everything is poured into a cooking-pot. To be presented for carving. (Bottéro 2001, 57)

Pancakes, as reported by the Roman physician, Oribasius:

Pancakes are prepared by putting olive oil into a frying pan, which is placed over a smokeless fire. Onto the heated olive oil is poured meal mixed with hot water. As the mixture is fried briskly in the olive oil, it sets and thickens like soft cheese. At which point those preparing it turn it over at once, causing the upper surface to be bottom, so that it is in connection with the frying pan. (Alcock 2006, 111)

The following two recipes are modernized versions prepared by the scholar-chef Cathy Kaufmann:

Barley and Fish Soup from Pre-Dynastic Egypt (c. 3000 B.C.E.):

½ cup barley

3 cups water

4 scallions, sliced

1 clove garlic, minced

1 whole tilapia, gutted [but not boned],

2 tablespoons butter

salt to taste

1. Rinse barley under cold running water to remove surface starch. Place barley in saucepan with water. Bring to a boil and simmer 30 minutes, skimming off foam that rises to the top.
2. Add scallions and garlic and boil another 10 minutes.
3. Cut the fish through the backbone into chunks, keeping on the skin and fins. Add the chunks to the barley base and cook 10 minutes more. Stir in butter and salt to taste (Kaufman 2006, 53).

Grilled Lamb or Mutton Chops from Attic Greece

4 tablespoons olive oil

1 tablespoon chopped fresh rosemary

4 lamb or mutton shoulder chops each about ¾ inch thick

½ head white cabbage, cored & thinly sliced

salt to taste

1. Combine 1 tablespoon olive oil with rosemary and rub over the chops.
2. Heat remaining olive oil in frying pan over low heat and add the sliced cabbage. Cook, stirring often until soft, about 20 minutes. Season with salt and set aside.
3. Preheat a grill over high heat. Season chops with salt and place on the grill, cooking about four minutes per side for rare to medium-rare chops, a bit longer for well done. Serve the chops on the cabbage (Kaufmann 2006, 101).

TEXTILES AND CLOTHING

Like food, dress offered a domain in which status and power could be expressed in most ancient civilizations, and, as in the case of food, the basic materials and techniques used for producing clothing, table coverings, toweling, mats, rugs, and so on in early civilizations were established long before the time of writing, probably by around 6000 B.C.E. However, the cultivation of plant materials and, in the Chinese case, silkworms, changed the character of dominant forms of dress and other textile uses. Animal skins, felted animal fibers, and coarsely woven plant materials gave way to increasingly fine woven flax (in Egypt, Mesopotamia, Greece, and Rome), cotton (in Harappan civilization and Mesoamerica), wool (in Mesopotamia, Greece, and Rome), and silk and hemp (in China) as the dominant materials for clothing among the wealthy and powerful. In Egypt, from which both the earliest and the greatest amount of evidence survives, around 3000 B.C.E. linen cloth woven out of flax fibers had about 20–25 warp threads and 25–30 weft threads per inch. By 2600 B.C.E., linens with a count of 160 by 120 threads were being produced, and by 1300 B.C.E., cloth with thread counts of 280 by 80 and 340 by 61 were being made (Crowfoot 1954). Because flax fibers do not accept dyes well, linens were almost always simply bleached or left a natural off-white color and designs were printed on the fabric, rather than woven into the cloth.

Coarsely woven loincloths remained the normal dress for common male workers almost everywhere in the ancient world, but only in Harappan civilization were women, regardless of class, normally portrayed as wearing only a mid-thigh length skirt held up by a kind of beaded belt or girdle. In one case, a shawl is wrapped around a female figure's arms, but her breasts remain bare (Mackay and Mackay 1976). In Harappan culture, however, women were distinguished by their jewelry and sometimes by elaborate headdresses or ribbons.

In other early civilizations, clothing varied both by gender, status, and, frequently, by family, tribal, or local group membership. In Mesoamerica, for example, a woman would usually wear a rectangular-shaped light cotton blouse called a *huipil* woven in a color and design that indicated her place of origin over a loose, calf-length cotton skirt. Wearing a *huipil* from some other village while at home was a sign of disrespect, but wearing a *huipil* from another village while visiting that village was to honor one's hosts.

In Han China, government officials wore a blue jacket with a design woven into the front and/or back. The colors and form of the design indicated both what ministry the official was assigned to and what rank he held in it (Harris 1993). Almost everywhere, members of the priesthood wore the most elaborate clothing seen in the civilization for ceremonial purposes. Since the Chinese emperor was, from the Shang dynasty into the Han, also the chief priest, he alone was allowed to wear saffron-died yellow robes interwoven with gold threads at ceremonial functions (Priest and Simmons 1934).

In some civilizations, most cloth was made in homes or in small weaving establishments attached to the residences of the wealthy. Thus, in Mesoamerica, Harappan civilization, and Greece, homespun cloth was the norm, but in Mesopotamia, Egypt during the New Kingdom, China during the Han Dynasty, and in Imperial Rome, textile production was at times concentrated in industrial style workplaces employing large numbers of women and men as spinners, weavers, and dyers. In one Mesopotamian wool cloth facility, for example, 127 slave girls and 30 children cleaned the wool and spun the yarn to provide raw materials for 165 female weavers. In Rome, there were woolen cloth making establishments that employed up to 300 workers, but home-spun cloth was judged appropriate for all but the wealthiest citizens (Wilson 1979), and some Roman political leaders, including Caesar Augustus (ruled 27 B.C.E.–13 C.E.), made a special point of wearing homespun woolens and de-nouncing the luxury and idleness associated with purchased clothing.

Steps in Producing Woven Textiles

Though processes such as felting and knitting were also employed, the vast majority of cloth in all ancient civilizations was woven, so we shall focus now on how woven cloth was produced. The initial series of steps, regardless of the kind of material used, were designed to remove accumulated contaminants from the source of natural fibers or to remove the fibers from their natural environment and prepare them for spinning. For flax fibers, which provided most cloth in ancient Egypt, this meant removing the seeds from the stem by using a comb or by threshing (i.e., beating the flax with a heavy tool) and then soaking the stem to decompose the gums and pectin that held the fibers in the stem. Next, the stem was pounded to free the fibers from the woody portion of the stems. The fibers were then pulled through a series of boards with different sized nail-like pins and were collected and loosely packed in a single strand around a stick called a distaff, ready for spinning.

For cotton, which was the dominant fiber in both Harappan civilization and Mesoamerica, the first step was to remove the fibers, or seed hairs, from the boll, or seedpod. Each cotton fiber is a single cell stretching out from a single seed, which may send out up to 20,000 fibers anywhere from three-eights of an inch to two and one half inches long, and any boll may have up to eight seeds; therefore, each boll could have up to 160,000 fibers. As the fibers dried, their cell walls collapsed and twisted, creating up to 300 convolutions per inch, which is what allowed the cotton fibers to hold together in spite of their relatively short length. After workers removed the cotton fibers from the bolls, they removed dirt, leaves, trash, and the seeds by hand. (It was not until the Middle Ages that a roller gin that allowed the fibers to go through but stopped the seeds was developed in India.) Finally, cotton was carded by hand in order to align the fibers and overlap them, and then the cotton was piled in a strand around a distaff.

According to legend, the Chinese princess Luo Zu, who lived around 2700 B.C.E., dropped a cocoon from a mulberry tree into her tea one day and found that when she tried to pick it out, it came out as a single, long strand that could be woven into silk cloth (Wilson 1979). Little is known about silk production until the Han dynasty, by which time silk cloth was not only worn by people of all classes, it had become the single greatest trading material produced in China and the material that gave its name to the trade route, or the Silk Road, which developed between China and the Near East, with ten-tacles extending into and through India. Silk yarn was produced by boiling the silkworms' cocoons in water to release the fibrous protein, *fibroin,* from the binding material, or *sericin,* that held the cocoon together. Workers would either whip the water with a stick, to which the fibers would adhere, or they would run the ends of the fibers from several cocoons through small holes in a porcelain disk in a process called reeling, which produced raw silk, in which individual filaments may be up to 1,000 yards long. The leftover shorter silk fibers were carded, combed, and worked into a loose strand around a distaff much like cotton to produce a heavier and duller textile than that made from raw silk.

Wool, which dominated cloth making in Mesopotamia, Greece, and Rome, comes from the soft inner coats of sheep. Its scaly microstructure allows the individual short fibers to interlock, producing extremely strong yarns. The first steps in processing wool involved cleaning it with water or sand to eliminate grease, sweat, and extraneous matter like leaves. Next, the wool was picked by hand to remove additional debris and to fluff it. Carding then aligned the fibers, which were placed on a distaff, ready for spinning.

Except for the case of raw silk, the loose fibers collected in parallel on a distaff had to be spun into tightly bound long strings, or yarns, in order to prepare them for weaving into cloth. First, the strand on the distaff was stretched and then it was twisted to bind the fibers to one another. As far as we know, these two processes were accomplished everywhere by the beginnings of civilization using a spindle, which was a stick around 18 inches long with a symmetrically weighted end that functioned as a kind of flywheel to keep the spindle rotating once it had begun to spin. As the loose strand of fibers was pulled off the distaff with one hand, it was simultaneously stretched by the weight of the spindle and twisted into a single strand of yarn, called a single-ply yarn, by rotation of the spindle. In some cases, single-ply yarn was not strong enough to use by itself. In that case, two or more single-ply yarns were re-spun into two-ply, three-ply, and so on yarns, or cords. Spinning wheels were not invented until around 750 C.E. in India (Wilson 1979).

Weaving yarn into cloth was and continues to be done on a device called a loom, the first picture of which appears on an Egyptian dish dated to around 4400 B.C.E. (Wilson 1979). The loom holds one set of threads or yarns, called the warp, evenly spaced and under some degree of tension so they do not become tangled, allowing a second set, the weft, woof, or crosswise yarns, to be interlaced with the warp. The earliest form of loom, the horizontal ground loom, which is still used by Bedouin tribes in North Africa, uses two straight poles, each of which is fixed to two short, upright posts embedded in the ground to hold the warp threads, which are fixed at equal distances from one another. At this point, some of the warp threads are lashed to a stick, called the heddle rod. When that rod is raised, the attached warp threads are raised. Next, on the side of the warp threads opposite where the cloth is to be woven, a shed rod is inserted below the relaxed warp threads and above the lifted ones, producing the situation shown in Figure 9.5a. The weft thread is then passed through the space—the shed—between the raised warp threads and the relaxed ones, and a thin rod is used to pound the weft until it is tightened

Figure 9.5
Shedding—Weft Alternates between Going above and below a Given Warp Thread.
Nick Livingston.

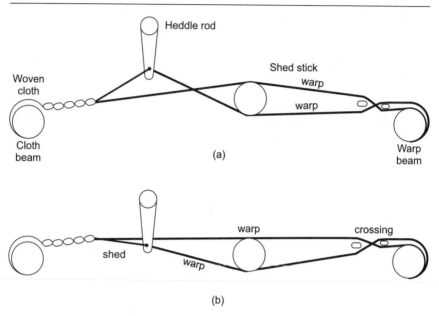

relative to the previous weft thread. At this point, the heddle rod is lowered so that the warp threads that were previously on top are now on the bottom and the shuttle carrying the weft thread is sent back between the two sets of warp threads, having been looped over the outside warp thread, as indicated in Figure 9.5b. The weft tread is again pounded down and the entire process repeated.

Though the orientation, size, and method of maintaining tension in the warp threads varied in producing other early looms, the basic process of weaving was identical in all types. In Mesopotamia and Greece, the warp-weighted loom, which first appeared around 2500 B.C.E., was most common. In this type of loom, the warp threads were hung from a horizontal bar and each warp thread or small group of warp threads was attached to a weight, which maintained the tension. The backstrap loom, or belt loom, was often used in China and Mesoamerica from pre-civilized times. Though it limited the size of weavings that could be done, this loom had the advantage of being both portable and easy for a single person to use. One bar, to which warp threads were affixed, was attached through two cords fixed near its ends to some solid object, such as a tree, the other bar fixed to the warp threads was attached to the weaver's waist. Thus, leaning forward or backwards resulted in varying the tension in the warp threads. This system made it easy to vary the tightness of the weave to adjust to weft threads of different character, and some of the most complex patterns found were done on backstrap looms. Large patterns were accomplished by stitching together segments of fabric done on backstrap looms. More complex pattern looms may have come into existence in the ancient world, especially in China, but there is inadequate archeological evidence to make them a certainty.

For the simplest plain-weave fabric, or tabby weave, a single heddle rod attached to alternate warp threads was used. For a stiffer and heavier fabric, two warps were raised and then two were relaxed and the weft thread was doubled for each pass. This created what is called the canvas weave, which was used for sails and tent coverings. More complex pattern weaves were produced when two or more heddle rods were used in some regular sequence or when yarns of two or more different colors were used either for sequences of warp threads or sequences of weft threads. Pattern-woven textiles using different colored yarns in the warp appeared as early as 2600 B.C.E. in Egypt, and pattern weaves that used multiple heddles appeared as early as circa 2160 B.C.E. (Crowfoot 1954). By the time of the Han Dynasty, Chinese silks incorporating complicated polychrome plant and animal motifs were common, as were loose weave silks that had a translucent gauze-like background with tightly woven patterns in the foreground (see Wilson 1979, 173, plate 52). Additional features of cloth could be added by using different yarns for warp and weft so that one or the other stood out in the pattern.

Mention of the use of different colored yarns in the last paragraph raises a final set of issues with respect to the preparation of woven cloth: the coloring and finishing. With the exception of linens made from flax, most cloth in ancient civilizations was colored using either dyes or by printing, and most cloth was finished in some way to make it stronger or softer than it would otherwise have been. Though there are a few recipes for dyes and instructions for finishing in Mesopotamian and Roman records, little is known about ancient processes and much has to be inferred from medieval records that are presumed to mirror older practices or from pictorial representations that demand extensive interpretation.

When colored patterns were to be woven into a piece of cloth, the yarn had to be dyed before the cloth was woven. More often, and especially in connection with plain-weave cloths and monochrome patterned weaves, it seems that dyeing was done to whole pieces of cloth. Before it was dyed, yarn or cloth was cleaned using agents such as potash, natron, alkaline plant solutions, or stale urine, whose breakdown produced ammonia, the cleaning agent. Next, the yarn or cloth was probably bleached. Vegetable fiber cloth was soaked in buttermilk, steeped in lye, washed, and spread out for exposure to the sun to whiten it. In early modern Europe, this process was frequently repeated several times, taking several months to complete, but we are not certain about the process in the ancient world. Animal fibers such as wool and silk yellowed in the sun, so they were treated differently. Silk was sometimes simply soaked in water, which left subtle, wave-like patterns in the cloth because different portions of the clumped silk were subjected to slightly different pressures. In other cases, silk was spread on racks and exposed to the heat of a sulfurous candle or fire. Wool was also bleached with sulfur fumes, and rubbing gypsum, or fuller's earth, into the cloth to provide a more uniform white, mitigated the lack of uniformity in bleaching.

After bleaching, the yarn or cloth might be dyed (i.e., treated with a material that chemically bonded with the fibers, producing a permanent or long lasting color). Some dyestuffs dissolved in water and combined directly with fabrics, but others demanded the presence of a third material, or mordant, that combined with both the dye and the fiber. These mordants were usually salts of aluminum, iron, tin, or chrome, applied to the fabric before the dye. The same dye would often produce different colors with different mordants. Finally, some of the oldest and most frequently used dyestuffs, including both woad and indigo, which produced blue cloth, were not water soluble. They had to be dissolved in a dilute alkali, which caused them to be reduced to a colorless substance that bonded with the fabric. As the fabric dried, sites on the dyestuff molecules were oxidized in the air, reproducing the initial color of the dyestuff.

Among the earliest and most widely used dyestuffs were mineral dyes; these will be discussed in the next chapter. Saffron, which came from the stigmas of the crocus flower and produced a brilliant yellow color, was used in Egypt by 2000 B.C.E. It became one of the most favored dyes in China and India as well as in Greece and Rome. Weld, a grassy plant found in the Mediterranean Basin, produced a solid yellow. Madder, which comes from the ground roots of the family *Rubiaceae,* was widely used from around 2700 B.C.E. in the Harappan civilization and soon after in Mesopotamia and Egypt to produce different shades of red, depending on how the plants were grown and how the fabrics were prepared. Additional vegetable dyes came from redwoods (red), logwood (blacks and dark blues), gum resins (browns), lichens (soft colors from greens through purple, depending on which lichens were used and how they were prepared), and walnut hulls (black and dark brown). Frequently used animal-based dyes came from mollusks (reds and purples), oak tree lice (reds), and cochineal (a louse-like bug from Mesoamerica that produced a brilliant red). To achieve colors not available from any single dyestuff, ancient dyers combined dyes. Thus, one of the earliest recipes for green combines the blue of indigo and the yellow of weld (Wilson 1979).

Sometimes, designs were dyed into fabrics by treating only appropriate portions of the fabric with either mordants or with materials such as wax, clay, or starch, which kept the fabric from accepting the dye. The latter process, called resist dyeing, produced fabrics called batiks, which became very popular after the period covered by this work in China, Egypt, and India. Few textiles were printed (i.e., colored with pigments that did not chemically bond with the fabric) in the ancient world, though there is some evidence of block-printed textiles in both China and India by around 400 B.C.E.

After fabrics were cleaned and bleached and/or dyed, they were often finished. Indian texts from around 200 B.C.E., for example, describe the use of rice water to strengthen the warp threads of cotton, and Pliny the Elder, writing in the first century of the Common Era, discusses the use of cereal starch and clay to strengthen wool fabrics. Ancient Egyptians finished linen fabric by pounding it with wooden mallets and rubbing it with stone or glass balls flattened on one side in order to soften it, and they used a wooden press to pleat it for making robes and skirts. Wool was fulled in ancient Rome (i.e., the woven cloth was again cleaned, usually with water, and then it was shrunk and shaped by drying it on an adjustable tenter frame to which it was attached by tenterhooks. Finally, it was pounded to force the fibers into an interlocking pattern like felt, which made it both softer and more water resistant). Even homespun wools were usually sent to fulling factories for finishing. A specially soft finish was sometimes given to fulled wool by raising any loose fibers (the nap) using a wooden frame set with closely spaced teeth (usually the buds of the teasle, a form of thistle) and then cutting them to a uniform short length with special shears.

Ten

Minerals, Metals, Pigments, Glazes, and the Origins of Alchemy

Chinese interest in identifying the properties of different materials and in the fabrication of new substances by combining and/or manipulating pre-existing substances was clearly evidenced in connection with medicine by the Han period, and the correspondence notions associated with *wuxing* allowed Chinese scholars to offer a theoretical framework within which to understand the properties and transformations of materials. Modern scholars often identify theorizing of this kind as alchemical because of its parallels with an Islamic tradition of al-*kîmîya*, which involved attempts to understand phenomena associated with the transformation of materials. This term, in turn, was probably derived from the Greek term *chyma*, which was initially used to characterize the casting of an ingot of metal (Forbes 1955). As a theoretical structure, alchemy was generally the last science to develop in most regions of the ancient world, if it emerged at all, but the technological activities that provided both the data and the stimulus for alchemical analyses were among the oldest and most widely distributed in all ancient civilizations, for they included food production, the production of soaps and detergents, the production of perfumes and cosmetics, the production of paints and of glass and glazes, the dyeing of textiles, the production of lubricants and mastics, and above all, the mining, manipulation, and uses of metals and other minerals.

Many of the terms for alchemical processes—cooking, roasting, fermenting, cupellating (i.e., heating in a sealed container to avoid contact with the air), distilling, separating, dyeing, and washing—ultimately derive from prior traditions of food or textile production. Martin Levey has even argued that virtually all alchemical apparatus known to the Islamic and European Middle Ages "might well have come from the utensil cupboard of a second millennium [Mesopotamian] kitchen" (1959, 135). Since food preparation and cloth making were primarily women's work in most ancient civilizations, it should not be surprising that women played a more extensive role in alchemy than in any other ancient science, with the possible exception of obstetrical and gynecological medicine, throughout antiquity and the Middle Ages (Levey

1959). In fact, two of the earliest Hellenistic alchemical treatises were associated with the names of Maria the Jewess and Cleopatra (Forbes 1955).

In this chapter, we will emphasize technologies associated with minerals and metals because they were of tremendous aesthetic, economic, and ritual importance in ancient civilizations and because minerals and metals played a central role in the emergence of alchemical *theories* wherever they became explicit, even though alchemical *practices* probably initially owed as much to kitchen activities. What seem to be the core recipes of the earliest alchemical documents, the Leiden and Stockholm papyri found at Thebes and datable to around 200 B.C.E. (Forbes 1955), derive from a set of practical recipes for creating the artificial or counterfeit gold, silver, emeralds, and lapis lazuli, which were used principally to produce what we would now call costume jewelry in Mesopotamia at least a millennium, and probably two millennia, earlier.

Though the term, mineral, may apply today to any homogeneous inorganic material, including a metal, it is currently usual to insist that a mineral should have a definite chemical composition (Forbes 1963). It has become common in the modern world to set aside certain substances and their alloys, or mixtures, which we designate as metals, for special treatment. Perhaps most important for our purposes, the ancients did not often distinguish between what we might call pure metals and certain alloys. For example, while we identify gold as a single element, most ancient civilizations used their term for gold to identify several naturally occurring gold alloys as gold. In fact, the most valuable form of gold in ancient Mesopotamia was red-gold—what we would call an alloy of gold and copper (Levey 1959)—and among the most frequently used kinds of gold was white gold or electrum—an alloy of gold and silver. Thus, from our perspective, ancient metals did not have a determinate chemical composition as other minerals did. By as early as the Old Babylonian period, it was well understood that human-produced mixtures of different, naturally occurring metals could create homogeneous alloys that at least mimicked, and perhaps even reproduced, such naturally occurring metals as red gold and white gold (Levey 1959). The metals known to the ancient world were generally lustrous, malleable, and ductile; they had unusually high tensile strength relative to organic materials, and they did not appear to the naked eye to have a crystalline structure as other minerals often did.

Color was extremely important in the ancient world everywhere, both for aesthetic and symbolic reasons. We have seen, for example, that Chinese correspondence theories included an important set of five colors that were used, among other places, in court costumes to symbolize status in a political regime. Moreover, color was clearly important in the creation of early ornamentation for its visual appeal. We know, for example, that Greek statuary was painted with vivid colors, and the jewelry associated with ancient Egypt and the Royal Tombs at Ur incorporated materials chosen for their color. Colors were sometimes simply intrinsic features of the materials used in the creation of objects—thus the distinction between red gold and white gold in Mesopotamia and the use of lapis lazuli, carnelian, and turquoise in jewelry almost everywhere that they became available. But in many other cases, color was added to objects by the use of pigments in some form of binding agent like a volatile vegetable oil (paints), by the use of gazes (thin films of glass, often colored by the presence of trace amounts of minerals or metals and adhering to the surface of objects), by mechanically covering a surface with a thin layer of some metal (usually gilding with gold), or, somewhat later, by plating objects with a metal to create a desired color.

Though a few important pigments were organic, many of the most highly prized were associated with naturally occurring minerals or were produced by combining naturally occurring minerals under controlled conditions. Natural blue pigments, for example, included powdered lapis lazuli from Afghanistan, Italy, or East Africa, and Azurite, a copper carbonate-based mineral widely distributed in outcroppings of copper deposits. Among the most important manufactured blue pigments was one called Egyptian Blue, which was distinguished because it could be compressed and molded into amulets, bowls, and pieces of statuary. Analyses of Egyptian Blue shows that it was composed of about 65 percent powdered sand, 7 percent natron (sodium carbonate), 15 percent powdered malachite (another copper carbonate based mineral), and 13 percent powdered lime (Dayton 1978). Natural green pigments included malachite, while manufactured greens were produced after around 1350 B.C.E. by adding iron or antimony-bearing materials to powdered azurite. Naturally occurring reds and yellows included ochres (clays colored by the existence of iron compounds), but the most desirable natural red in China, the Near East, and in Rome, came from cinnabar, or mercury sulphide (HgS), which appears in small amounts throughout the world, sometimes in crystalline form.

Because of its importance as a correlate of the heart and of fire in the Chinese *wuxing* correspondence system, cinnabar red became associated with immortality in China. Cinnabar also became an extremely important material in the West. The Romans painted the faces of conquering generals with it, for example, and it became associated with the Christ child in Christian art. The Roman author, Pliny the Elder, tells us that the pigment made from ground cinnabar was as expensive as gold. Thus, much of the alchemical theory in both China and in Hellenistic Egypt and Greece was directed at creating vermilion, or what was thought to be artificial cinnabar.

The creation of glazes and, eventually, of faience (a self-glazed mixture of powdered sand or quartz and potash or sodium carbonate) and glass was also closely connected to metallurgy and mineralogy in the ancient world. Glazing was almost certainly discovered when molten copper was poured into molds of sandstone or soapstone. Under appropriate conditions, the heat of the copper melted the inner surface of the mold, and the presence of copper oxides produced a bright blue color so that when the copper object was removed from the mold, the inner surface was smooth and brightly colored. Beads of blue glazed soapstone appear in Egypt by 3500 B.C.E. and Egyptian molded faience figurines date from the period between 1900 B.C.E. and 1800 B.C.E. (Dayton 1978).

As glazing became more common, sometime before about 1550 B.C.E., artisans in southern Europe and Egypt found that heating a paste of sand or quartz, natron, and a coloring agent at temperatures well below that of melting drove off volatile impurities, leaving an intermediate material called a frit, which could then be melted, producing a superior glaze or faience. Glass, which is essentially a frit melted through its entire volume, could be found in Egypt and Mycenaean Greece by around 1300 B.C.E. Texts dealing with glass manufacturing appeared in Mesopotamia during the seventh century B.C.E. (Levey 1959), but glass making does not seem to have reached China until the late Han period and did not reach Mesoamerica before Columbus.

Though glazes eventually became important in the production of clay-based ceramics, clay does not bond easily with the glazes produced before 1000 B.C.E., after which lead oxides began to replace natron in the production of glazes. The new glazes had a coefficient of expansion more compatible with that of clay pots, so they did not tend to separate from the clay as it cooled.

We saw in chapter 8 a few nonmetallic minerals, such as gypsum, were known, modified, and used in construction even before the rise of civilizations and many kinds of stone—especially flint and obsidian—were flaked to make tools long before the creation of permanent settlements of any kind. Naturally occurring metallic copper and meteoric iron were both used in small amounts for creating utilitarian objects such as needles, awls, fish hooks, saw teeth, harpoon and spear heads, and knives beginning as early as the eighth millennium B.C.E. in many parts of the world (Craddock 1995). However, evidence suggests that, with the exceptions of obsidian, flint, and a few other forms of stone, mineral materials, as well as many metals including gold, silver, copper, and alloys such as bronze and brass, were initially used in ancient civilizations primarily for human adornment, the creation of secular art objects, and in connection with magical and religious rituals before they were turned to the large scale making of tools, weapons, and other utilitarian products. Amulets, vases, and statues made of such hard materials as alabaster and granite appear in Egypt around 3500 B.C.E., nearly 750 years before stone masons began quarrying blocks of granite for use in constructing mastabas, pyramids, and temples. Jade beads, discs, and animal figurines have been found in the earliest Shang graves in great numbers (Fong 1980). Similarly, copper was used in Harappan civilization in the production of jewelry and sculpted animals and human figures that were probably used in religious rituals earlier than it was used for the construction of axes and adzes.

In what follows, we will begin by considering how ancient minerals and metals were acquired, starting with procedures for mining and quarrying minerals, metals, and metallic ores. We will then move on to the processes of making minerals and metals suitable for use. We will consider how mineral and metallic objects were fabricated, and finally we will discuss how the processing of metals and minerals gave rise to alchemical theorizing. As usual, because we have the earliest and the greatest extent of textual and archeological material from ancient Mesopotamia, Egypt, and China, we will emphasize those civilizations, making comparisons with other civilizations where evidence permits.

THE FORMATION OF MINERAL AND METAL DEPOSITS
AND EARLY MINING TECHNIQUES

In order to get an idea of how early minerals and metals were found and extracted, it is useful to understand how different kinds of mineral deposits were formed in the first place. Most mineral and metal deposits began in connection with volcanic activity. Fissures and fractures were created in the local rock, and these filled with mineral-bearing aqueous solutions at high temperatures and pressures. As pressures and temperatures decreased, various portions of the dissolved materials precipitated out, creating veins of rock such as quartz, calcite, and so on, within which minerals, including precious and semi-precious stones as well as metals and metallic ores, were embedded. It is often the case that iron ores were present in these deposits, but at least until around 1200 B.C.E., techniques for extracting metallic iron from its ores had not been well developed because of the high temperatures required, so other minerals and metals were initially extracted then the veins were sometimes re-visited at later dates to get the iron.

Alternatively, in some places where strata of easily flaked materials such as shale or loose gravels were covered by mineral-bearing soft rock, water precipitating through the upper layers of rock leached out minerals and deposited them in nearly horizontal beds within the layered material, creating thin but broad flats of highly concentrated, mineral-bearing rock. Further geological activity, including erosion, glacial scouring, and upheavals with folding sometimes exposed the veins or flats of mineral-bearing material to the surface action of water and wind.

In a few cases, weathering and/or water flow over the surface of an exposed mineral-bearing vein slowly broke down the matrix and released small particles of desirable material that were carried by a stream and deposited as part of the alluvium in the stream bed where and when the flow slowed down. Most ancient gold was almost certainly recovered from such stream, or placer, deposits. Tin oxides were also frequently found in alluvial deposits, and much placer gold contains traces of tin. Occasionally, small flakes of native metals, especially gold, became cold welded together as they bumped along, creating substantially sized nuggets. In other cases, when ore bodies were exposed at the surface, the chemical action of the air and percolating water oxidized the predominantly sulfurous minerals. In the case of copper-bearing ores, this produced the familiar blue and green copper minerals malachite and azurite, which in turn were reduced in the watery regions common in the upper parts of ore-bearing strata, creating pieces of metallic copper.

Since mineral-bearing veins often have striking visual characteristics, they are likely to be noticed, and in some cases aesthetically appealing materials could simply be mechanically mined by breaking them out of the matrix using stone hammers (Craddock 1995). This, for example, seems to be the way in which pieces of deep blue lapis lazuli were extracted from deposits in the mountains of what is now Afghanistan beginning around 4500 B.C.E., the way that red crystals of cinnabar (HgS) were mined even before the rise of civilizations, and the way that pieces of reddish carnelian were extracted in the Harappan region by no later than 2500 B.C.E. Indeed, evidence of simple stone-hammer mining exists worldwide. It seems that the earliest mining of gold was probably done by crushing the ambient material and simply picking out the small flakes of native metal (usually some alloy of gold with copper, silver, or tin), and copper was mined in this way in the western highlands of Egypt and in the Sinai region of what is now southern Israel between 5000 and 4000 B.C.E. (Silverman 1997). In general, early mines were worked simply through shallow caves or trenched along the veins of ore.

In a few places where mines were located near the tops of relatively steep hills or cliffs, ventilation could be achieved by creating a horizontal tunnel that linked up with a vertical shaft from which several galleries departed. Elsewhere, mines tended to be very small with very short galleries departing from near vertical shafts that were rarely more than 10 meters deep because deeper shafts and longer galleries made for severe ventilation problems. At the Wadi Timna, in the Sinai, for example, where copper was the primary target material and the surrounding rock was soft sandstone, the Egyptians developed over 9,000 independent mine shafts within about 10 meters of one another during the 14th century B.C.E. (Craddock 1995). The earliest Timna mines were cold-worked, first with stone and later with metal-tipped hammers.

In many cases, the matrix containing desirable materials was hard enough that the immediate mechanical extraction of the valuable material was impractical or inefficient. In such cases, fires were often set at the face of the vein. The heat produced cracks and flaking in the matrix—sometimes to a depth of 30 cm when a fire was allowed to burn overnight (Craddock 1995). The softened matrix could then be mechanically broken apart to extract the valuable material. Throughout the world, native metallic copper was mined in this way from no later than 4000 B.C.E.

With rare exceptions, because the geological activities that created deposits of metals and minerals occurred in connection with volcanic activity and were thus in mountainous regions at some distance from the river valleys in which early civilizations developed, the earliest mining activities and the earliest use of metals, minerals, pigments, and glazes occurred outside of the great civilizations in the highland regions of the Americas, Europe, North and East Africa, and Asia. For this reason, most metals and minerals came into civilizations with the initial settlers, as in Egypt, or through trade. Mesopotamian texts, for example, refer to silver from Cappadocia (in modern Turkey) and metallic ores from the Kurdish regions of northern Iraq, Iran, and Afghanistan (Forbes 1963). Once civilizations gained access to minerals and metals, however, they tended to create new technologies for manipulating and using them. Moreover, the more imperial civilizations of Mesopotamia and China frequently sought and gained military and political control over relatively distant mining sites to ensure their supplies of raw materials.

THE EARLY USE OF NATIVE COPPER, GOLD, AND IRON

In spite of the fact that metals are a major constituent of the earth's crust in the form of mineral compounds, only three metals, copper, gold, and iron, exist in significant amounts in metallic form on or near the surface of the earth. Of these three, iron, largely in the form of meteorites, was both relatively rare and very difficult to work. With a melting point of approximately 2,804° F it could not be melted until the development of special high temperature furnaces around 1100 B.C.E. in China and later elsewhere. Thin pieces of iron could sometimes be broken off a meteorite's surface with stone hammers. These pieces were then usually softened by heating and shaped by hammering, thus explaining the small number of iron knife blades and spear points that have been found near places where large meteors struck the earth.

Metallic copper is the most abundant naturally occurring metal, and though its melting point, at 1,981° F, is high enough that it cannot be melted in an ordinary campfire, it can be softened enough in a campfire to allow for hammering into relatively thin sheets and different shapes. Moreover, heating, hammering, and slowly cooling (i.e., annealing) copper hardens it and toughens it so that it wears slowly and is not brittle. Thus, copper can be used in making both ornamental objects and tools. Sometime around 2700 B.C.E. in the Harappan region, in North America, in Europe, and in the Sinai region, temperatures of around 2,012° F were reached in fires aided by strong drafts, making it possible to melt native copper. This melting probably occurred first within mines as fire-setting became a common way to break up the veins of quartz or other matrix material in which bits of copper were trapped. In this case, melted copper was probably found in the ashes of the fires.

Metallic gold is less commonly found than metallic copper and it is too soft to be useful in tools. It has a melting point very close to that of copper (pure gold melts at 1,945° F), but gold is much softer and more ductile, so it is much more easily worked. Even at ordinary atmospheric temperatures, it can be beaten into very thin sheets, so it can be applied as a finish to objects made of almost anything, and once in metallic form it is almost completely non-reactive, so it retains its luster almost indefinitely.

SMELTING

In North America, the melting and casting of native copper never led to further developments in metallurgy, but virtually everywhere else it led very rapidly to smelting, or the extraction of metals from their ores. There is debate about precisely how this happened, though it is clear that it happened independently and at different times in different places. Furthermore, it is clear that smelting occurred in two distinct phases. In the first phase, metallic copper was produced by the direct reduction of copper oxide ores at high heat in a very low oxygen environment, usually produced by the presence of charcoal, which removed oxygen from the atmosphere. This process was probably discovered accidentally very quickly after fire-setting became common. Even though ancient mines tended to be very shallow, the chimney effect of a 10-meter mining pit was probably enough to create a sufficiently rapid air flow to allow the fire to reach temperatures in excess of 1,832° F, high enough to melt any small bits of metallic copper in the vein and to roast the malachite and azurite ores to produce metallic copper or copper oxides that were then reduced when they dripped into the fire and came in contact with the residual charcoal produced by the burning wood. This accidental smelting process created puddles or ingots of molten copper in the fire. Once cooled, these ingots could then be re-melted in crucibles to be poured into molds, or cast.

Alternatively, at many mines, the metal- and ore-bearing rock was first beneficiated (crushed with rock hammers or grindstones and then sorted by hand or washed) near the mine head to separate the concentrated metal and incidental mineral material from the matrix. This concentrated material was hauled away to be heated in crucibles in furnaces created for that purpose at sites where fuel was available. At Zawar, in northern India, for example, ore was crushed near the mines and the enriched material was taken into the valley below to be heated in the presence of charcoal, which had been found to help remove impurities in the metal. At some point it was recognized that not only was the metal being melted, but that the ores that could not be easily separated from the metal were producing additional metal. Soon, ores were being heated in crucibles to produce metal even when there was little or no associated native metal present (Craddock 1995). Similar scenarios almost certainly led to the development of smelting independently and almost simultaneously in several places around the world.

The good news about copper produced in the early phase of smelting is that it tended to have very little iron content—usually below 0.05 percent—so the copper was very easily worked. On the other hand, this early smelting process only worked well with very high grade ores, which comprised a small fraction of the ores available in most places. During this phase of smelting it also became clear that other metals could be produced from different mineral ores—thus silver, tin, lead, and zinc were added to copper and gold to form the inventory of metals available to ancient civilizations at the beginning of the third millennium (3000 B.C.E.) in Egypt, Mesopotamia, and Harappan Civilization, by the Shang period (1600 B.C.E.) in China, and much later in Central America, depending on what particular ore deposits were locally available and what trading networks could be developed. Indeed, it is not clear that any other phase of smelting ever occurred in Mesoamerica, where gold and copper remained the only metals in use to the time of Columbus. It is probable that the Maya, so advanced in mathematics and astronomy, had no metallurgical tradition at all.

New methods of smelting developed relatively rapidly in the Near East, but more slowly elsewhere. I have already mentioned that iron-containing ores—frequently in the form of silicates—often accompanied copper ores where

Figure 10.1
Types of Early Smelting Furnaces. Nick Livingston.

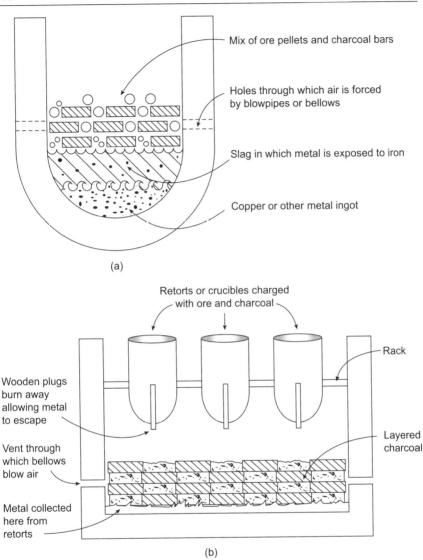

Mix of ore pellets and charcoal bars

Holes through which air is forced
by blowpipes or bellows

Slag in which metal is exposed to iron

Copper or other metal ingot

(a)

Retorts or crucibles charged
with ore and charcoal

Rack

Wooden plugs
burn away
allowing metal
to escape

Layered
charcoal

Vent through
which bellows
blow air

Metal collected
here from
retorts

(b)

copper was present. Iron silicates melt at temperatures well below that at which iron melts, and even below that at which copper ores are normally reduced, producing copper. Furthermore, iron silicates have a specific gravity substantially lower than that of any of the common metals of antiquity, so when iron silicates were present in an ore containing copper or other metals as they were heated, the iron silicate tended to melt first, creating what is called a slag, through which the molten metal then dripped, removing many impurities. Initially, for copper smelting, the furnace was filled with layers of relatively coarse ore pellets and chunks of charcoal. The charcoal was lit and air was forced into the mix through blowpipes or other methods to promote combustion (see Figure 10.1a). This process could use vastly lower grade ores than the earlier one, but in the copper case, the resulting metal tended to have a larger percentage of dissolved iron that it picked up while dropping through the slag—typically about 0.3 percent, but sometimes up to 3 percent iron— which made the copper much harder to work.

Though lead does not occur naturally in metallic form, it has a relatively low melting point at 621° F and its principle ore, galena, is widely distributed and was used throughout the ancient world as an eye paint. There is general agreement that if a lump of galena had been accidentally dropped into a campfire or hearth, it would have been reduced, producing lead.

Lead is very soft and not very lustrous. It was, nonetheless, intentionally produced by about 3500 B.C.E., for lead drinking vessels and ornaments appear in Mesopotamian graves by around that time and lead bars have been found in pre-dynastic Egyptian sites. Moreover, some sheets of lead appear in the royal graves at Ur from around 2000 B.C.E. Sheet lead rolled into sections of pipe became common in the Near East by around 700 B.C.E., and lead was certainly one of the metals smelted at Laurion, the great silver mine established about 480 B.C.E. near Athens. Lead pipe was probably appropriated by the Romans from the Assyrians in Mesopotamia to become the most common form of small diameter water pipe throughout the Roman Empire.

For other metals that did not occur naturally in metallic form, including zinc at Zawar in North India, jars were filled with a tightly packed ore and charcoal mix. These jars were stopped up with wooden plugs and inverted in a rack in a furnace. The metal formed in the jar and passed through a slag near the mouth of the jar before the plug burned away, allowing the molten metal to flow onto the furnace floor (see Figure 10.1b). We know relatively little about the shapes of most of these furnaces because the high heats destroyed most after a few smelts, but fragments suggest that most were shaft-shaped with a circular cross section somewhat larger in the reaction region than above or below where they were reduced to about half a meter in diameter. They were probably about 2 to 3.5 meters high and made out of clay or brick and clay with the lower, ingot-collecting, region often below grade level.

The earliest mining and smelting furnaces may have been fueled with wood and brush, but people everywhere where metal was smelted rapidly discovered that charcoal both produced a hotter fire and provided what we now recognize as a powerful reducing atmosphere, so that metals were much more efficiently produced in charcoal-fueled furnaces than in wood-fueled ones. Generally, charcoal was produced by burning wood in very limited supplies of air—in pits or in large, tight stacks. Typically, it took about 100 kilograms of wood to make 20 kilogram of charcoal and between 20 and 50 kilograms of charcoal to produce 1 kilogram of copper. In some dry regions, such as that near Timna in the Sinai and in Northern China, that meant that mining produced almost complete deforestation in the region, but most early mines were in heavily forested regions, so sustained-yield timber harvesting provided adequate fuel. Even where timber supplies were very short, there is no indication that fossil fuels such as coal were used in antiquity. Coal seems to have been used first for iron production in China in the fourth century c.e. (Craddock 1995).

Air was supplied to some furnaces simply by directing the openings into the reaction region toward the prevailing winds at places where winds were common and strong, but in most cases air entered the furnace through short clay tubes called tuyeres. These, in turn, were fed by a variety of devices. The earliest seem to have been blowpipes, which are depicted in Egyptian tomb paintings from the third millennium and which have remained in use for small furnaces in Central and South America, Africa, and Southeast Asia to the present day. It is likely that bag bellows made of animal skins with a nozzle at one end and an opening that could be closed by gathering the material together by hand at the other were also used very early. The bag was opened to allow air to enter, then the material was gathered together to keep air from escaping through the opening. When the bag was squeezed, air escaped through the nozzle into the tuyere. These bag bellows are depicted in Greek and Roman bas-reliefs from the sixth century to the end of antiquity and they remained in use in some places in Africa and India into the 19th century, but they are relatively inefficient.

Pot bellows replaced bag bellows and supplemented blowpipes almost everywhere except in Europe and possibly China by the late Bronze Age, and they too remain in wide spread use in Africa and south Asia into the 21st century. Pot bellows were composed of ceramic pots about 30 cm in diameter and 5–10 cm high with an air exit hole in one side. These were topped with leather skins, including flap valves, which could be opened and closed manually. Typically they were used in pairs. The operator shifted his weight from the leather top of one pot to the other, holding the flap valve closed on the down stroke, so air was forced out of the side and into the tuyere (see Figure 10.2a). Experiments have shown that one pair of pot bellows operated by an experienced person could have provided all of the air needed by one of the furnaces at Timna in the 14th century b.c.e. (Craddock 1995).

By the early first millennium, Concertina bellows (see Figure 10.2 b) essentially like those used by 19th-century blacksmiths began to be used in Europe, the Middle East, and Northern India. In China, by the early Warring States Period, around 450 b.c.e., double acting box piston bellows (see Figure 10.2c) were in use. These very efficient bellows provided an advantage in smelting iron, which melts at around 2,804° F, giving rise to an extensive early iron industry in China.

Figure 10.2
Types of Bellows. Nick Livingston.

(a) Pot Bellows.
(b) Accordion Bellows.
(c) Chinese Double-Acting Box Bellows.

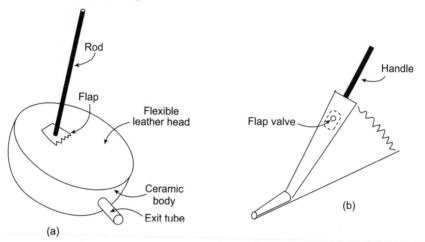

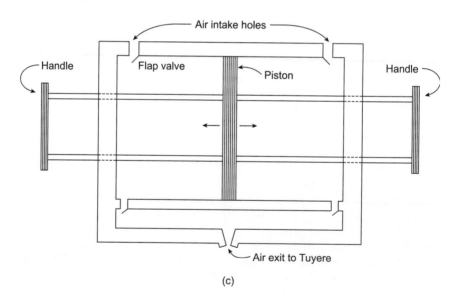

REFINING METALS

Most naturally occurring and smelted metals contain at least small amounts of other substances, including other metals mixed in with them. We have seen, for example, that copper objects produced by early, pre-slagging smelting can be distinguished from later copper objects by the percentage of iron in them. In many cases, the included materials seriously affected the properties of the metal, making it unusually brittle, for example. In other cases, there were other practical reasons to want purified metals. Copper, for example, became an extremely important medium of exchange throughout the Mediterranean region and Near East by the late third millennium, and there was often concern that the copper being traded met some standard of purity. Similarly, during the seventh century B.C.E., initially in Lydia, pure gold and silver became standard metals for coinage, and since much native gold contained substantial amounts of silver, it became important to be able to separate the silver from the gold and to purify each metal. In theory, the purity of any metal can be determined by measuring its specific gravity, but there is no indication that such a measure was used in practice, even after Archimedes's famous discussion of how to determine the composition of Hiero's crown around 250 B.C.E. at Syracuse.

According to the legend reported by Vitruvius, a certain amount of gold was given to a craftsman to make a crown for the king. After an appropriate time, the craftsman presented a crown weighing exactly the same as the gold given him, but someone claimed that some of the gold had been taken by the man and replaced by silver. Archimedes had crowns fabricated of equal weights of gold and silver and measured the volume of each by measuring the overflow of a filled vessel with water. The heavier gold displaced a smaller volume of water. When the volume of the suspect crown was measured in the same way it was found to have a greater volume than that of the gold crown, showing that the craftsman was, indeed, a thief (Vitruvius 1960).

Instead of measuring specific gravities, starting around 600 B.C.E. at Sardis and extending well through the Renaissance, metal workers judged the purity of gold based on the color of a mark left on a smooth black stone called a *touchstone* (Dayton 1978); there was virtually no way to assess the purity of other metals except by their color and mechanical properties (i.e., their hardness and ductility).

The simplest form of refining—used almost everywhere for copper, and called cupellation—involved re-melting the native or smelted metal in a cleaned crucible and stirring it to bring the reactive impurities to the surface where they could be oxidized and either evaporate or form a surface layer (sometimes a slag) that could be skimmed off. Separating silver from gold was a much more complex operation, and though some Mesopotamian texts suggest that copper was removed from gold as early as the late third millennium, the separation of gold from silver is not well attested until the late seventh century B.C.E. at Sardis and until the end of the Han period (c. 220 C.E.) in China. The processes in the two places were somewhat different, but both depended on the fact that silver reacts with the chlorine in salt so that the silver in electrum could be extracted as silver chloride, leaving pure gold. In a separate operation, the silver could then be smelted out of the silver chloride.

In the Near East, the electrum was hammered into thin sheets in its solid state. These sheets were placed in a cooking pot and packed in a mixture of salt and brick dust. The pot was heated to slightly below the melting point of the electrum alloy sheets for an extended period of time, during which the silver slowly bonded with the chlorine in the salt, which in turn formed a cement with the brick dust (Craddock 1995). Once cooled, the sheet of electrum had become pure gold. One sample from Egypt, datable to around 500 B.C.E. was, for example, found to be 99.8 percent gold, whereas earlier native gold typically contained between 60 and 90 percent gold with up to 40 percent copper and/or silver (Aitchison 1960). In China, the gold-silver alloy was melted in a crucible and powdered salt was stirred into the melt. The silver-chloride slag rose to the top and was skimmed off using a thornwood stick. This process was repeated until no slag formed, at which point the remaining gold was very nearly pure (Needham 1969).

The separation of silver from lead was also a major problem in antiquity because the principle sources of both after around 2500 B.C.E. were ores that were mostly galena (lead sulfide, PbS) mixed with varying amounts of argentite (silver sulfide, Ag_2S). Simple cupellation, in which the lead was oxidized by blowing air across the surface of the melt to produce litharge, was adequate to reach levels of silver purity that were widely acceptable until the rise of silver coinage and the nearly simultaneous discovery of a huge galena-based silver and lead mine at Laurion, just outside of Athens about 490 B.C.E. Up until that point, objects that we identify as silver tended to have anywhere from about 60 percent elemental silver to 95 percent silver content. As silver became used for coinage, however, much higher levels of purity were sought. Athenian coins, for example, ranged from 98.98 to 99.40 percent silver, and Roman silver was routinely 99 percent or more elemental silver (Aitchison 1960). Cupellation could probably not have provided that level of purity, and it is likely that the Romans, and possibly the Athenians, followed cupellation with a second process involving amalgamation in mercury.

The Romans certainly knew that gold and silver, but not lead, can be dissolved in, or amalgamated with mercury, which in turn can be produced from cinnabar in a process to be discussed below. Amalgamation involved bringing small particles of solid, impure silver into contact with the mercury, which dissolved the silver, leaving the residual metal in solid form. The silver was then removed from solution by placing the amalgam in a leather or canvas bag and squeezing. The mercury dripped through the bag and the pure metal remained (Dayton 1978).

THE PRODUCTION OF MERCURY

The production of mercury from cinnabar is discussed in the earliest Chinese medical treatise from the Han dynasty. It was probably known in Turkey and Attic Greece by around 500 B.C.E., and there is textual evidence of it in Greece from 312 B.C.E. In one of the methods, powdered cinnabar was mixed with water into a kind of dough that could be formed into small bricks. These were alternated with equal numbers of similarly sized charcoal blocks and heated in a furnace with a domed lid that contained a small hole in the middle. An iron or vitreous condensing tube was closely sealed to this hole at one end and inserted into a water-containing jar at the other. The furnace was then fired for about 10 hours. Mercury vapor was released as the sulfur and carbon reacted to form a gunky residue. The mercury vapor condensed in the tube, dripping through the cool water and forming a pool of liquid mercury in the bottom of the jar (Ch'iao p'ing 1948). Driving vaporous materials off a mixture of solid materials (sublimating) or liquids (vaporizing) by heating and then capturing some fraction of the materials by condensation is the principle behind all distilling practices.

A second method of producing mercury from cinnabar was described by Theophrastus in his *On Stones* (c. 300 B.C.E.). It involves mixing powdered cinnabar with vinegar and pounding it with a copper pestle in a copper mortar (Takacs 2000).

ALLOYING

Just as the purification of copper began sometime before 2000 B.C.E. in the Middle East, the intentional mixing of metals to create alloys—initially bronzes (alloys of copper, especially with tin and/or lead) in order to improve desirable qualities such as hardness also began in Mesopotamia by around 2000 B.C.E., in Egypt by around 1750 B.C.E., and in China around 1600 B.C.E. It would perhaps be more proper to say that bronzes were first imported to Mesopotamia, Egypt, and China by these dates, probably from Europe in the Mesopotamian and Egyptian cases (Dayton 1978) and from Siberia in the Chinese case. The ingots of metal that came from elsewhere were worked locally in the major civilizations, however. There is, for example, evidence of a large-scale bronze casting industry at Zhengzhou, less than 50 kilometers south of Anyang and far from any mines, from the early Shang period (c. 1600 B.C.E.). Though it is very likely that the earliest bronzes everywhere were naturally occurring, there is written evidence that the conscious alloying of tin with copper to create bronzes with different features was being practiced in China well before about 1000 B.C.E. The *Kao kung chi* from the eighth century of the Common Era outlines six different types of bronze for six different purposes, moving from those that required relatively soft metal to those that demanded increasing hardness:

There are six kinds of *chi* [alloys]—those containing five parts of metal [copper] and one part of tin are used for making tripods and bells; four parts of metal and one part of tin, for axes; three parts of metal and one of tin for spears and lances; two parts of metal and one of tin for larger knives; four parts of metal and two [this should probably be three] parts of tin for smaller knives and arrows; one part of metal and one of tin for mirrors. (Ch'iao p'ing, 1948, 32)

Modern analysis shows that, at least from Zhou times (c. 1100 B.C.E.), the percentage of tin in different bronze objects follows the sequence discussed in the *Kao kung chi* (Ch'iao p'ing 1948).

Brasses, which combined copper with zinc rather than tin, probably appeared as naturally occurring alloys in eastern Turkey sometime in the eighth century B.C.E. (Craddock 1995). Because zinc boils at a temperature below the melting point of copper, artificial brass cannot be made by simply mixing melts of the two metals. A process in which finely divided copper was heated in the presence of zinc oxide and charcoal in a closed crucible below the melting point of copper (1,981° F) but above the boiling point of zinc (1,683° F) was developed no later than about 30 B.C.E. in or near Pergamum, off the western coast of modern Turkey, for brass coinage came into existence around 27 B.C.E. there and 23 B.C.E. in Rome (Craddock 1995). Artificial brass objects were made starting in about 9 C.E. in China (Ch'iao p'ing 1948).

IRON AND STEEL PRODUCTION AND WORKING

The production of iron and steel, which is a form of processed iron, is more complex than that of the other solid metals known in antiquity, so smelted iron came later and the means of smelting were quite different in Europe and the Near East than they were in China. Largely because of the use of the box piston bellows, furnace temperatures in China were capable of reaching those necessary to produce impure iron in liquid form by the Warring States period. Though pure iron melts only above 2,802° F, iron containing 2–5 percent carbon will melt at between 2,102° F and 2,192° F, depending on exactly how much carbon is present, so by the Han period, China had developed an extensive iron industry based on the production of pig, or cast, iron. Cast iron, averaging about 4 percent carbon is hard but quite brittle, so it cannot be worked by hammering. In order to produce a more workable iron, the Chinese removed the carbon impurities from the molten iron by a puddling process like that used to refine copper. That is, they ran the molten iron into a vat where it was stirred while dried earth was sprinkled on the surface. The carbon impurities tended to combine with substances in the earth, producing a scum that could be removed. Iron produced in this way became wrought iron, which was much more malleable than cast iron, but not nearly as hard.

At some point—but still during the Han period—the Chinese began to produce steel, which is hard but not brittle. They did this by combining pig and wrought iron, which we now know produced an iron alloy with a carbon content of between about 0.5 and 2 percent. Wrought iron was beaten into thin sheets and covered with thin casts of pig iron. The wrought and pig irons were tied together, placed in a furnace, and heated just below the temperature at which the pig iron would melt. The pig iron gradually fused with and then diffused through the wrought iron, creating steel (Ch'iao p'ing 1948). This material could be worked at red heat, and it was extremely strong and could maintain a sharp edge, making it ideal for making tools and weapons.

In Europe and western Asia, large-scale iron smelting started sometime after 1200 B.C.E. This was initially done at temperatures well below the melting point of iron in furnace pits like that of Figure 10.3a. The process produced smallish, spongy blooms of solid iron that usually weighed less than 20 kilo-

Figure 10.3
Cross Sections of Early European Furnaces for Making Iron. Nick Livingston.

(a) Early Pit Furnace.
(b) Roman Shaft Furnace.

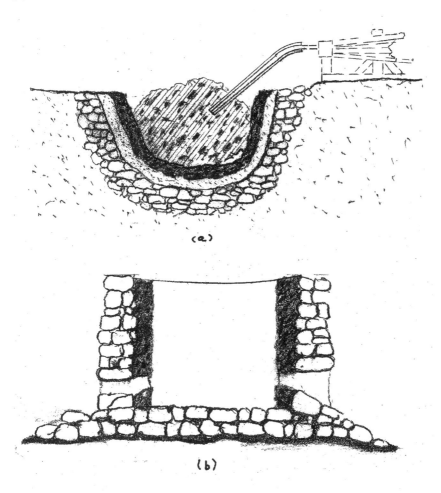

(a)

(b)

grams and were shot through with veins of slag. These blooms were left in the bottom of the furnaces when they cooled. Repeated hammering and annealing of the bloom forced out most of the slag and other impurities, producing a very pure wrought iron that was quite soft and malleable. By around 300 B.C.E., shaft furnaces such as that depicted in Figure 10.3b were in use. Air was forced in on one side and the slag was drained off on the other, leaving the bloom to form in the reaction area above the openings and to settle slowly to the bottom of the furnace. In general, large pieces of iron were produced by welding (i.e., by heating small blooms to about 2,012° F in a forge and hammering multiple blooms together).

Most steel produced outside of China in antiquity was probably accidentally produced when thin bars of wrought iron were welded together to form the blades of weapons. Carbon was probably first introduced into the surface of the iron during the hammering process, making it harder than the wrought iron. There is some evidence, however, that at a relatively late date, Roman smiths intentionally carburized the edges of iron weapons and tools to make them hold an edge (Aitchison 1960). Little or no iron casting was done outside of China until after the period covered by this book. Indeed, two of the most spectacular early iron objects produced just before 300 c.e.—North-Indian pillars, one 23 feet, 8 inches in length with a circular cross section that ranged from 16.5 inches in diameter at the base to 12.5 inches in diameter at the top, and the other, 42 feet long with a roughly square cross section with about an 18-inch diagonal—were not cast but were made by hot welding plates of wrought iron on top of one another until the final height was reached (Aitchison 1960).

CHANGES IN MINING DURING THE FIRST MILLENNIUM B.C.E.

The form of mines changed substantially in several parts of the world during the first millennium as systems for ventilating and draining allowed for the creation of deeper and more extensive mine systems, which, in turn, demanded systems of timbering to keep galleries from collapsing. The new forms appeared first in China, where galleries as long as several hundred meters connected to multiple shafts that extended below the water table. These were created during the Warring States period and into the Han period (c. 450 B.C.E.–200 C.E.). Work at the faces of the galleries remained relatively unchanged, with fire-setting and the use of hammers, picks, and chisels supplemented now by the use of iron-headed battering rams to break up the veins of ore.

The simplest method for improving ventilation was to create shafts in pairs not too distant from one another and then to run galleries between the two so that air could move through the galleries. In other cases, long galleries with shafts at their ends fanned out from a central shaft. When a fire was set in the central shaft, air was drawn down from the extremities and sometimes diverted using shutters into shorter side galleries. The Tonglushan copper mine at Daye in the Hubei province of China operated from about 450 B.C.E. to 200 C.E. (Fong 1980). This mine had multiple shafts, galleries, and drifts (side excavations off main galleries), and there is substantial evidence of shuttering to control air flow (Craddock 1995).

Drainage could also be a significant problem. Where mines were high above nearby valleys, channels called adits were tunneled in from the valley side to drain mines. Some Roman drainage tunnels (which also provided ventilation) reached three kilometers in length (Craddock 1995). In other cases, a ladder of ponds was created in one of the deepest shafts. Water was directed from the galleries to be drained through troughs of wood, or channels cut in the tunnel floors into a pool at the lowest point, and a ladder of pools was built up the side of the shaft. In the most primitive systems, miners would dip a bucket from one pool and pour it into a higher pool. Once it was at the top of the shaft, it could be directed away along a ditch. At Rio Tinto, in Spain, Roman miners developed a system of water wheels, the buckets of which scooped up water at one level and deposited it into a pool about 3–5 meters higher, through a series of 8 different levels, raising the water a total of approximately 30 meters or almost 100 feet (Craddock 1995).

THE SPIRITUAL DIMENSION OF MINING AND METALLURGY

In chapter 4, I argued both that the citizens of ancient civilizations lived in a vastly more participatory relationship with the natural world than we do and that important events and enterprises almost always involved some ritual elements intended to promote the success of the activity. So far, I have discussed mining, metallurgy, and mineralogy in ancient civilizations as if they emerged in a completely objective way, but Egyptian, Chinese, Indian, and Mesopotamian documents make it clear that these practices had an important spiritual dimension as well. Here, for example, is a translation of a portion of a text from the library of Assurbanipal (600 B.C.E.), which sets forth the rituals involved in building a furnace for smelting ore in Mesopotamia:

When thou settest out the [ground] plan of a furnace for minerals, thou shalt seek out a favorable day in a fortunate month, and thou shalt set out the ground plan of the furnace. While they are making the furnace, thou shalt watch them and thou shalt work thyself: thou shalt bring in embryos [born before time?]. Another, a stranger, shall not enter, nor shall one that is unclean tread before them; thou shalt offer the due libations before them. The day when thou puttest the mineral into the furnace, thou shalt make a sacrifice before the embryos; thou shalt set a censer with incense of pine, thou shall pour *kurunna*-beer before them. (Eliade 1978, 72)

There is great disagreement regarding whether "embryos" in this text should be taken literally or as a term for the pieces of ore placed in the furnace, but regardless of which translation is chosen, there is no question that the text places smelting in a participatory context, treating both furnace and ores as living beings needing to be appropriately treated so that the furnace would do its work on the ore. One reason for the ambiguity regarding how "embryos" is to be understood is that all metallurgical traditions that have left a written trace—those of Mesopotamia, China, Egypt, and India—treat the natural production of precious stones and metals as a process of slow growth in the belly of the earth—which, given time, would yield the most mature or perfect stone, diamond, or metal, gold. The miner and metallurgist intervened in this process to both speed it up and to abort it at some appropriate place, producing whatever metal was sought. From this perspective, it is easy to understand the ore pieces as embryos that grow into the metal. Evidence suggesting a literal interpretation comes from a number of African traditions in which human embryos were offered as sacrifices in the process of creating a furnace (Eliade 1978).

The linkage of metallurgy with growth and birth is strongly suggested by another set of relationships that existed among pre-civilized peoples and were evidenced in China during and after the Han Dynasty. Both metal workers and shamans—the semi-divine men responsible for spiritual medicine—were known as "masters of fire." Indeed, in many early cultures, the art of the metal worker was identified with shamans. Thus, metallurgy and health often became linked in the same person and processes. One of the early Han texts that demonstrates this connection is focused on both the production of gold and the indefinite prolongation of life. It simultaneously emphasizes the spiritual dimension of metallurgical/medical practice:

Sacrifice to the furnace and you will be able to summon (supernatural) beings. When you have called forth these beings, the powder of cinnabar can be transformed into yellow gold; when the yellow gold is produced, you will be able to make of it utensils for drinking and eating and in doing so you will have prolonged longevity. When your longevity is prolonged you will be able to see the blessed of the island of *P'eng Lai*, which is in the mist of the seas. When you have seen them and have made the *feng* and *chan* sacrifices, then you will not die. (Eliade 1978, 112–113)

As we shall see later, practices and theories of alchemy grew out of this ritualized and participatory form of metallurgy in China, India, and Alexandrian Egypt. In these places, spiritual metallurgy combined with local philosophical doctrines, and when it did, it everywhere carried forward the presumptions that metals grew slowly to perfection in the earth, that the alchemist had to carry out certain propitiatory rituals to succeed in his activities, and that metallurgy and mineralogy are intimately connected with human health. As an Indic text attributed to Nâgârjuna (fourth century B.C.E.) states: "Mineral preparations act with equal efficacy on metals and on the human body" (Eliade 1978, 134).

METHODS OF FABRICATING DECORATIVE
OBJECTS FROM MINERALS AND METALS

Once a mineral or metal was extracted from the ground or smelted from its ores, it had to be worked in some way to create a useful and/or beautiful object. This working was, in all civilizations, done by a different group of people than those who prepared the metal in the first place, and sometimes there was a division of labor among those who worked with different metals. Thus, in Mesopotamia, smiths, who worked to shape metal objects, were distinguished from the miners and smelters who produced the metal, and goldsmiths, silversmiths, and coppersmiths were also distinguished from one another.

Perhaps the earliest decorative object associated with a settlement that would become part of an early civilization is a necklace composed of six ob-

Figure 10.4
Obsidian and Shell Necklace from Northern Mesopotamia, circa 5000 B.C.E.
Nick Livingston.

sidian flakes, roughly 1.5 centimeters thick and 5 centimeters in diameter, plus a dark clay piece shaped to match the obsidian. Each of these was made into a bead by drilling a hole from one edge to the opposite edge. Between each pair of these large beads were threaded two or three cowrie shells that had been filled with red ochre. This necklace (see Figure 10.4), which is dated to about 5000 B.C.E., was found at Arpachiya, near Nippur in Mesopotamia (Tait 1986).

Several things about the necklace are of special interest. First, neither the obsidian nor the shells could have been be found near Arpachiya. The stone came from northern Turkey, and the shells came from the Mediterranean shore or the Persian Gulf, so both must have been traded for, even at this very early and pre-literate date. Second, the obsidian beads were not left in their natural state, but were carefully shaped and polished before being drilled. Third, it seems likely that the clay bead was intended to imitate the obsidian in order to have seven large beads (seven, remember, was a particularly powerful number in Mesopotamia). Each of these features is typical for jewelry made throughout all early civilizations: the raw materials often came from far away, they were extensively modified, and imitations were sought and fabricated when rare and expensive materials were not available.

Many of the early pieces of jewelry found in Egypt and Mesopotamia and in the cities of the Harappan culture incorporated beads that almost certainly originated at Lothal, a seaport near the head of the Indus River, or at Chanhudaro, which lay between Lothal and Mohenjo-daro. These sites were inhabited from around 3500 B.C.E. to around 1750 B.C.E., and they were the locus of large and famous bead-making industries (Chattopadhyaya 1986). Local materials, including soapstone, carnelian, limestone, and jasper, as well as gold and copper, were used, but other raw materials, including lapis lazuli, jade, turquoise, onyx, and silver were imported. Furthermore, the most common beads were made of soapstone and then glazed with green and blue glazes, probably to imitate the rarer, more expensive, and much harder to shape jade, turquoise, and lapis lazuli. Beads of many shapes—including cylindrical, tapered with a larger diameter at the middle than at the ends, disk shaped, and globular—were made, and some—especially those of carnelian—had etched designs in them. Virtually all of those that did not have a glaze on them were polished.

Though slightly different processes were used to produce different shapes, the most common cylindrical and disk-shaped beads were produced in the following way. A piece of stone was cut into rods with roughly square cross-sections either by using a hammer and chisel to crack and split them longitudinally or by using a saw (probably a toothless piece of metal or metal wire used with an abrasive such as powdered quartz or emery). Then, the rod was flaked using bone or metal tools into a bar with roughly round cross section. At this point, it was probably polished by rubbing on sandstones with successively fine abrasive qualities. Next, it was cut crosswise into sections small enough to drill along the axis of the cylinder. Drilling was done using stone-tipped bow drills in which the tip had a small, cup-like cavity containing an abrasive. When shorter, disk-like cylinders or double tapered cylinders were desired, the longer cylinders were again cut and possibly abraded to produce the final shape. Those beads that would be glazed were then covered with the appropriate mineral paste and fired in an oven to create the desired color.

Bead making did not remain solely an Indus based industry beyond the mid-second millennium B.C.E. There is a wall painting from Thebes, around 1420 B.C.E., for example, that shows Egyptians making beads. In this case, the workers drilling the holes operate three drills with a single bow (Tait 1986). Though it seems very likely that Egyptian, Mesopotamian, and probably Chinese bead making techniques were derived from the Harappan industry, the existence of bead making in Mesoamerica at a much later date indicates that it could develop independently in multiple places.

Some of the most spectacular decorative arts of antiquity are associated with the royal cemetery at Ur, which dates from sometime between 2500 and 2200 B.C.E. Necklaces found there (see Figure 10.5) include many shapes of beads, some imported and some fabricated locally from imported materials, including gold. Gold was also used to form a variety of shapes, many created by curling, twisting, and plaiting gold wires into two- or three-dimensional configurations (filigree). In the earliest examples, as at Ur, the wires were not

Figure 10.5
Sample Necklaces from the Royal Tombs at Ur, circa 2500–2200 B.C.E.
Nick Livingston.

(a) With Carved Beads from Lothal.
(b) With Alternating Gold and Lapis Lazuli Leaf Pattern.

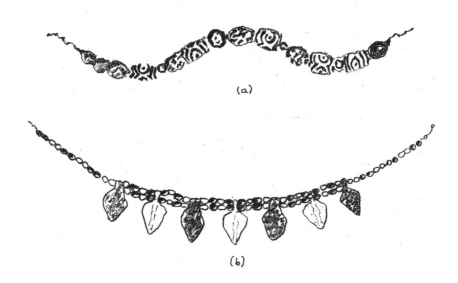

(a)

(b)

solidly joined to one another, but soon they were soldered (i.e., molten gold was drawn by capillary action into the spaces between wires to form a solid joint) to produce more stable forms. Wires were not drawn but were produced by cutting sheets of gold that had been beaten very thin (to approximately 0.01 cm) into long strips that were twisted into small tubes and then delicately hammered until the material had become pressure welded. It is possible, but not certain, that filigree techniques came from India where itinerant gold and silversmiths still create fine filigree jewelry in a client's courtyard from measured amounts of gold or silver. In some cases, a filigree pattern was made on a sheet of gold or silver backing and then the spaces bounded by wire or edge-mounted thin strips of gold were filled with gemstones or glass (cloisonné). In the glass case, a frit of appropriate color was placed in each space and the piece was then heated to a temperature high enough to melt the frit, but too low to melt the metal. Regardless of where it originated, filigree work almost certainly moved from Mesopotamia into the Mediterranean Basin, where it reached an amazing state of sophistication among the Minoans during the 13th century B.C.E. and the Greeks during the 7th century B.C.E. Cloissonage was more widely developed by the Egyptians who had greater experience with glass-making.

Sheets of gold were also formed by placing them over either concave or convex patterns made of stone, bone, metals, or wood and then pushing them from the back side using hammers and appropriately shaped tools into the shape of the pattern (repoussé). After basic shapes were created, details could be produced by stamping, by chasing (in which the surface of the piece is pressed into indentations in the pattern which is applied to the back), by engraving (i.e., by cutting grooves in the surface), or by granulation (allowing small drops of gold to fuse to a gold surface). Granulation was relatively crudely done in Mesopotamia, but it became a highly developed specialty in Greece and even more so among the Etruscans and Romans.

Gold, electrum, copper, and both precious and semi-precious stones were used in three other ways to make objects found in the Royal cemetery at Ur and elsewhere in Egypt and the Mediterranean basin. In the first, chips or formed pieces of minerals and metal were inlayed into bitumen to create both two dimensional pictures and three dimensional statuettes. In the second, gold was used instead of paint or glazes to "gild" objects constructed from cheaper materials including wood. In the third, gold was cast (i.e., poured into a mold) to make rings and small pendants—usually in the shape of animals. Because of the expense of producing solid gold objects, it was almost never cast into larger pieces.

Many Egyptian artifacts taken from tombs during the 19th and early 20th centuries are of gold and the images and caskets of pharaohs were gilded with gold because gold was associated with immortality, so we have experience with large numbers of gold artifacts from Egypt. The Egyptians used all of the techniques found in mid-to-late third millennium Mesopotamia for creating jewelry, adding the lost wax, or investment, process of casting, which allowed the creation of complex shapes for which a mold could not have been extricated from a solid pattern. In this technique, a pattern was made of beeswax, a mold composed of a semi-fluid material such as plaster was used to surround it, and after the mold hardened, the mold was heated to melt the wax, which was poured out through the same hole that the metal was poured into. In some cases, the mold was then cut into sections and re assembled for use. For unusually complex shapes, the mold could only be used once. Unlike the case with Egyptian mathematics or medicine, Egyptian metalwork became increasingly sophisticated over time, with periods of stagnation when society was disrupted.

While there were clear connections and continuities among Indian, Mesopotamian, Egyptian, Greek, and Roman jewelry making, both China and Mayan Mesoamerica developed traditions that remained largely independent until the Han Dynasty in China and until European contact in Mesoamerica. Very little metal was used for personal ornamentation in either Shang or Zhou China (c. 1700–450 B.C.E.) or among the Maya throughout their history. In both places, jade was the most commonly used material for making pendants and other amulets, often in the shape of animals. Sometimes, in China, the figures were fully three dimensional, but often they were made out of flat pieces of jade that had been sawn off a relatively large block to a thickness of 0.25–0.5 centimeters. One surface was then cut and/or abraded into a shallow- or bas-relief. Chinese women tended to wear hairpins and combs beginning during the Warring States period and continuing into the 20th century C.E. In the most ancient period, these were usually made of bone or jade; by the Han Dynasty, gold had become the material of choice, though some silver was used. Bronze, which had been used to cast a variety of vessels and bells by the early Shang period, was very rarely used for ornamentation until the Han period, and then, when used for belt hooks, it was usually gilded with gold or inlaid with jade or turquoise. Gold was very rarely used by the Maya, who made beautiful jade beads, pendants, nose pins, and ear and lip plugs.

MAKING TOOLS, WEAPONS, AND OTHER LARGE OBJECTS

Though small items for personal adornment or religious use constitute the greatest number of objects made of gold, silver, and minerals in most ancient civilizations, copper, bronze, and iron were often used to produce objects of greater secular utility and/or size. Native copper and iron, which had been of importance to pre-civilized peoples, played a minimal role in civilizations, where the populations were large enough that only the volumes of metal made possible by smelting allowed for significant metal use. In spite of the fact that metals, including copper, were used by North and South American populations well before the Mayan civilization came on the scene, Mayan artifacts include almost no metal, and those that do were probably imported from other American cultures. As such, the discussion of human-produced metal use will be restricted to the Harappan, Mesopotamian, Egyptian, Chinese, Greek, and Roman civilizations, always with an awareness that metalworking techniques in all but the Harappan civilization were probably initially imported from nearby groups.

Copper was the earliest metal to be used to produce tools and weapons. The techniques used to form copper objects all predate the emergence of civilizations, and those techniques constitute virtually all of the techniques available to create objects of gold, silver, lead, and their alloys such as electrum, bronze, and brass, though they were refined over time as a consequence the specialization allowed by urbanization. Native copper may have been cold hammered, or cold forged, as early as the sixth millennium B.C.E., but sometime between about 5000 B.C.E. and 4500 B.C.E., metalworkers discovered that the brittleness and difficulty of shaping that seemed to follow from extensive cold hammering could be controlled by alternately hammering and heating the metal to a dull red heat (Forbes 1964, vol. 9). This process, called annealing, allows the metal grains, which deform to follow the shape of the part when it is being pounded, to reorient themselves, producing greater ductility. Annealed metal is thus easier to shape, but a final cold-hammering produces a tough edge or surface, allowing even relatively pure copper, which is quite soft, to be fashioned into effective tools, such as those used by Egyptian stone cutters and carpenters as early as 2600 B.C.E. Since copper ores were often found mixed with other metallic ores, and since almost any accidental alloying made the alloy tougher than copper, the natural bronzes that resulted were almost always harder and tougher than pure copper.

Sometime between 4000 and 3500 B.C.E., copper began to be produced in crucibles in permanent furnaces. Then, the molten metal was poured into molds, or cast. Open mold copper casting first appeared in Mesopotamia at Susa around 3500 B.C.E. Between 3000 and 2700 B.C.E., a very strong copper-working tradition emerged. Socketed axes created with cores inside of multiple-piece molds appeared first, but soon picks, double axes, bowls, rings, tubes, mirrors, fish hooks, and forks appeared, followed by complex castings of animal forms that were almost certainly produced using molds created by the lost wax method. New written terms that distinguish between copper and bronze also appeared in Mesopotamia during this period, though it is not clear until around 2200 B.C.E. that smiths were intentionally creating bronze alloys (Forbes 1964, vol. 9).

Because it is highly ductile, copper, like gold and later, lead, was often beaten into thin sheets and either rolled into tubes or formed over other materials. Some early copper statues were even produced by shaping a skin of copper over a wooden frame. Copper pots were also often given spouts and handles created from separate pieces. In these cases, it was often necessary to join two edges or pieces of copper together. At the beginning of the copper-working period, copper rivets (or nails when there was a wooden form underneath) were most commonly used. This practice was continued until the end of antiquity, but for fine work, soldering became common in classical times (c. 500 B.C.E.). Soldering was probably adopted from the gold and silversmiths, as were the use of copper filigree and granulation. Copper objects, including axes and adzes made with two-piece molds, were found at Mohenjo Daro no later than 2800 B.C.E., but compared with Egyptian and Mesopotamian artifacts, Harappan copper objects remained relatively crude.

Though bronzes were being intentionally created in the Near East by 2200 B.C.E., the most spectacular bronzeworking culture developed in China starting no later than 1700 B.C.E. Bronze swords and three-legged drinking cups, cast in molds made out of several porous ceramic pieces, appear first in the archeological evidence, but based on the preponderance of tool molds found at the Zhengzhou foundry, scholars agree that agricultural implements such as adzes and hoes were made equally early in very large numbers and later melted down to reuse the metal (Fong 1980). Ritual vessels made of bronze and initially based on prior pottery shapes were a sign of wealth and power in Shang China, and these were generally buried in the graves of the ruling class, so many of these have been preserved. The practice continued throughout antiquity, and the ornamentation became increasingly ornate, with highly stylized real and fictional animal masks, dragons, and ideographs as well as complex geometrical patterns predominating. The frequency of animal designs is explained in an early story about nine great cauldrons cast before the Shang dynasty:

Anciently, when the *Xia* rulers were the inheritors of virtues, creatures of different regions were depicted. The metals of the nine provinces were used to cast tripods with representations of these creatures on them. All the myriad creatures were represented to teach the people about the spirits and evil forces. Thus, the people, when they went among the rivers, marshes, hills, and forests did not meet with injurious things, and the spirits of the hills, monstrous things, and water spirits did not meet with people [to do them injury]. (Fong 1980, 10)

Though very fine piece mold casting, including cores, was done as early as the Shang period, lost wax casting did not begin in China until around 475 B.C.E. Some very early bronze artifacts include riveted seams, but even during the Shang period, in order to avoid unsightly joins, when a Chinese vessel was going to have a protruding spout or handle, that piece was pre-cast and set in place so that when the main piece was cast the molten metal softened the edge of the pre-cast piece and fused with it, creating the equivalent of a weld. Han advances included the incorporation of gold and silver inlays on bronze vessels and the incorporation of more realistic depictions of animals.

A unique feature of the Chinese bronzeworking tradition that began in the Shang period and continued through the Han was the casting of sets of bells of varying sizes to produce different sounds. Within the earliest set of five bells from around 1300 B.C.E. is one standing 35 centimeter high, with a 58-centimeter diameter at the mouth and weighing over 150 kilograms (Fong 1980). By Han times, bells of up to several tons in weight were being cast.

THE RISE OF ALCHEMY

As we have seen in chapters 7 and 9, and in the earlier portions of this chapter, the knowledge of how to make various medicines, dyes, and metallic and mineral products as well as how to fabricate imitations for many expensive and rare materials was well established in virtually all ancient civilizations. For the most part, this knowledge remained unrecorded and the property of members of craft guilds, although in Mesopotamia by the 8th century B.C.E., cuneiform tablets giving recipes for manufacturing synthetic lapis lazuli, synthetic copper, synthetic silver, and blue frit were produced (Forbes 1955, vol. 1). Within a century, recipes for medicines and glassmaking also appear, often with warnings that such recipes should only be communicated to those with special qualifications.

In both Han China and Hellenistic Egypt, this craft lore, which contained many disconnected elements, met up with self-conscious philosophical traditions that attempted to bring order and coherence to both the natural and human worlds as well as to their interactions. Out of these confrontations of craft lore and philosophical traditions, alchemy was born. Chinese and Hellenistic alchemy emerged nearly simultaneously, developing between about 200 B.C.E. and 300 C.E. They shared an interest in transmuting metals and a focus on qualitative rather than quantitative concerns—especially on color—as well as a secretive orientation and a focus on the ethical purity of the true alchemist. However, they seem to have had quite different origins and initial aims.

Chinese alchemy originated in Daoist philosophy, with its special concern for prolonging life. It incorporated craft knowledge from metallurgical traditions largely to serve a goal—immortality—drawn from the philosophical tradition, though there were certainly some self-proclaimed alchemists who sought to use theories regarding the transmutation of base metals into gold simply to curry favor at court or to seek personal riches. The alchemy that developed at Alexandria, on the other hand, seems to have begun with practical recipes from traditions of metallurgy, bead making, dyeing, and food preparation. These texts interacted with philosophical traditions that sought to bring order and unity into the phenomena associated with many crafts. Initially, Alexandrian alchemy showed little interest in medicine or health and it drew upon several philosophical traditions—especially those of Aristotle and the Stoa—finding its paradigmatic phenomena in the transmutation of metals. Like Chinese alchemy, the core doctrines developed at Alexandria linked alchemical success with the purity of the alchemist, but also like Chinese alchemists, those in the Hellenistic tradition included a fair number of office seekers and seekers of wealth to complement the seekers of knowledge.

By the time that Western alchemy was incorporated into Islamic thought, an emphasis on medicine was grafted onto the Hellenistic tradition, almost certainly as a consequence of interactions with the Chinese tradition (Needham 1981). When that happened, the extensive Chinese emphasis on correspondences among many levels of phenomena was grafted onto the more limited Western notion that different metals corresponded with different celestial objects drawn from Babylonian astrology and to the ubiquitous idea that the structure of the human body mirrored the structure of the cosmos.

From its emergence in the writings of Lao zu and Zhuang zu, daoist philosophy had emphasized that the dao was an "eternal and infinite principle which produces and maintains all creation." Furthermore, the man who could come to fully possess the dao would be "exempt from all danger of decay . . . . because there is in him no place of death" (Johnson 1928, 37–38). Within the dao, the yang principle was the "living force," so the way to achieve longer life—even immortality—was to accumulate yang properties. Initially, this doctrine was a small part of daoist philosophy, but by the beginning of the second century B.C.E., it had become the central consideration for one important branch of daoist thought (Johnson 1928). A variety of strategies were developed to attain the dao. Typically, these included a regimen of physical and mental disciplines, with an emphasis on proper breathing and gymnastic exercises as well as on mental exercises intended to achieve a state of complete tranquility and indifference to the events of the world. In addition to the regimen of exercise, the dao seeker was charged with eating a proper diet of yang foods and with using medicines containing vitalizing qualities.

Here, at the level of medicines and dietary supplements, alchemical theory and metallurgical practices entered the daoist project of seeking long life and immortality, for of the nine most vitalizing substances, eight were minerals or metals. The most comprehensive treatment of early Chinese alchemy, the *Nei P'ien*, written by alchemist Ko Hung (281–322 C.E.), under the pseudonym Pao Pu Tzu, includes the following: "The medicine of the immortals, of the highest rank is cinnabar, next is gold, next is silver, next are the various species of the '*chih* [plant]', and next are the five species of jade" (Johnson 1928, 59).

Cinnabar seems to have been at the top of the list by virtue of both its color, which was associated with the blood and the heart, and by virtue of the role it played in producing mercury, which was known as the living metal. Its efficacy was frequently attested to as in the following recipe from the *Nei P'ien:*

Take three pounds of genuine cinnabar, and one pound of white honey. Mix them. Dry the mixture in the sun. Then roast it over the fire until it can be shaped into pills. Take ten pills the size of a hemp seed every morning. Inside a year, white hair will grow black, decayed teeth will grow again, and the body will become sleek and glistening. If an old man takes this medicine for a long period of time, he will develop into a young man. The one who takes it constantly will enjoy eternal life, and will not die. (Johnson 1928, 63)

In addition to cinnabar itself, daoist alchemists sought to create an elixir, *chin tan,* which contained cinnabar as well as mercury, sulfur, lead, and other secret ingredients, which was not only reputed to prolong life but also to transmute other metals into silver and gold (Ch'iao-p'ing 1948).

Because silver and gold were powerful, life-prolonging substances in their own right daoists spent substantial effort discussing the "art of yellow and white," or the transmutation of baser metals into gold and silver. One might reasonably ask why not use naturally occurring silver and gold rather than trying to produce it alchemically. The *Nei P'ien* gives us a simple answer:

Native gold and silver are both excellent. But the professors of *Dao* are all, without exception, poor. There is a proverb to the effect that no saintly man is corpulent, and no professor of the *Dao* is rich. Perhaps the master and disciples are ten in number, perhaps five. Yet how shall gold and silver be obtained for them? They cannot travel afar to find these commodities for themselves. Therefore it is expedient that they make them! (Johnson 1928, 71)

That transmutation was a natural process occurring in the earth over substantial periods of time was widely held in China, as elsewhere. A second-century B.C.E. Chinese *materia medica* offers the following account:

It is said . . . that copper, gold, and silver have a common origin. The exhalation of the red *Yang* gives birth, through concentration, to certain filaments which, after two hundred years, become transformed into rock, in the center of which copper is formed. But there are those who say that red sulphide of mercury through absorbing the exhalations of the green *Yang* gives birth to a mineral called '*kung shih*' [probably marcasite], which at the end of two hundred years becomes native cinnabar; . . . at the end of three hundred years this cinnabar is changed into lead, which in turn, after two hundred years is changed into silver. Finally, this silver, after having been subjected to the action of the spirit of the Grand Harmony for two hundred years, becomes gold. (Johnson 1928, 75)

The art of the yellow and the white sought to bypass or accelerate this natural growth of silver and gold.

When we turn to Hellenic Greece, all of the major philosophical schools developed matter theories capable of incorporating notions of transmutation, and at least that of Aristotle explicitly addressed the origins of minerals and metals. Furthermore, as we shall see, Theophrastus's *On Stones* even incorporated information about metallurgical practices. It was not, however until around 200 B.C.E., at Alexandria, that these philosophical theories about matter were systematically applied to the problems of manufacturing dyes and silver and gold (i.e., to alchemical problems).

Aristotle had theorized that all material substances were made of a qualityless prime matter and a form. Furthermore, the most fundamental forms were hot, cold, wet, and dry. Earth was matter imbued with nothing but dryness and coldness; water was wet and cold; air was wet and hot; fire was hot and dry. In order to transform fire into earth, then, one simply had to induce a change from hot to cold, leaving the dryness alone. Precisely how this was to be accomplished is unclear, though Aristotle did make the point that of all qualities, hotness, coldness, wetness, and dryness had the special properties that bodies containing any of them could communicate their qualities to other contiguous bodies. Thus, for example, exposing any body to fire would make it hotter and exposing a body to water would usually make it moister. Applied later to alchemical practices, this theory was capable of explaining why heating, cooling, solution in water, and drying were central alchemical processes.

Aristotle explicitly turned his attention to the origins of minerals and metals in his *Meteores*, which dealt with sublunar phenomena. There, he argued that minerals and metals are formed from two kinds of exhalations. One is moist and cold and is produced when the sun falls on water; the other is hot and dry and is produced when sunlight falls on earth. The second predominates in minerals (i.e., stones that cannot ordinarily be melted), while the first predominates in metals, which are fusible and malleable to varying degrees depending on how predominant the moist, cold exhalation is (Aristotle, 378a–389a). When alchemists appropriated this theory, they identified the cold-wet exhalation with mercury and the hot–dry one with sulfur, thus both acknowledging the importance of mercury and sulfur in the tradition of metallurgical recipes and promoting continued experimentation using sulfur and mercury (Lindsay 1970). Since mercury is a shiny, silver-colored fluid and sulfur is a yellow, dull, and crumbly solid, both the color and malleability of different metals could at least qualitatively be accounted for depending on the relative amounts of mercury and sulfur.

Aristotle's student, Theophrastus, included more detailed accounts of specific craft practices, but with less theoretical structure. Here, for example, is his discussion of Athenian methods of processing cinnabar and producing mercury:

[At a place near Ephesos] a sand which glows like the scarlet kermes-berries is collected and thoroughly pounded into a very fine powder in stone vessels. It is then washed in copper vessels and the sediment is taken, pounded, and washed again. There is a knack in doing this, for from an equal amount of material some workers secure a great amount of cinnabar, and others, little or none. However, use is made of the washings that float above, especially as wall paint. The sediment which forms below is found to be cinnabar, while all that is above, which is the great part, is merely washings.

The process is said to have been invented by Kallias, an Athenian from the silver mines, who collected and studied the sand, thinking it contained gold owing to its glowing appearance. But when he found it contained no gold, he still admired its fine color and so came to discover the process, ... From these examples it is clear that *technē* imitates nature, *physis,* and yet produces its own peculiar substances, some for utility, some merely for their appearance like wall paint, and some for both purposes, like quicksilver [mercury]—for even this has its uses. It is made by pounding cinnabar with vinegar in a copper mortar with a copper pestle. (Lindsay 1970, 19)

At Alexandria, Greek philosophy and Near Eastern craft knowledge drawn largely from metallurgy and dyeing practices were joined with a mystical, religious dimension associated both with long-standing spiritual practices among metallurgists and with the Gnostic obsession with astral influences to form the major stream of Western alchemy. A key doctrine unified the earlier Babylonian association between metals and the various planets and the Gnostic assent of the human soul through the various planetary spheres to reach the transcendent deity, creating an identification of the soul's passage through the planets to God with the transmutation of metals from lead through the other metals into gold. For those who entered fully into the idea that alchemical transmutation and the purification of the soul were intertwined, which included the vast majority of later Christian and Islamic alchemists, alchemy became simultaneously the path by which the alchemist could purify herself and achieve salvation, the path to create a universal elixir to treat all illness, and the path to create silver or gold.

Bibliography

Citations from the works of Aristotle and Plato are indicated by "Becker numbers," which allow one to find passages in any scholarly edition from the mid-19th century to the present.

Aaboe, Asger. 1964. *Episodes from the Early History of Mathematics.* New York: Random House.

Adams, Robert M. [*Scientific American.*] [1960] 1979. "The Origin of Cities." Reprint, *Hunters, Framers, and Civilizations: Old World Archaeology,* 171–177, ed. C. C. Lamberg-Karlovsky. San Francisco: W. H. Freeman and Company.

Aeschylus. 1926. *Aeschylus.* Trans. Herbert Wier Smyth. Cambridge, MA: Harvard University Press.

Aitchison, Leslie. 1960. *A History of Metals.* Vol. 1. New York: Interscience Publishers.

Alcock, Joan P. 2006. *Food in the Ancient World.* Westport, CT: Greenwood Press.

Allchin, F. R. 1995. *The Archeology of Early Historic South Asia: The Emergence of Cities and States.* Cambridge: Cambridge University Press.

Aristotle—Since the mid 19th century all passages in Aristotle's works have been identified by their "Becker numbers," which allow passages to be found in all scholarly editions. I follow this tradition by indicating the name of the work (in English) and the Becker numbers.

Bacon, Francis. 1960. *The New Organon.* Indianapolis: Bobbs-Merrill.

Barber, Bernard. 1952. *Science and the Social Order.* New York: Macmillan.

Barrow, R. H. 1949. *The Romans.* Harmondsworth, England: Pelican Books.

Bates, Don, ed. 1995. *Knowledge and the Scholarly Medical Traditions.* Cambridge: Cambridge University Press.

Bernal, J. D. 1971. *Science in History, Volume 1: The Emergence of Science.* Cambridge, MA: MIT Press.

Bigelow, Jacob. 1929. *Elements of Technology: Taken Chiefly from a Course of Lectures Delivered at Cambridge on the Application of the Sciences to the Useful Arts / Now Published for the Use of Seminaries and students.* Boston: Hilliard, Gray, Little, and Wilkins.

Bijker, Wiebe and John Law. 1992. *Shaping Technology/ Building Society: Studies in Sociotechnical Change.* Cambridge, MA: MIT Press.

Bijker, Wiebe, Thomas P. Hughes, and Treor Pinch, eds. 1989. *The Social Construction of Technological Systems: New Directions in the Sociology and History of Technology.* Cambridge, MA: MIT Press.

Blofeld, John, trans. and ed. 1965. *I Ching: The Book of Changes.* New York: Penguin Compass.

Bodde, Derk. 1991. *Chinese Thought, Society, and Science: The Intellectual and Social Background of Science and Technology in Pre-modern China.* Honolulu: University of Hawaii Press.

Bottéro, Jean. 2001. *Everyday Life in Ancient Mesopotamia.* Baltimore, MD: Johns Hopkins University Press.

Bottéro, Jean, et. al. 2000. *Ancestor of the West: Writing, Reasoning, and Religion in Mesopotamia, Elam, and Greece.* Chicago: University of Chicago Press.

Bradford, John. 1954. "Building in Wattle, Wood, and Turf." In *A History of Technology, Volume 1: From Early Times to Fall of Ancient Empires,* eds. Singer, Holmyard, and Hall, 299–326. New York: Oxford University Press.

Britton, J. P. 1992. *Models and Precision: The Quality of Ptolemy's Observations and Parameters.* New York and London: Hubner.

Brothwell, Don and Patricia Brothwell. 1969. *Food in Antiquity: A Survey of the Diet of Early Peoples.* New York: Praeger.

Brown, R. and E. Lenneberg. 1954. "A Study in Language and Cognition." *Journal of Abnormal & Social Psychology* 49: 454–462.

Bush, Vannevar. 1945. *Science—The Endless Frontier: A Report to the President.* Washington, D.C.: U.S. Government Printing Office.

Bushnell, G.H.S. 1961. "The Crimson Tipped Flower: The Birth and Growth of New World Civilization." In *The Dawn of Civilization,* ed. H. Stuart Pigott, 359–386. New York: McGraw-Hill.

Chang, K. C., ed. 1977. *Food in Chinese Culture: Anthropological and Historical Perspectives.* New Haven, CT: Yale University Press.

Chattopadhyaya, Debiprasad. 1986. *History of Science and Technology in Ancient India: The Beginnings.* Calcutta: Firma KLM Private Limited.

Chattopadhyaya, Debiprasad. 1996. *History of Science and Technology in Ancient India: III, Astronomy, Science, and Society.* Calcutta: Firma KLM Private, Limited.

Ch'iao-p'ing, Li. 1948. *The Chemical Arts of Old China.* Easton, PA: Journal of Chemical Education.

Childe, V. Gordon. 1950. "The Urban Revolution." *Town Planning Review,* 21: 1–17.

Childe, V. Gordon. 1951. *Man Makes Himself.* Rev. ed. New York: New American Library.

Childe, V. Gordon. 2004. *Foundations of Social Archeology: Selected Writings of V. Gordon Childe.* Ed. Thomas C. Patterson and Charles Orser, Jr. Walnut Creek, CA: Altimira Press.

Chopra, Ananda. 2003. "Ayurveda." In *Medicine across Cultures: History and Practice of Medicine in Non-Western Cultures,* ed. Helaine Selin, 75–83. Dordrecht, Netherlands: Kluwer Academic Publishers.

Clagett, Marshall. 1989. *Ancient Egyptian Science, Volume I: Knowledge and Order.* Philadelphia: American Philosophical Society.

Clagett, Marshall. 1995. *Ancient Egyptian Science, Volume II: Calendars, Clocks, and Astronomy.* Philadelphia: American Philosophical Society.

Clagett, Marshall. 1999. *Ancient Egyptian Science: A Source Book, Volume III: Ancient Egyptian Mathematics.* Philadelphia: American Philosophical Society.

Closs, Michael. 1986. "The Mathematical Notation of the Ancient Maya." In *Native American Mathematics,* ed. Michael P. Closs, 291–369. Austin: University of Texas Press.

Cohen, Morris R. and I. E. Drabkin. 1966. *A Sourcebook in Greek Science*. Cambridge, MA: Harvard University Press.

Comte, Auguste. 1855. *The Positive Philosophy*. Ed. and trans. Harriet Martineau. New York: C. Blanchard. Comte liked Martineau's editing so much that when he published his collected works he had Martineau's version re-translated into French rather than use his original text.

Cottrell, Brian, and Johan Kaminga. 1990. *Mechanics of Pre-industrial Technology*. Cambridge: Cambridge University Press.

Craddock, Paul T. 1995. *Early Metal Mining and Production*. Washington, D.C.: Smithsonian Institution Press.

Cramer, Frederick H. 1954. *Astrology in Roman Law and Politics*. Philadelphia: American Philosophical Society.

Crowfoot, Grace. 1954. "Textiles, Basketry, and Mats." In *A History of Technology*. Vol. 1, ed. Charles Singer, et al., 413–451. New York: Oxford University Press.

Cullen, Christopher. 1996. *Astronomy and Mathematics in Ancient China: The Zhou bi suan jing*. Cambridge: Cambridge University Press.

Curtis, Robert I. 2001. *Ancient Food Technology*. Leiden, The Netherlands: Brill.

Daumas, Maurice. 1969. *A History of Technology and Invention: Vol. 1, The Origins of Technological Civilization*. New York: Crown.

Dayton, John. 1978. *Minerals, Metals, Glazing and Man: Or Who Was Sesostris I?* London: George G. Harrap & Co.

Donadoni, Sergio, ed. 1997. *The Egyptians*. Chicago: University of Chicago Press.

Drower, M. S. 1954. "Water-Supply, Irrigation, and Agriculture." In *A History of Technology*. Vol. 1, ed. Charles Singer, et al., 520–557. New York: Oxford University Press.

Dudley, Donald R. 1962. *The Civilization of Rome*. New York: New American Library.

Dumas, Maurice, ed. 1969. *A History of Technology and Invention: Progress through the Ages. Volume 1: The Origins of Technological Civilization*. Trans. Eileen B. Hennessy. New York: Crown.

Eberhard, Wolfram. 1977. *A History of China*. Berkeley: University of California Press.

Edelstein, Emma J., and Ludwig Edelstein. 1998. *Asclepius: Collection and Interpretation of the Testimonies*. Baltimore, MD: Johns Hopkins University Press.

Eliade, Mircea. 1964. *Shamanism: Archaic Techniques of Ecstasy*. Princeton, NJ: Princeton University Press.

Eliade, Mircea. 1978. *The Forge and the Crucible*. 2nd ed. Chicago: University of Chicago Press.

Epicurus. 1964. *Letters, Principal Doctrines, and Vatican Sayings*. Indianapolis: Bobbs-Merrill.

Estes, J. Worth. 1993. *The Medical Skills of Ancient Egypt*. Sagamore Beach, MA: Science History Publications.

Evans, James. 1998. *The History and Practice of Ancient Astronomy*. New York: Oxford University Press.

Farrington, Benjamin. 1961. *Greek Science*, Rev. ed. Baltimore, MD: Penguin Books.

Finley, M. I. 1979. *The World of Odysseus*. Harmondsworth, England: Penguin Books.

Fong, Wen, ed. 1980. *The Great Bronze Age of China*. New York: Metropolitan Museum of Art.

Forbes, R. J. 1955–1964. *Studies in Ancient Technology*. 9 vols. Leiden, The Netherlands: Brill.

Frankfort, Henri, H. A. Frankfort, John A. Wilson, and Thorkild Jacobsen. 1949. *Before Philosophy: The Intellectual Adventure of Ancient Man*. Harmondsworth, England: Penguin Books.

Friberg, Jöran. 2005. *Unexpected Links between Egyptian and Babylonian Mathematics*. New Jersey: World Scientific Publishing.

Gillings, Richard. 1972. *Mathematics in the Time of the Pharaohs*. Cambridge, MA: MIT Press.

Hardy, Grant and Behnke Kinney. 2005. *The Establishment of the Han Empire and Imperial China*. Westport, CT: Greenwood Press.

Harris, Elenore L. 1998. *Ancient Egyptian Divination and Magic*. Boston: Weiser Books.

Harris, Jennifer, ed. 1993. *Textiles: 5,000 Years: An International History and Illustrated Survey*. New York: Harry N. Abrams.

Harris, William V. 1989. *Ancient Literacy*. Cambridge, MA: Harvard University Press.

Harrison, John A. 1972. *The Chinese Empire: A Short History of China from Neolithic Times to the End of the Eighteenth Century*. New York: Harcourt, Brace Jovanovich.

Hawass, Zahi. 2000. *Silent Images: Women in Pharaonic Egypt*. New York: Harry N. Abrams.

Hawkes, Jacquetta, and Sir Leonard Woolley. 1963. *History of Mankind, Vol. I,: Prehistory and the Beginnings of Civilization*. New York: Harper and Row.

Hayek, Friedrich A. von. 1979. *The Counter Revolution of Science: Studies on the Abuse of Reason*. Indianapolis: Liberty Press.

Heath, Sir Thomas L. 1921. *A History of Greek Mathematics, I: From Thales to Euclid*. Oxford: Oxford University Press.

Heath, Sir Thomas L. 1956. *The Thirteen Books of Euclid's Elements*. 3 vols., 2nd ed. New York: Dover.

Hippocrates, 1978. *Hippocratic Writings*, ed. G. E. R. Lloyd. London: Penguin Books.

Ho, P.Y. and F. P. Lisowski. 1993. *Concepts of Chinese Science and Traditional Healing Arts: An Historical Review*. Singapore: World Scientific Publishing.

Hodges, Henry. 1970. *Technology in the Ancient World*. New York: Barnes and Noble.

Hooykaas, Reijer. 1972. *Religion and the Rise of Science*, Grand Rapids, MI: Eerdmans.

Høyrup, Jens. 2002. *Lengths, Widths, Surfaces: A Portrait of Old Babylonian Algebra and its Kin*. New York: Springer—Verlag.

Huff, Toby E. 1993. *The Rise of Early Modern Science: Islam, China, and the West*. Cambridge: Cambridge University Press.

Humphrey, John W. 2006. *Ancient Technology*. Westport, CT: Greenwood Press.

Humphrey, John W., John P. Oleson, and Andrew N Sherwood, eds. 1998. *Greek and Roman Technology: A Sourcebook*. London: Routledge.

Jaki, Stanley. 1978. *The Road of Science and the Way to God*. Chicago: University of Chicago Press.

Jingfeng, Cai, and Zhen Yan. 2003. "Medicine in Ancient China." In *Medicine Across Cultures,* ed., Helaine Selin, 49–73. Dordrecht: Kluwer Acfademic Publishers.

Johnson, Obed Simon. 1928. *A Study of Chinese Alchemy*. Shanghai, China: Commercial Press.

Johnston, Sarah Iles, and Peter T. Struck eds. 2005. *Mantikê: Studies in Ancient Divination*. Leiden: Brill.

Jonas, Hans. 1963. *The Gnostic Religion: The Message of the Alien God and the Beginnings of Christianity*. Boston: Beacon Press.

Joseph, George Gheverghese. 2000. *The Crest of the Peacock: Non-European Roots of Mathematics,* New ed. Princeton, NJ: Princeton University Press.

Jouanna, Jacques. 1999. *Hippocrates*. Baltimore, MD: Johns Hopkins University Press.

Kaufman, Cathy K. 2006. *Cooking in Ancient Civilizations*. Westport, CT: Greenwood Press.

Kirk, G. S., and J. E. Raven. 1963. *The Presocratic Philosophers: A Critical History with a Selection of Texts.* London: Cambridge University Press.

Kitto, H.D.F. 1957. *The Greeks.* Baltimore, MD: Penguin Books.

Knorr, Wilbur. 1975. *The Evolution of the Euclidean Elements: A Study of the Theory of Incommensurable Magnitudes and its Significance for Greek Geometry.* Dordrecht-Holland: D. Reidel.

Knorr, Wilbur. 1986. *The Ancient Tradition of Geometrical Problems.* Boston: Birkhäuser.

Kramer, Samuel Noah. 1959. *History Begins at Sumer.* Garden City, NJ: Doubleday.

Kramer, Samuel Noah. 1963. *The Sumerians: Their History, Culture, and Character.* Chicago: University of Chicago Press.

Krebs, Robert E. and Carolyn A. Krebs. 2003. *Groundbreaking Scientific Experiments, Inventions, and Discoveries of the Ancient World.* Westport, CT: Greenwood Press.

Lakshmiantham, V., and S. Leela. 2000. *The Origin of Mathematics.* Lantham, New York: University Press of America.

Langdon, Stephen. 1935. *Babylonian Menologies and Semitic Calendars.* London: Oxford University Press.

Lao-tzu. 1963. *Lao tzu.* Trans. D. C. Lau. Harmondsworth, England: Penguin Books.

Lasserre, François. 1964. *The Birth of Mathematics in the Age of Plato,* Larchmont, NY: American Research Council.

Le Blank, Charles, and Susan Blader, eds. 1987. *Chinese Ideas about Nature and Society: Studies in Honor of Derk Bodde.* Hong Kong: Hong Kong University Press.

Lenzer, Gertrude. 1975. *Auguste Comte and Positivism: The Essential Writings.* New York: Harper and Row.

Levey, Martin. 1959. *Chemistry and Chemical Technology in Ancient Mesopotamia.* Amsterdam: Elsevier Publishing.

Li, Yan, and Dù, Shíràn. 1987. *Chinese Mathematics: A Concise History.* Oxford: Clarendon Press.

Lindsay, Jack. 1970. *The Origins of Alchemy in Graeco-Roman Egypt.* New York: Barnes and Noble.

Lloyd, G.E.R. 1996. *Adversaries and Authorities: Investigations into Ancient Greek and Chinese Science.* Cambridge: Cambridge University Press.

Lloyd, G.E.R. 2002. *The Ambitions of Curiosity: Understanding the World in Ancient Greece and China.* Cambridge: Cambridge University Press.

Lloyd, G.E.R., and Nathan Sivin. 2002. *The Way and the Word: Science and Medicine in Early China and Greece.* New Haven, CT: Yale University Press.

Lloyd, Seton. 1954. "Building in Brick and Stone." In *A History of Technology, Volume 1: From Early Times to Fall of Ancient Empires,* eds. Singer, Holmyard, and Hall, 456–494. New York: Oxford University Press.

Lounsbury, Floyd G. 1978. "Maya Numeration, Computation, and Calendrical Astronomy." In *Dictionary of Scientific Biography, Vol. 15: Supplement 1,* 759–818. New York: Scribners.

Luck, Steve. 1999. *International Encyclopedia of Science and Technology.* New York: Oxford University Press.

Lucy, J., and R. Shweder. 1979. "Whorf and His Critics: Linguistic and Nonlinguistic Influences on Color Memory." *American Anthropologist* 81: 581–615.

Mackay, Ernest and Dorothy Mackay. 1976. *Early Indus Civilization.* New Delhi: Indological Book Corporation.

Majano, Guido, 1975. *The Healing Hand: Man and Wound in the Ancient World.* Cambridge, MA: Harvard University Press.

Martzloff, Jean-Claude. 1997. *A History of Chinese Mathematics*. Berlin: Springer-Verlag.

Marx, Karl. 1983. *The Portable Karl Marx*, ed. Eugene Kamenka. Harmondsworth, England: Penguin Books.

Maziarz, Edward A. and Thomas Greenwood. 1968. *Greek Mathematical Philosophy*. New York: Frederick Ungar.

McClellan, James E. III, and Harold Dorn. 1999. *Science and Technology in World History*. Baltimore, MD: Johns Hopkins University Press.

Mukhopadhyaya, Grindranath. 1922–1929. *History of Indian Medicine, Containing Notices, Biographical and Bibliographical, of the Ayurvedic Physicians and Their Works on Medicine: From the Earliest Ages to the Present*. 3 vols. Calcutta: University of Calcutta.

Murray, William Breen. 1986. "Numerical Representations in North American Rock Art." pp. In *Native American Mathematics*, ed. Michael P. Closs, 45–70. Austin: University of Texas Press.

Nakayama, Shigeru. 1969. *A History of Japanese Astronomy: Chinese Background and Western Impact*. Cambridge, MA: Harvard University Press.

Nakayama, Shigeru, and Nathan Sivin. 1973. *Chinese Science: Explorations of an Ancient Tradition*. Cambridge, MA: MIT Press.

Needham, Joseph. 1954–2004. *Science and Civilization in China*. 7 vols. Cambridge: Cambridge University Press.

Needham, Joseph. 1969. *The Grand Titration: Science and Society in East and West*. London: Allen and Unwin.

Needham, Joseph. 1981. *Science in Traditional China*. Cambridge, MA: Harvard University Press.

Neugebaur, Otto. 1942. "The Origin of the Egyptian Calendar." *Journal of Near Eastern Studies*, 1: 396–403.

Neugebauer, Otto. 1955. *Astronomical Cuneiform Texts*. 3 vols. London: Lund Humphries.

Neugebauer, Otto. 1957. *The Exact Sciences in Antiquity*, 2nd ed. Providence, RI: Brown University Press.

Neugebauer, Otto. 1983. *Astronomy and History: Selected Essays*. New York: Springer-Verlag.

Nissen, Hans J., Peter Damerow, and Robert K. Englund. 1993. *Archaic Bookkeeping: Early Writing and Techniques of Economic Administration in the Ancient Near East*. Chicago: University of Chicago Press.

Noegel, Scott, Joel Walker, and Brannon Wheeler, eds. 2003. *Prayer, Magic, and the Stars in the Ancient and Late Antique World*. University Park: Pennsylvania State University Press.

Nye, David. 2006. *Technology Matters: Questions to Live With*. Cambridge, MA: MIT Press.

Oldenziel, Ruth. 2006. "Signifying Semantics for a History of Technology." *Technology and Culture* 47: 477–485.

Olson, Richard. 1982. *Science Deified and Science Defied: The Historical Significance of Science in Western Culture, Volume 1, From the Bronze Age to the Beginnings of the Modern Era ca. 3500 B.C. to ca. A.D. 1640*. Berkeley: University of California Press.

Olson, Richard. 2004. *Science and Religion from Copernicus to Darwin: 1450–1900*. Westport, CT: Greenwood Press.

Oppenheim, A. Leo. 1977. *Ancient Mesopotamia: Portrait of a Dead Civilization*. Chicago: University of Chicago Press.

Pannekoek, A. 1961. *A History of Astronomy*. London: George Allen and Unwin.

Parker, R.A., and Waldo Duberstein. 1942. *Babylonian Chronology: 626 B.C.–A. D. 45.* Chicago: University of Chicago Press.

Piggott, Stuart, ed. 1961. *The Dawn of Civilization: The First Survey of Human Cultures in Early Times.* London: Thames and Hudson.

Pinch, Geraldine. 1994. *Magic in Ancient Egypt.* Austin: University of Texas Press.

Plato. 1959. *Timaeus.* Trans. F. M. Cornford. New York: Macmillan.

Porter, Theodore M. 1995. *Trust in Numbers: The Pursuit of Objectivity in Science and Public Life.* Princeton, NJ: Princeton University Press.

Prakash, Gyan. 1999. *Another Reason: Science and the Imagination of Modern India.* Princeton, NJ: Princeton University Press.

Priest, Alan, and Pauline Simmons. 1934. *Chinese Textiles: An Introduction to the Study of Their History, Sources, Technique, Symbolism, and Use.* New York: Metropolitan Museum of Art.

Ptolemy, Claudius. 1998. *Ptolemy's "Almagest,"* ed. G. J. Toomer. Princeton: Princeton University Press.

Randall, John Herman. 1970. *Hellenistic Ways of Deliverance and the Making of the Christian Synthesis.* New York: Columbia University Press.

Ray, P. C. 1916. *A History of Hindu Chemistry,* Rev. ed. Vol. 1. Calcutta: Chuckerverttey, Chatterjee, & Co.

Reiner, Erica. 1999. "Babylonian Celestial Divination." In *Ancient Astronomy and Celestial Divination,* ed. N. M. Swerdlow, 21–37. Cambridge, MA: MIT Press.

Reingold, Nathan. 1964. *Science in Nineteenth Century America: A Documentary History.* New York: Hill and Wang.

Rostovtzeff, M. 1963. *Greece.* London: Oxford University Press.

Roux, Georges. 1992. *Ancient Iraq,* New ed. New York: Penguin Books.

Sapir, E. 1929. "The Status of Linguistics as a Science." *Language* 5: 209

Sarton, George, 1952. *A History of Science: Ancient Science through the Golden Age of Greece.* Cambridge, MA: Harvard University Press.

Schlesinger, I. M. 1991. "The Wax and Wane of Whorfian Views." In *Influence of Language on Culture & Thought,* eds. R. Cooper and B. Spolsky, 7–37. New York: Mounton de Gruyter.

Schoeser, Mary. 2003. *World Textiles: A Concise History.* London: Thames and Hudson.

Selin, Helaine, ed. 1999. *Encyclopedia of the History of Science, Technology, and Medicine in Non-Western Cultures.* Dordrecht, Netherlands: Kluwer Academic Publishers.

Selin, Helaine, ed. 2003. *Medicine across Cultures: History and Practice of Medicine in Non-Western Cultures.* Dordrecht, Netherlands: Kluwer Academic Publishers.

Shafik, Ahmed and Waseem Elseesy. 2003. "Medicine in Ancient Egypt." In *Medicine across Cultures: History and Practice of Medicine in Non-Western Cultures,* ed. Helaine Selin, 27–47. Dordrecht, Netherlands: Kluwer Academic Publishers.

Shermer, Michael. 1997. *Why People Believe Weird Things: Pseudoscience, Superstition, and Confusion.* New York: Henry Holt.

Sigerist, Henry E. 1951. *A History of Medicine, Volume I: Primitive and Archaic Medicine.* New York: Oxford University Press.

Sigerist, Henry E. 1961. *A History of Medicine, Volume II: Early Greek, Hindu, and Persian Medicine.* New York: Oxford University Press.

Silverman, David P. 1997. *Ancient Egypt.* London: Duncan Baird Publishers.

Singer, Charles, E. J. Holmyard, and A. R. Hall, eds. 1954. *A History of Technology, Volume 1: From Early Times to Fall of Ancient Empires.* New York: Oxford University Press.

Sivin, Nathan. 1995. *Science in Ancient China: Researches and Reflections.* Aldershot, England: Ashgate.

Smith, David Eugene. 1923. *History of Mathematics.* Vol. 1. Boston: Ginn and Co.

Smith, Norman. 1975. *Man and Water: A History of Hydro-Technology.* New York: Charles Scribner's Sons.

Swerdlow, Noel, ed. 1999. *Ancient Astronomy and Celestial Divination.* Cambridge, MA: MIT Press.

Szabó, Árpád. 1978. *The Beginnings of Greek Mathematics.* Dordrecht, Holland: D. Reidel Publishing Company.

Takacs, Laszlo. 2000. "Quicksilver from Cinnabar: The First Documented Mechanico-chemical Reaction?" *Journal of Metals* 52: January, 12–13.

Tait, Hugh, ed. 1986. *Seven Thousand Years of Jewellery.* London: British Museum Publications.

Tambiah, Stanley Jeyaraja. 1990. *Magic, Science, and the Scope of Rationality.* Cambridge: Cambridge University Press.

Tarn, W. W. 1952. *Hellenistic Civilization.* 3rd ed. Cleveland: World Publishing.

Taub, Laba Chaia. 1993. *Ptolemy's Universe,* Chicago: Open Court.

Tick, Edward. 2001. *The Practice of Dream Healing: Bringing Ancient Greek Mysteries into Modern Medicine.* Wheaton, IL: Theosophical Publishing House.

Tod, Marcus Niebur. 1979. *Ancient Greek Numerical Systems.* Chicago: Ares Publishers.

Trawick, Margaret. 1995. "Writing the Body and Ruling the Land: Western Reflections on Chinese and Indian Medicine." In *Knowledge and the Scholarly Medical Traditions,* ed. Don Bates, 279–296. Cambridge: Cambridge University Press.

Unschuld, Paul U. 1985. *Medicine in China: A History of Ideas.* Berkeley: University of California Press.

Van der Waerden, B. L. 1963. *Science Awakening: Egyptian, Babylonian, and Greek Mathematics.* New York: John Wiley and Sons.

Van der Waerden, B. L. 1974. *Science Awakening, II: The Birth of Astronomy.* Leyden, Netherlands: Noodhoff International Publishing.

Viesca, Carlos. 2003. "Medicine in Ancient Mesoamerica." In *Medicine across Cultures: History and Practice of Medicine in Non-Western Cultures,* ed. Helaine Selin, 259–283. Dordrecht, Netherlands: Kluwer Academic Publishers.

Vitruvius. [c. 27 B.C.E.] 1960. *The Ten Books on Architecture.* Trans. Morris Hicky Morgan. New York: Dover Books.

Vlastos, Gregory. 1949. "Religion and Medicine in the Cult of Asclepius, a Review Article," *Review of Religion,* 13: 269–290.

Volti, Rudi. 1995. *Society and Technological Change.* 3rd ed. New York: St. Martin's Press.

Wang, Aihe. 2000. *Cosmology and Political Culture in Early China.* Cambridge: Cambridge University Press.

Watson, William. 1961. "China: The Civilization of a Single People." In *The Dawn of Civilization: The First Survey of Human Cultures in Early Times. Ed.* Stuart Piggott, 254–276. London: Thames and Hudson.

Whorf, B. 1956. *Language, Thought & Reality: Selected Writings of Benjamin Lee Whorf.* Ed. John B. Carroll. Cambridge, MA: MIT Press.

Wilson, David Sloan, 2002. *Darwin's Cathedral, Evolution, Religion, and the Nature of Society.* Chicago: University of Chicago Press.

Wilson, Kax. 1979. *A History of Textiles.* Boulder, CO: Westview Press.

Winner, Langdon. 1977. *Autonomous Technology: Technics-out-of-control as a Theme in Political Thought.* Cambridge, MA: MIT Press.

Wittfogel, Karl. 1957. *Oriental Despotism: A Comparative Study of Total Power.* New Haven: Yale University Press.

Wright, G.R.H. 2000. *Ancient Building Technology: Volume 1, Historical Background.* Leiden, Netherlands: Brill.

Wright, G.R.H. 2005a. *Ancient Building Technology: Volume 2, Materials, Part 1, Texts.* Leiden, Netherlands: Brill.

Wright, G.R.H. 2005b. *Ancient Building Technology: Volume 2, Materials, Part 2, Illustrations.* Leiden, Netherlands: Brill.

Yosida, Mitukuni. 1973. "The Chinese Concept of Nature." In *Chinese Science: Explorations of an Ancient Tradition,* eds. S. Nakayama and N. Sivin, 71–89. Cambridge, MA: MIT Press.

Young, Charles, et al. 1976. "Computation with Roman Numerals," *Archive for History of Exact Science* 15: 141–8.

Zimmerman, Francis. 1995. "The Scholar, the Wise Man, and Universals: Three Aspects of Ayurvedic Medicine." In *Knowledge and the Scholarly Medical Traditions,* ed. Don Bates, 297–319. Cambridge: Cambridge University Press.

Index

Academy: Imperial, 71, Plato's, 158
Acumoxibustion, 157
Acupuncture, 134, 135, 157
Addition, 29, 32–34, 38
Adze, 170, 178, 212, 234
Aeschylus, on ancient technologies, 3, 13
Agglutinative languages: and characteristics of science, 63–66; and education, 66–72
Agricultural calendar(s), 83, 93, 100, 108, 109, 122
Agriculture: dry land, 7; flood plain, 8, 16, 17, 21, 81, 171, 183. *See also* Irrigation
Ahtarvaveda, 133
Air: as element, 147, 158, 159, 160, 161, 238; in alchemy, 209; in medicine, 146; in metallurgy, 216, 218, 219, 222, 225; in mines, 23, 154, 176, 182, 192, 206, 226
Akkadian, 9, 14, 65
Alchemy: Alexandrian, 235, 239; Chinese, 141, 209, 210, 211, 235–37; defined, 209; documents, 210; late emergence of, 209; practices, 210, 236, 238; processes, 209, 238; theories, 210–12, 236, 239; women in, 209–10
Alcmaeon, 161
Alexander The Great, 14, 22, 94, 109, 185
Alexandrian astronomy, 116–23
Alloys, 210, 212, 223–24. *See also individual metals*

Almagest. See Ptolemy
Alphabetic language: education and literacy, 31, 75–79, 80, 81
Amulet(s), 72, 137, 139, 211, 212, 232
Anatomy, 131, 163, 164
Anaximander, 158
Anaximenes, 158, 161
Anuyoga Dwara Sutra, 48
Anyang, 18, 223
Aperon, 158
Appian: historian, 94; way, 180
Aqueduct(s): Mesopotamian, 172; Roman, 180–81
Arch, 166, 175. *See also* Arches
Archeological: evidence, 2, 6, 7, 9, 17, 30, 165, 166, 171, 187, 234; investigations, 13
Arches: corbelled, 172, 175; Roman, 181; true, 175, 176
Area measurements: Chinese, 43; Egyptian, 44–45, 50; Greek, 54–55; Indian, 46–47, 48; Mesopotamian, 50–51, 172, 181
Aristotle: and alchemy, 236, 237–38; *Metaphysics*, 5, on elements, 159, 162–63, 238; *Meteores*, 238; on *episteme* (sciences), 56, 76; on origins of mathematics, 5, 48; *Posterior Analytics*, 56; *Prior Analytics*, 56; 54, 55, 131, 151, 159, 163, 164
Art of yellow and white. *See* Transmutation
Asclepiad medicine, 141–43. *See also* Medicine

About the Author

RICHARD G. OLSON is Professor of History and Willard W. Kieth Jr. Fellow in the Humanities at Harvey Mudd College and Adjunct Professor of History at Claremont Graduate University. His publications include *Science Deified and Science Defied: The Historical Significance of Science in Western Culture* (University of California Press, 2 vols, 1982 & 1992) and *Science and Religion, 1450—1900: From Copernicus to Darwin* (Greenwood Press, 2004).